Peace Clan

Peace Clan

Mennonite Peacemaking in Somalia

Peter M. Sensenig

Foreword by
David W. Shenk

☙PICKWICK *Publications* · Eugene, Oregon

PEACE CLAN
Mennonite Peacemaking in Somalia

Copyright © 2016 Peter M. Sensenig. All rights reserved. Except for brief quotations in critical publications or reviews, no part of this book may be reproduced in any manner without prior written permission from the publisher. Write: Permissions, Wipf and Stock Publishers, 199 W. 8th Ave., Suite 3, Eugene, OR 97401.

Pickwick Publications
An Imprint of Wipf and Stock Publishers
199 W. 8th Ave., Suite 3
Eugene, OR 97401

www.wipfandstock.com

PAPERBACK ISBN: 978-1-4982-3101-5
HARDCOVER ISBN: 978-1-4982-3103-9

Cataloguing-in-Publication data:

Sensenig, Peter M.

Peace clan : Mennonite peacemaking in Somalia / Peter M. Sensenig.

xxvi + 260 pp. ; 23 cm. Includes bibliographical references.

ISBN 978-1-4982-3101-5 (paperback) | ISBN 978-1-4982-3103-9 (hardback)

1. Mennonites—Somalia. 2. Peace—Religious aspects—Mennonites. I. Title.

BV3625.S56 S478 2016

Manufactured in the U.S.A.   02/23/16

Biblical quotations are from the New Revised Standard Version Bible, copyright 1989, Division of Christian Education of the National Council of the Churches of Christ in the United States of America. Used by permission. All rights reserved.

Several paragraphs in chapters 1 and 5 were first published in David W. Shenk and Peter M. Sensenig, "The Somali Conundrum: Christian Presence in Turbulence and Peace," in *Freedom of Belief and Christian Mission*, edited by Hans Aage Gravaas, Christof Sauer, Tormod Engelsviken, and Knud Jorgensen, Regnum Edinburgh Centenary Series. Oxford: Regnum, 2015. Used by permission.

Several paragraphs in chapter 5 were first published in Peter M. Sensenig, "A Leg to Stand On: Ahmed Haile, Glen Stassen, and Elicitive Peacemaking," *Christian Ethics Today* vol. 22, no. 4 (fall 2014). The full text from which this excerpt comes can be found at http://christianethicstoday.com/wp/wp-content/uploads/2014/11/CE-95_final.pdf. Used by permission.

To Christy—your faith inspires me.

To Moses—it is my great hope that you find joy and purpose as a member of God's peace clan.

A light to guide us in the brightness of the day when hopes are fulfilled and circumstances are favorable, and a light to guide us in the darkness of the midnight when we are thwarted and the slumbering giants of gloom and hopelessness rise in our souls.

— MARTIN LUTHER KING JR, *STRENGTH TO LOVE*

Contents

Foreword by David W. Shenk | xi
Acknowledgments | xvii
Abbreviations | xix
Introduction | xxi

1. Clans Converge, 1953–1976 | 1

    Establishing the Mission in Somalia | 3
    Mission and Mentors | 7
    Core Convictions | 15
    A Communal Way of Seeing | 26
    Taking the Long View: Patience as a Way of Reasoning | 36

2. Shifting Sand: Religious, Political, and Interfaith Changes, 1976–1990 | 41

    Religious Shift: Nonresistance to Peacemaking | 42
    Political Shift: Somalia's Failing Government | 49
    Interfaith Shift: Islam as Peacemaking Partner | 60
    Finding Footing | 73

3. Salt, Light, and Deeds: Tensions in Mennonite Involvement | 77

  The Colonialist Moment | 78
  Evangelism, Development, and Peacemaking | 83
  Salt, Light, and Deeds as Witness, Elicitation, and Service | 92
  Living in the Borderlands | 100

4. Strength is Weakness: The Appeal and Failures of Intervention | 102

  Imagining Intervention | 105
  Why Intervention Failed | 119
  Contesting Intervention | 130

5. A Salt and Light Alternative: Mennonites and Somali Peacemaking Practices During the Civil Conflict | 136

  The Elicitive Method | 138
  Kinship and Clan | 144
  Peace from the Ground Up: Mennonites and Somali Peacemaking | 159
  Ahmed Ali Haile, a Mennonite Peacemaker in Action | 171

6. Saints and Soldiers: Somali Islam and Peacemaking | 177

  Islams in Tension: Sufism and Islamism in Somalia | 181
  Somali Sufi Saints | 196
  Conclusion | 199

7. Bridge-Builders: Mennonite Peacebuilding Education and Women Peacemakers | 202

   EMU and Somali Peacebuilding | 204
   Women as Peacemakers in Somali Culture | 208
   Women's Peacebuilding Leadership Program | 212
   Breathing Peace: Dekha Ibrahim | 217

8. Peace Clan Past and Present | 220

   A Good Name | 221
   The Task of Renewal | 222
   Security in Relationships | 224
   Without Knowledge there is No Light | 228
   A Welcoming Peace Clan | 230

Appendix: List of Interviews | 237
Bibliography | 239
General Index | 251
Scripture Index | 259

Foreword

PETER SENSENIG'S REMARKABLE STUDY explores the engagement of diverse peace movements within the Somali experience. Although Somali-inhabited regions in northeastern Africa have acquired notoriety as a perceived haven for pirates and jihadists, Sensenig's study gives special attention to Somali peacemaking practices and aspirations. The Somali practice of peacemaking emerges wherever responsible decision makers find space to develop peacemaking alternatives. In recent decades Somali peacemakers have struggled within sometimes powerful countervailing forces that oppose peacemaking. A Mennonite role has been to encourage peacemaking themes within the indigenous Somali matrix. Somalis have sometimes referred to the Mennonite presence as the "Peace Mission."

Sensenig's book is an exploration of a variety of peacemaking approaches within the Somali experience. These are both indigenous within the Somali society as well as interventions from outside. Especially noteworthy are the traditional pre-Islamic themes. All traditional peacemaking is centered in the quest for restoration of relations. The institution of clan-based consensual decision-making is vitally significant and deeply embedded within the culture. This study explores the enormous asset of such traditional approaches to peacemaking.

Also significant is the Islamic engagement with a vision of the *umma* (Muslim community) as a universal community of peace. In Somali societies where clan systems might be disintegrating, the *umma* that transcends clan systems is an asset in the quest for peace; for example, the Friday prayers unite the various clans in prayerful submission to God.

In these modern times both the *umma* and the clan are pressed with enormous stressors. Some Somali peacemakers view the clan as the most viable foundation for authentic peacemaking. Others look to the *umma*. And others have feet planted firmly in both worlds; they believe that it is feasible and right for the *umma* and the clan to function as complementary communities of peace.

The Mennonite community has been a presence within both the Muslim community and the clan systems. Mennonites have been invited into Somalia as community developers and educationalists. These service workers view themselves as an expression of the church demonstrating the love of God. The Mennonite engagement with Somali people commenced about sixty years ago. That engagement has been intermittent and often tenuous. Nevertheless, it has been a real and sustained engagement.

Sensenig observes that these Mennonite service workers have been viewed by the Somali people as a "peace clan" engaged in cultivating approaches to peacemaking. Within the Somali/Islamic context the distinctive gift the Mennonite presence offers is a peace centered in the reconciliation and forgiveness revealed in Christ. The Mennonite "peace clan" is viewed as a people of prayer; they gather regularly for times of worship. Although Mennonite presence is numerically small and tenuous and teams of Mennonites are not always physically present in Somalia, the "salt" of that presence has been appreciated and in fact seems to be quite significant.

Mennonite spirituality contributes in various ways to the Somali notion that Mennonites are a peace clan. The Mennonites brought a sensitive and lively theological engagement into their presence in Somalia. In this study Sensenig invites readers to lively engagement with Islamic theology. All of this happens within the context of peacemaking within Islam and within traditional pre-Islamic Somali culture.

The Sufi mystical streams of Muslim theology are especially pertinent. The Sufis are viewed as communities of inter-clan peace within mainstream Islam. Therefore, it makes good sense for Somalis to consider Mennonites as a peace clan serving among the Somali clans or within the *umma*. Peace clan is a good niche for the Somali interpretation of the Mennonite presence within their regions.

Each community has a gift to offer in the peace process. This is not a syncretistic amalgam of all the communities and theologies. Rather each community selects those values and commitments that are perceived to be pertinent. Selection happens. The respective faith centers inform believers as they select and critique their respective approaches to peacemaking.

For example, the Muslim *umma* and the Somali clan systems are influenced in positive ways by the presence of the Mennonite peace clan. These communities are complementary in the peace process: the Muslim *umma;* the indigenous Somali clans; the Mennonite clan. The Somali clan leaders will most likely recruit the insights and authority of the Muslim imams who are committed to cherishing the authority and universality of the Muslim *umma*. Likewise, the forgiveness themes in the Christian faith are honored by Somali clan leaders.

By way of illustration, a Somali follower of Jesus convened a weekly gathering under the great tree in his yard. For some years this gathering of imams, clan leaders, and a follower of Jesus met regularly for serious conversations about the Somali peace process. They were among the carriers of the peacemaking process. They concluded their gathering with a goat meal. That was a respectful and serious conversation. They were a peace-questing gathering somewhat analogous to the peaceful Sufi communities within the widespread network of Somali clans.

However, the peace process is not always so respectful. Peacemaking is also touched with travail. The path of peacemaking has within it the blood-stained foot prints of those who have showed the way. Peacemakers are sometimes martyrs to that calling. One of the key peacemaking leaders, whose story is told in these pages, lost his leg in a rocket attack. His friends nicknamed him the One-legged Peacemaker.

This study weaves into the narrative various peacemaking accounts and reflections. Sensenig is impressed with the reservoir of wisdom for peacemaking that is present within the Somali systems. These peace themes seem to be so helpful. What, then, has gone so wrong in the Somali experience? Alas, grist has gotten into these complementary systems. The Somali people have a common language, religion and ethnicity. How, then, can it be that large regions of Somali-inhabited North Eastern Africa have descended into intermittent conflict?

Sensenig argues that the culprit is outside interventions. He describes the interventions with considerable depth. His observation is that the interventions, such as UNOSOM (United Nations Operation in Somalia) in southern Somalia, short circuited the normal indigenous ways of resolving conflict. Sensenig's study describes a century of multiple interventions, including the interventions of the Western colonial era. He observes that there is a pattern to the interventions. They all fail in establishing the peace!

Sensenig's conviction is that interventions undercut the tradition approaches to peacemaking. He argues that interventions throw into confusion time-tested institutions for peacemaking. For example, could it be that *sharia* law is more effective in establishing the peace in an Islamic Somali society than is the extension of international rule with its statement on human rights? Sensenig's response is that none of the interventions that have sought to establish peace among the Somalis has succeeded. Even as I am writing this paragraph, southern Somalia is occupied by three interventions. The alternative is for the interventions to desist. Sensenig counsels to let traditional approaches in their rich and sometimes confusing varieties flourish.

The peacemaking engagement within the Somali experience attracts interest, reaching even beyond the Somali experience. For example, recently I was asked to speak in a Chinese university in Shanghai on the theme "Mennonite Peace Witness among the Muslim Somalis." I was astonished and asked, "Why this theme?"

My hosts responded, "Chinese academics consider the Mennonite church to be a church with a peace witness. There is also keen interest in Islam and the emerging jihadist movements in some areas. We want your lecture to combine insights into peacemaking and Islam. Include observations on the Christian role in peacemaking."

There is much to commend in the concept of a people nicknamed as a peace clan. That is what our Chinese hosts were reaching for in the request for a lecture on Mennonite peace witness. The Somali peace clan concept suggests a people of peace among other clans. This is not a top-down or interventionist approach to peacemaking. Rather the concept of peace clan suggests a community cooperating with other communities as they cultivate together approaches to peacemaking. It is the Abraham calling to be a people of blessing to all peoples. That is the calling of the Mennonite peace clan within the Somali context. At a time when Christians are often perplexed as to the nature of their mission in a sometimes terroristic world, the mission of a people to be a peace clan within the Somali context is quite remarkable.

Indeed the themes of this study are right in line with many discussions globally on peacemaking. In all the conversation this book will foment, it is essential for communities to be nurtured by the commitment to peacemaking. Actually that might be less complex than we have assumed, as this story demonstrates.

A Somali friend told me this story which he said summarizes his approach to peacemaking:

> An illiterate mother, with small children in tow, was carrying her basket of figs to the market to sell. Then on the path in front she saw her enemy coming up the trail toward her. She unloaded the basket of figs and gave them to her enemy. Her enemy gladly accepted the gift of figs.
>
> Thereafter the fig-giver and the fig-receiver became friends.

David W. Shenk, PhD

Global Consultant with EMM for Christian/Muslim Relations

Adjunct Professor in Several Graduate Schools Teaching Courses on the Religions and Peacemaking

Acknowledgments

I AM GRATEFUL TO Glen Stassen, who worked to sharpen, broaden, and improve in myriad ways my academic abilities. Glen's passion for peacemaking was infectious, and his loyalty to his students unmatched. I could not have asked for a better mentor. I thank also my dissertation committee members, John Paul Lederach and David Shenk. David has modeled for me and many others what it means to engage Muslim neighbors with respect, integrity, and a deep desire for peace.

My deep gratitude extends to friends among the faculty and students of University of Hargeisa's Institute of Peace and Conflict Studies. Their courage and patience gives me hope that better days are imminent.

I am grateful to my parents J. Carl and Julia Sensenig; my commitment to Anabaptist faith and to Africa owes much to their influence. Many members of the Mennonite family in Somalia, both North Americans and Somalis, have graciously agreed to take part in this research. Their comments have greatly improved what follows, while I take full responsibility for any shortcomings. Even in retirement many are deeply invested, in prayer and otherwise, in the peace of Somalia. Their words are featured here, but their lives speak even louder. May those whose lives have been cut short in Somalia—by war, persecution, or illness—also continue to speak through these stories.

Abbreviations

al-Itihaad al-Islamiya	Somali Islamist group
al-Shabaab	Somali Islamist group
baraka	grace or blessing
AMISOM	African Union Mission in Somalia
AU	African Union
BBC	British Broadcasting Corporation
CJP	Center for Justice and Peacebuilding
diya	payment for bloodshed
EMBMC	Eastern Mennonite Board of Missions and Charities
EMC	Eastern Mennonite College
EMM	Eastern Mennonite Missions
EMU	Eastern Mennonite University
guurti	assembly of elders
ICU	Islamic Courts Union
MCC	Mennonite Central Committee
qat	narcotic plant
SIM	Sudan Interior Mission

SNM	Somali National Movement
SPI	Summer Peacebuilding Institute
tariqa	Sufi order
TFG	transitional federal government
TNG	transitional national government
UNITAF	Unified Task Force, code-named Operation Restore Hope
UNOSOM	United Nations Operation in Somalia
USAID	United States Agency for International Development
USC	United Somali Congress
wadaad	Sufi sheikh
WPLP	Women's Peacebuilding Leadership Program
xeer	customary law

Introduction

WHEN MY FAMILY ARRIVED in Mogadishu in 1986 for an assignment with Eastern Mennonite Missions (EMM), we were joining a work that was already thirty-three years in the making. In just six decades Mennonites have walked with Somalis through colonial rule, independence and transition to democracy, a military coup and dictatorship, civil war and anarchy, foreign military intervention, mass migrations, and famines. The Mennonite work in Somalia required constant attention to the ever-shifting political situation, which in one moment could mean abrupt dismissal from the country and in another an invitation for deeper involvement in health care or education.

In the sand-swept capital city along the Indian Ocean, my parents met Somalis who called themselves Mennonites. A few were Christians, but many were Muslims. What can it possibly mean when a Somali Muslim identifies himself as a Mennonite? It is an astounding statement that defies the given identity boundaries. For most, it meant that they were educated in the Mennonite schools by foreigners who demonstrated loving care for them. Their experiences in the schools shaped them and represented something good in their lives. They understood that Mennonites believed in peace, and on some level they identified with that way of being in the world.

This book is my effort to respond to the question of what it might mean to proclaim peace in a Somali context. I contend that the Mennonite presence in Somalia represents the initiation of a peace clan, a family composed of people who have been drawn to the same divine gift, whose lives are thrown out of control by their love for strangers.

Part of what it means to live lives that are out of control is to resist the temptation to understand peace as something one can own or secure. In that sense, attempts to define peace or peacemaking invariably run the risk of domesticating the radical nature of the peace God offers. Chris Huebner describes the peace of the church as a vulnerable exchange of gifts, which is precisely what places it out of our control. Peace cannot be defined as a future goal that we might reach, because that would imply that we have the means to control history.[1]

The term *peacemaking* in the subtitle of this book, however, implies action, or at least movement. Jesus calls peacemakers blessed and promises that they will be called the children of God (Matt 5:9). How does one work for what one cannot define? The answer is that peace can only be defined in terms of relationships. Huebner's caution in defining peace is about allowing our understanding of peace to become too small, trapped by goals that justify our search for security and settlement. Peace is far bigger than the absence of war or violence. The concept of shalom in the Hebrew Bible always calls for responsibility to one another. Shalom refers most often to wholeness within the community, a quality of relationship that can only be described by an encounter, not abstractly or idealistically.[2]

Peace, therefore, is about how one sees oneself in relation to one's neighbor. In this sense peace is bound up in identity, which is why the precariousness of peace is incompatible with a stable identity. Huebner writes, "The pursuit of a stable identity works against the call to remain charitably open to the stranger. A Christian conception of peace is better captured by metaphors of fluidity and ambiguity than by those of solidity and stability."[3] The call to love enemies and strangers results in fragmented identities that resist domestication. Somalia has been a dangerous place for many, including Somali women, men, and children, as well as foreign soldiers and aid workers. Mennonites in Somalia have faced that danger on many occasions. In 1959 a Mennonite worker was attacked and injured in her home at night. EMM faced opposition throughout the 1960s because of some Somali converts. The martyrdom of Merlin Grove in 1962 was only a precursor to the many Somali believers martyred in the 1990s and following. But for Christians, risk is at the heart of their faith because their discipleship is rooted in patience and in the cross of Christ. John Rempel writes, "The distinctive charism of Mennonitism is

---

1. Huebner, *Precarious Peace*, 30.
2. Westermann, "Peace (Shalom)," 22–30.
3. Huebner, *Precarious Peace*, 37.

its combination of two convictions: that the church . . . is already the bearer of the kingdom and that one of the most astonishing evidences of this new reality is the possibility of loving one's enemy."[4]

The "peace clan" as I have defined it—a family drawn together by love for strangers—is necessarily a precarious identity. Yet I think it aptly describes the attachments Mennonites and Somalis have formed with one another despite the broader context of violence, colonial and neocolonial domination, and cultural barriers.

If peace is precarious because it is a gift, not a state that one can establish and preserve, then Mennonites need Somalis at least as much as Somalis need Mennonites. Somalia is not where Mennonites go to do peacemaking. Somalia is where Mennonites learn to be peacemakers, along with their fellow peace clan members. In Somalia, peace is precarious indeed. Perhaps this is why Somalia has served as one of the most significant places for Mennonites to work out what it means to follow Jesus in an uncertain world.

The academic sources on the Mennonite history in Somalia are limited. I therefore engage publications in Mennonite periodicals as well as unpublished primary sources, including files on the history of Eastern Mennonite Missions (EMM) and Mennonite Central Committee (MCC), in addition to the secondary sources already available. Much of this information is found in the archives of the Lancaster Mennonite Historical Society.

Because this subject has received so little academic attention, the experts are the intergenerational tribe of Mennonites who have served in Somalia, now scattered across North America but concentrated in Pennsylvania. I rely heavily on interviews with them and with Somalis living in the United States and Canada who are connected to the Mennonite work. In some cases, I employ pseudonyms to protect identities.

What theological differences or continuity exist across the six decades of Mennonite mission and peacemaking work in Somalia? As one might expect, significant shifts occurred in language and practices over time. Yet the Mennonite presence maintained a distinctive emphasis on unobtrusive, culturally sensitive work from the ground up. This approach is informed by a particular theology of peoplehood in which the goal is to invite others into an inclusive peace clan. In order to understand the nature of the changes in the Mennonite approach as well as the continuity across those shifts, I work somewhat chronologically beginning in the 1950s, and propose constructive responses along the way.

4. Rempel, "Ambiguous Legacy," 361.

In the chapter that follows I interrogate how a peace clan from rural North America interacts with a foreign cultural setting. The focus of this chapter is the question of how Mennonites applied their peace commitments in a Somali context, even as they were being changed through the interaction with Somalis. I apply the holistic character ethics framework in order to identify four key dimensions that contributed to the Mennonite ability to sustain their peace emphasis in the early period of their involvement in Somalia. First, the community loyalty of Mennonites informed their sense of calling to mission, but also allowed the deepest values and commitments of their tradition to be transmitted into a new cultural setting. Second, the content of those basic commitments emphasized following Jesus, love, and forgiveness, as well as the costly nature of discipleship. The Mennonites found creative ways to live out these convictions in the difficult circumstances presented by life in Somalia. Third, the Mennonite communal worldview also impacted the way in which they interacted with Somali conceptions of community, including kinship, traditional Somali peacemaking, and Somali authority systems. And finally, their work was infused with a sense that only a long-term commitment would have any lasting impact among Somalis. Patience required building deep friendships, a foundation God could use to establish the church. The cultural sensitivity of the early Mennonite missionaries was the precursor to the elicitive peacemaking approach that followed.

In chapter 2 I argue that the Mennonite mission in Somalia began with an emphasis on establishing Christian fellowships and on service through education and medical work. In the ensuing decades, however, the emphasis shifted to include justice and peacemaking. Three factors facilitated this shift. First, broader theological patterns in the Mennonite church paid increased attention to activism over quietism and justice over nonresistance. Second, the changing political context in Somalia made questions of justice and peace more acute. Finally, the attitude toward and descriptions of Islam on the part of Mennonites became more positive as deeper interfaith relationships developed, setting the stage for the elicitive approach to peacemaking that followed in later work.

At this juncture it is possible to identify two related tensions in the Mennonite presence in Somalia. The third chapter discusses the context of colonialism and the issue of evangelism and peacemaking. Internal Mennonite disagreements on these issues cannot be entirely reconciled, but I argue that Jesus' calling to salt, light, and deeds in the Sermon on the Mount allows and even requires a variety of approaches. Each of these three metaphors corresponds to a term that Mennonites have used to describe their peacemaking presence in Somalia. Salt refers to the mandate to *witness* to Jesus Christ the Prince of Peace through communal practices that are different from the wisdom of the world. Light means pointing the nations toward God's saving work, *eliciting* the cultural treasures that can glorify God. Deeds are acts of *service* that glorify God by reflecting God's concern for the wellbeing of each person.

In chapter 4 I analyze how a peace clan responds to the dominant methodology of military intervention in a time of crisis. As the situation in Somalia deteriorated, the issues of intervention and appropriate response perplexed Mennonites, along with others in the broader church and in Christian non-governmental organization (NGO) circles. I explore the contours of these debates before turning to the military operations to argue that the decision-making in the period leading up to intervention, actions during operations, and the results of the operations all indicate grave failures with regard to effectiveness and respectful engagement with Somalis.

The fifth chapter continues to develop what it might mean for Mennonites to be *salt* and *light* in a Somali context, particularly in the circumstances following the collapse of the government in 1991. The Mennonite presence in the preceding decades laid a foundation for an alternative response to the dominant mode of intervention. The elicitive approach articulated by John Paul Lederach builds on the conviction that the tools for peacemaking are not manufactured externally but emerge from within a culture. Somali culture has a wealth of resources for peacemaking that can strengthen security as well as provide for the needs of everyone. Kinship performs both the positive social function of ensuring that all have their needs met and the positive political function of resolving conflict through the traditional channels of authority, the elders. The traditional social contract *xeer* is a vital tool in moving conflict from the vicious cycles of retaliation toward restitution and even reconciliation. Mennonites, whose peacemaking is centered on reconciliation rather than simply coexistence, engaged these Somali traditions in a number of ways. MCC and EMM supported ground-up peace initiatives led by Somalis, such as the peace group *Ergada* and the successful Borama Peace Process, rather than assuming the necessity of a highly centralized government at the expense of traditional forms of governance.

I close chapter 5 with the story of Somali Mennonite peacemaker Ahmed Haile. His remarkable journey demonstrates that moral imagination, reconciliation, and peacemaking are possible. That the Somali-Mennonite relationship can yield someone like Ahmed Haile gives me hope that God indeed is at work in the world to reconcile warring people. His earthly sojourn, which ended in 2011, was utterly devoted to strengthening the peace clan.

Chapter 6 continues the task of eliciting peacemaking resources from within Somali culture, particularly Somali religion. Religious values, like the cultural values of the previous chapter, cannot be imposed from above but must emerge from the most profound part of people's religious identity. I propose that three elements—historical analysis of the tensions within Somali Islam, constructive readings of the Qur'an that promote peace, and peacemaking examples within Somali Sufism—are essential ingredients in the articulation of a peace-oriented Somali Islam.

The most recent Mennonite connections to Somalia, particularly the work of the Center for Justice and Peacebuilding at Eastern Mennonite University (EMU), have been focused on peacebuilding education. The seventh chapter therefore demonstrates how the elicitive approach to peacemaking is central to contemporary Mennonite work in the Horn of Africa. Many of the most significant theorists and practitioners are women because of their unique peacemaking positions in Somali society.

Each generation of Mennonites who works in Somalia observes that they are standing on the shoulders of those who came before. In the concluding chapter I outline the continuity between the past and present work in Somalia. Mennonites operate as a welcoming peace clan within wider society, seeking out peacemaking partners in every context and finding security in relationships. The good name that Mennonites have established in Somalia requires the constant renewal of relationships. Mennonites are continually drawn back into education, which holds promise as the basis for ongoing Somali-Mennonite partnership in the future.

This story represents an all-out challenge to enmity, grounded in deep trust that God has a better future for peoples divided by what Martin Luther King Jr. called "the eternal accidents of race, religion, and nationality."[5] Accident is one way to describe how North American Mennonites found themselves in an arid Islamic land of camels, frankincense, and myrrh. Eternal may well describe the fruit of the friendships that were forged there.

---

5. King, *Strength to Love*, 27.

1

Clans Converge, 1953–1976

BERTHA BEACHY, A MENNONITE who spent many years working in and around Somalia, has noted remarkable overlap between traditional Somali and European Anabaptist cultures.[1] The emphasis on genealogy, the dependence on camels and cows, and the strength of oral tradition were mutually, if often subconsciously, recognized. Yet when Mennonites first set foot in Somalia in 1953, the cultural chasm was immense. How would white, North American, Anabaptist Christians relate to East African pastoralists who had been Muslim as long as anyone could remember?

In this chapter I examine what shaped the Mennonite approach to peacemaking in the early period of involvement in Somalia. The holistic character ethics[2] framework allows us to identify four key dimensions that contributed to a foundation for peacemaking.

1. Beachy, "My Pilgrimage," 208–12.

2. The term *holistic* can refer to two different but overlapping concepts. One is that the spiritual and material wellbeing of persons are inseparable. God cares deeply about the material aspects of people's lives, including health, education, and freedom from violence. Ronald Sider grounds his defense of a "holistic, biblical vision for empowering the poor" in both the Old and New Testaments, noting that work is not just to meet needs, but an avenue for loving God and neighbors (*Just Generosity*, 61–92). In this sense, the Mennonite Mission was holistic from the beginning, establishing schools and hospitals in response to the real needs of the Somali people for good health care and education. The emphasis on peacemaking heightened over time with the shifting political situation, but the later move toward more active conflict transformation was a natural one in light of the holistic approach that was already established.

The other sense in which I use the term *holistic* refers to the framework of holistic character ethics. Here *holistic* refers to the analysis of all the dimensions informing ethical decisions and practices, including loyalties and passions, the way of seeing, the way of reasoning, and the underlying convictions. My contention is that such analysis reveals the sources and strengths of peacemaking in Mennonites, and allows for

Glen Stassen and David Gushee formulated *holistic character ethics* in order to bring attention to dimensions of ethical thought and practice that are often ignored. In societies influenced by the individualism of the Enlightenment, ethics is often construed in terms of decisions. Focusing on decisions obscures the critical role that social context, the way in which we reason, and especially loyalties play in shaping character. As humans we are not simply autonomous beings who believe certain propositions and then act on those beliefs. As important as our theological convictions are, they are only one part of what informs our practices. We are also deeply shaped by where we were born, whom we admire and follow, and our loyalties to certain people, practices, or ideas. If our ethic fails to pay attention to any of these dimensions, "it either lacks the ability to take a clear stand on concrete ethical issues, or it takes the stand naively, unaware of and uncritical about its own crucial assumptions. It lacks the power to detect errors and weaknesses in that dimension of character, to know where to repent and change."[3]

The four dimensions of holistic character ethics are *basic convictions*, the way of *perceiving the social context*, the way of *reasoning*, and *loyalties and passions*. Each of these dimensions contains particular variables; for instance, one variable of perceiving is the way in which one views authority. Jesus' teachings and biblical ethics more broadly pay attention to all four dimensions and their variables. Here I argue that all four dimensions shaped the way in which Mennonites approached their foundational years in Somalia. My analysis often takes a narrative form because I am drawing from interviews with early Mennonite missionaries in Somalia. Moreover, narrative is a particularly powerful way both to convey an ethical message (like Jesus' parables) and to find windows into the manner in which the four dimensions shape practice.

This analysis performs two essential functions for a continued faithful Christian witness: affirming and sharpening the life-giving traditions of the past, and identifying areas where repentance and change are necessary.

---

repentance and change where necessary.

3. Stassen and Gushee, *Kingdom Ethics*, 59.

Establishing the Mission in Somalia

Rhoda Lind first felt called to be a missionary at age seven, a calling she received through reading books about missionaries. Some years later, she found herself in a scene straight from one of the dramatic mission stories. On January 16, 1953 Rhoda, her husband Wilbert, and their son Daniel disembarked in Mogadishu as the first Protestant missionaries ever to have begun Christian work in Somalia.[4] When the Lind family arrived in the city there was no dock, so they were precariously lowered from the ship in a basket attached to ropes. A tugboat then took the passengers in to shore. They stayed in a hotel for about a month during the construction of their house, which was a block from the Indian Ocean.[5]

Rhoda's calling was not unique; she came to faith in an environment that was deeply saturated in mission language and energy. Yet for many years the mission impulse lay dormant in North American Mennonites. The Mennonites of North America were relative late-comers in the modern overseas mission movement, organizing in the early twentieth century in the wake of the Sunday school movement. Mission was no foreign concept to the early Anabaptists; it was their primordial urge because they rejected the notion that one is a Christian simply by virtue of geographical or social location. The Anabaptist insistence that one could be saved only by believing the gospel and following Jesus made witness a duty of all believers, not just ordained leaders. The early Anabaptists regularly sent out missionaries, who met persecution from both Protestants and Catholics from the beginning of the sixteenth century. The attempt to find rest from the bitter opposition of fellow Christians led to migrations to the new world and to a communal mentality that earned Anabaptists the label "the quiet in the land." Nevertheless, Mennonites were not immune to the mission-oriented winds that swept through many Protestant churches in the late nineteenth century. Despite some opposition from traditionally minded Mennonites, convictions for missions developed and grew both from ecumenical influence and from "a dawning consciousness that this was an essential aspect of Biblical faith."[6]

---

4. Smoker and Eshleman, *God Led Us*, 19–20. The Roman Catholic Church began missionary work in Somalia in 1881. Swedish Lutherans entered what later became part of Somalia in 1898. They ended their work in 1935 at the request of the Italian authorities.

5. Rhoda Lind, interview by author, Lancaster, PA, December 3, 2012.

6. Erb, introduction to *Called to be Sent*, 6.

One aspect of the mission movement among North American Christians was the establishment of Sunday schools as a form of outreach. Mennonites picked up on this trend in the late nineteenth century. Eastern Mennonite Board of Missions and Charities (EMBMC, later Eastern Mennonite Missions) organized in 1914 as a mission in North America, and in a matter of a few years the idea of overseas missions came under discussion in the board. The Mission had already begun work in Tanganyika and Ethiopia by the mid-twentieth century.[7] The changing political situation in Somalia led Mission leaders to consider the Horn of Africa as a new field of work.

As southern Somalia, under Italian rule, was moving toward independence and unification with the British protectorate Somaliland in the north during the 1950s, the leadership of EMM sensed a unique opportunity. In January 1950 executive secretary Orie O. Miller suggested the possibility of sending workers to Somalia. That October Merle Eshleman and Mahlon Hess visited Somalia from Tanganyika in order to observe the prospects for establishing a mission there. The UN Trusteeship Charter under which Italy took over Somali in 1950 contained a religious freedom clause, but it was unclear what religious freedom meant in a context where nearly all citizens are Muslim and the governors are Catholic. The Mennonite explorers found some helpful contacts among the Italian administrators and the UN, but British officials discouraged them from establishing work in Somaliland. After their visit, they concluded that EMM should establish a mission in Italian Somaliland, a recommendation the mission board accepted in March 1951. A second investigative trip in February 1952 by Orie Miller and Merle Eshleman was met by a warm invitation from Dr. Spinelli of the Italian administration.

When the Linds moved to Mogadishu in 1953 they received a surprising welcome, and people seemed eager to receive medical and education help offered by the Mission. Learning the Somali language proved to be challenging, particularly because it was unwritten at the time, but the missionaries worked with language helpers. The first organized worship service was held on March 8, 1953 with the Linds, an Italian Protestant couple, and a Somali Muslim present. Muslim Somalis, sometimes as many as a dozen, regularly visited the worship services. One primary point of interaction with Somalis was evening English classes for young people. Students also expressed interest in the Bible and in spiritual

---

7. Wenger, *People in Mission*, 54–58.

teaching that compared the Old Testament stories to those found in the Qur'an. The Linds encountered some men who had become Christians under the Swedish Lutheran mission, who were still identifying as Christians even as they continued as Muslims, a mixture that the missionaries found confusing and troubling.[8]

In June 1954 the Mennonites visited the village of Mahaddei Uen, where they were generously welcomed by the eager chief and told to pick a location for the mission school and clinic, for which work started in 1955. The quiet work in health and education won the trust of Somalis, and some professed faith in Christ.[9] Other EMM staff arrived in the mid and late 1950s, including Carl and Leota Wesselhoft in 1956. The mission set up agricultural demonstrations in the village of Torda and schools and clinics in the towns of Mahaddei and Jamama.[10]

Italian Somalia and British Somaliland became independent and united on July 1, 1960 to form the Republic of Somalia. At this point there were Mennonite schools and clinics in three locations, in addition to a boarding school at Mahaddei Uen. The Mennonite work continued during the transition to independence, with a new hospital opening in Jamama in March 1961.[11] One year later, however, under the influence of conservative mullahs and Egyptian emissaries in protest of the propagation of the Christian faith, the government suspended all of the mission's activities. Three months later, in July 1962, the suspension was lifted and once again all of the mission schools and clinics could open. As he was registering students for the new school year, Merlin Grove was fatally stabbed by a Somali mullah who resented the foreign Christian presence the Mennonites represented. Grove's wife Dorothy was also stabbed but survived, expressing forgiveness and love for the Somali people. Grove's martyrdom and the ongoing work of the mission after his death became a seal of the special relationship between Somalis and Mennonites.[12]

One year later in 1963, however, the national assembly changed the 1961 constitutional article that had endorsed freedom of religion to now banning teaching any religion besides Islam. The government declared that the schools of mission agencies must also teach Islam. Sudan Interior

---

8. Smoker and Eshleman, *God Led Us*, 21–32.
9. Eby, "Triumph in Suffering," 125–26.
10. Eby, *Fifty Years, Fifty Stories*, 126.
11. Wenger, *People in Mission*, 62.
12. Eby, *Fifty Years, Fifty Stories*, 32–33.

Mission (SIM), an interdenominational mission organization not affiliated with the Mennonites, chose to close its schools rather than include Islam in the curriculum. EMM and the Bishop Board of the Lancaster Conference decided, at the encouragement of Somali Christians, to continue to operate the schools with Islam as a subject of study.[13] Although this decision appeased some Somali leaders, in 1964 the Minister of State told the mission that they must not teach the Christian faith to Somali citizens. Despite this official resistance, a core of Somali believers chose elders for their fellowships in 1966, and SIM completed a Somali translation of the New Testament in the same year (the Old Testament translation was completed in Ethiopia in 1977).[14]

A famine swept through central Somalia in 1965, and the Mennonites joined the Somali government in administering emergency medical care to those suffering in the town of Galkayo.[15] The medical ministry continued to expand with a new nurse training school in Jamama in 1968. The Mennonite Economic Development Association (MEDA) also began rural development projects in the Mahaddei region. A community development program was launched there in 1970. Work was also expanding on the education front; in 1969 the German Evangelical Churches donated two million shillings to build a secondary school in the town of Johar, which opened its doors to two hundred students in 1971.[16] The 1969 coup that put General Siad Barre into power left the future of the mission and of the Somali Christian community uncertain, but the Revolutionary government assured the mission that its contributions to education, development, and medicine in the country were welcomed. In 1972, however, the Somali government nationalized all the schools and medical facilities of the mission without compensation as part of President Barre's move toward scientific socialism. With the exception of eight teachers, all mission workers, including administrators, were dismissed from the country by 1974. In 1976 the remaining mission teachers were asked to leave, and some relocated to Kenya to continue to work with Somalis there.[17]

---

13. Wenger, *People in Mission*, 63.
14. Eby, *Fifty Years, Fifty Stories*, 127.
15. Leaman, "Mustard Seed," 2–5.
16. Eby, *Fifty Years, Fifty Stories*, 127–28.
17. Wenger, *People in Mission*, 63–64.

Mission and Mentors

One of the key insights of holistic character ethics is that the people who influence us—our community, mentors, and those to whom we have a sense of loyalty—play a profound part in shaping our ethical thinking. It is therefore pertinent to inquire into the people, ideas, and communal understandings that influenced the early Mennonite missionaries in Somalia, in order to comprehend how their approach took shape. The community loyalty of Mennonites, including a robust ecclesiology, informed their sense of calling to mission, but also allowed the deepest values and commitments of their tradition, particularly the commitment to peacemaking, to be transmitted into a new cultural setting. Analysis of the loyalties dimension will also encourage us to observe ways in which the present context differs from the milieu in which their work emerged.

The atmosphere in which early Mennonite missionaries in Somalia were born and raised was saturated with the idea of Christian mission, and reinforced by the presence of missionaries in the churches and communities. The Sunday school movement impacted the Mennonite Church at the end of the nineteenth century, and soon the idea of overseas mission provided the impetus for the organization of EMM in 1914. In 1933 Elam Stauffer and Orie Miller were sent on the first exploratory trip to Tanganyika. The mission took later trips to explore possibilities in Ethiopia and Somalia, leading to work in those countries and eventually in various parts of Europe, Honduras, and Vietnam (following MCC's relief efforts there).[18] EMM became the only district board of the Mennonite Church with an extensive overseas program, which grew quickly with strong support and high per capita giving from Lancaster Conference churches, an abundance of personnel, and cooperation with other burgeoning mission organizations like Mennonite Board of Missions and Charities in Elkhart.[19] By the end of the century, nearly every Lancaster County Mennonite had relatives who had spent time in mission work abroad. In the words of historian John Ruth, "Outreach had become a Lancaster Mennonite way of acknowledging that the entire earth is the Lord's."[20]

Along with a freshly ignited passion for mission, Mennonites also imbibed from other Christian groups a newfound sense of piety and

---

18. Sauder, "Witness Grows," 55–63.
19. Erb, introduction to *Called to be Sent*, 7.
20. Ruth, *Earth is the Lord's*, 1123.

devotion to God. Personal surrender to God's will became the hallmark of obedience. John Ruth writes, "Among mission-minded people, there was much emphasis on 'surrender,' the continual quest for the Keswick ideal of 'the deeper life' preached at many a Bible conference." Ruth adds, somewhat tongue in cheek, that "somehow, 'to be nothing' could often leave the will quite strong."[21] Responding to God's call at a deeply personal level required willingness to count the cost, recognizing hardship as a necessary part of Christian mission. The 1956 booklet *God Led Us to Somalia* intones, with a hint of foreshadowing the 1962 martyrdom of Merlin Grove, "The greatest opportunity of all is for men and women who love the Lord Jesus supremely and are ready to go for Him to one of the earth's hardest battlegrounds to live and die for Him. On behalf of Muslim Somalia, is the love of Christ constraining *you*?"[22]

A Mission Environment

For many early missionaries to Somalia, the orientation toward mission started at home. Mary Gehman describes her family as mission-oriented; her parents were involved with the church's mission in Reading, Pennsylvania, and all of her siblings taught Sunday school and Bible school.

They read about the lives of missionaries in the past, and interacted with the missionaries sent out from their home district. At Eastern Mennonite College (EMC, now EMU), Gehman studied mission and Islam, Bible, and other subjects with teachers like Otis Yoder and Chester Lehman.[23] Many of the early EMM workers studied at EMC either before or during their terms of service. Carl Wesselhoeft attributes his sense of call not to one person but to the mission-oriented atmosphere cultivated at EMC and in home congregations. Mission work was a concrete way to serve the Lord and to follow the mandate of Matthew 28.[24] Bertha Beachy, the first woman in her family to attend college, also experienced EMC as a mission catalyst. Beachy notes that the idea of overseas mission work was normalized not only by the number of returning missionaries but by the participation of young Mennonite men in Civilian Public Service (CPS), which her brother completed in Puerto Rico. Revival meetings in

21. Ibid., 922–23.
22. Smoker and Eshleman, *God Led Us*, 32.
23. Mary Gehman, interview by author, Lancaster, PA, October 1, 2012.
24. Carl Wesselhoeft, interview by author, Logan, OH, January 2, 2013.

Ohio and Iowa, as well as in other parts of the country, served to spark interest in mission activities. At those meetings Beachy sensed that God had a purpose for her that she must follow to the best of her ability. "For the gifts and the calling of God are irrevocable" (Rom 11:29) took on a special meaning that strengthened her commitment to obey the call to overseas mission.[25]

In some cases, missionaries were influenced by family members who were involved in mission. Ivan Leaman acknowledges that the mission calling he felt as a young boy likely derives from the fact that his uncle and aunt, Clyde and Alta Shenk, served for many years as missionaries in Tanganyika; "stirrings of those early years led me to think that I was called, turned into a strong conviction that I was going to be a missionary." Impacted by the book *Jungle Doctor*, Leaman went to medical school to prepare for his service on the field. Both Ivan and Mary Ellen grew up in homes and congregations that fostered an interest in missionary work, even to the point of idealizing it. After an EMM leader approached them about the need for a doctor in Somalia, they began to see signs that God was calling them there, including coming across a magazine article that described Somalis as "one of the most handsome races in the world."[26]

While Fae Miller was studying nursing at Lancaster General Hospital, she was offered an appealing teaching scholarship to Case Western Reserve. Simultaneously she received a letter from EMM, asking her to go to East Africa. She knew immediately what her choice would be. Her nursing director responded to Miller's decision with a furious racist rant, warning her, "You're going to lose your life there with those dirty heathen." But Miller knew that through the church God was calling her to Somalia, even though the decision required the sacrifice of other attractive opportunities and appeared foolish to some. Miller acknowledges that she, like many early Mennonite missionaries, entered her service with a fairly traditional mission framework. The missionary as the carrier of the gospel to unenlightened peoples, ideas of heaven and hell, and the assumption of male leadership had an impact on the way Mennonites practiced mission in a Somali context. Yet Miller recognizes that it was the influence of her conservative Mennonite background, including her family and a loving Sunday school teacher, that brought her to Somalia in the first place. Once on the field her assumptions about the perfection of

25. Bertha Beachy, interview by author, Goshen, IN, January 3, 2013.

26. Ivan and Mary Ellen Leaman, interview by author, Lancaster, PA, November 14, 2012.

missionaries, both herself and others, were quickly debunked. When she came home on furlough and faced the admiration of relatives and others at missionary meetings, she encouraged them also to consider mission work. But she stressed the importance of mentors on the field, especially for single workers.[27]

Communal Calling: Orie Miller and Paul Kraybill

The Mennonite emphasis on community served as a counterbalance to the more personal, pietistic understandings of God's call that influenced the church. The Mennonite ecclesiology held that surrender to God, in effect, meant surrender to God's will as it was understood by the church. Just as under the guidance of the bishops the local body of believers communally called and ordained church leaders, so too the community participated in the calling of missionaries. The authority of communal discernment was virtually unquestioned. Carolyn Plank, a nurse who arrived shortly after the Linds, did not feel called to Somalia but felt that she should go because the mission board asked her. She only stayed in Somalia for about a year before being called to Java, which turned out to be a much better fit.[28] When Clayton Keener's name was drawn for pastoral ministry in the lot, he and his wife Martha moved their family back to the United States from the mission field in Addis Ababa, Ethiopia, despite their desire to continue there.[29] As a member of the church, one's life was not one's own; it belonged to God and to one's fellow believers.

The calling of missionaries, however, was not a purely democratic activity; often an individual in a position of leadership played an important part in identifying how the gifts of people matched a particular need on the mission field. Two such important leaders in the Mennonite Church in the mid-twentieth century were Orie O. Miller and Paul N. Kraybill.

Orie Miller was a remarkable person with seemingly boundless energy. John Ruth writes of him: "Eventually secretary of both MCC and EMBMC, Orie Miller probably wielded a wider practical influence among American Mennonite activities than any other person of his time, including those living in much less restrictive conferences than Lancaster. He

---

27. Fae Miller, interview by author, Orrville, OH, January 1, 2013.
28. Lind, interview.
29. Ruth, *Earth is the Lord's*, 1058–59.

held at least sixty-seven positions in dozens of the most important agencies across the North American Mennonite fellowship and beyond."[30] A mentor to many, including a whole generation of protégés known as "Orie's Boys,"[31] Miller advised others that he had learned early in his career not to say no when God or the church was calling. In addition to providing the impetus for beginning work in Somalia, Miller served as a conduit for God's calling in the lives of many early missionaries. Miller sought out people with all sorts of gifts and skills, conjuring up for Mennonites the image of the Somali people awaiting with outstretched arms for help. "Opportunities in this land are almost unlimited," he wrote, "opportunities to do medical work, translation and literacy work, to help the youth of the country who are reaching out for new things and hoping to take their place in the world, and to reach the girls and through them the homes of the country."[32]

Miller saw the Bible as a source book for Christian mission, from creation to the call of Abraham to Jesus and the Holy Spirit. Abraham, Isaac, and Jacob were called out of their culture and home in order to be a chosen people with a special relationship to God. Jesus described people as sheep who need to return to the shepherd, and the church is the personal witness to Jesus as the Son of God. Although the church was captive to the state for a millennium, the awakening in Europe that revealed new freedom in Christ also brought back the biblical pattern of mission, the "pilgrim life of scattering and suffering."[33] Miller found a host of images and principles for mission in Scripture: the disciple as a pilgrim, ready on call; the world as a ripe harvest to which God calls laborers; the unity of Jesus and the Father in mission; and the love of Christ as the impetus for sharing the gospel.

Out of this ecclesiology emerged Miller's perspectives on calling. The draft was forcing young Mennonite men into 1-W and Pax service in different parts of the US and the world. As his peers were joining the military and losing their lives, Omar Eby recalls feeling that he should suffer also, not stay in a comfortable home setting. Miller wrote a letter inviting Eby to go to Vietnam as an English teacher. Then at Eby's graduation ceremony, Miller informed him that his service location had

30. Ibid., 919.
31. Ibid., 973.
32. Smoker and Eshleman, *God Led Us*, 32.
33. Miller, "Biblical Imperative," 23–30.

been changed to Somalia. Eby was not certain where Somalia was, and sat waiting for a clue in the conversation. Nevertheless, he agreed and was soon teaching in Mogadishu with EMM.[34] On a later occasion Miller approached Eby and asked him to go home, earn a graduate degree, get married, and return to Somalia to build the mission education program. "Brother Miller," Eby responded, "whenever I receive an invitation like this I never know whether I am hearing the voice of God or that of an old man." Miller replied, "I'll have you know, Omar, God uses old men like me to tell young men like you what to do."[35]

Rhoda Lind felt a calling at a very young age to go to China, a calling she intended to follow even before meeting her future husband Wilbert, who was serving in China. Orie Miller asked her to go to Tanganyika, however, and she served there for two years before getting married. Miller then asked them to go to Ethiopia, but changed his mind when he had a revelation regarding Somalia while flying over Africa. It was only a short time later that the Linds stepped off the boat in Mogadishu.[36]

Paul Kraybill also exerted considerable influence in calling Mennonites to mission enterprises. As EMM considered the possibility of Somalia, Kraybill noted that Christian mission in majority Muslim countries is not often successful in any quantifiable way, but the calling to all nations nevertheless includes those under influence of Islam. Kraybill saw the remarkable manner in which the door opened in Somalia as a "sign and seal" of God's leading Mennonites there.[37]

Kraybill had a part in Mary Gehman's calling to Somalia when he asked her during her senior year at EMC (where Kraybill was affectionately referred to as PK) whether she would consider the new mission site. But even earlier an elderly missionary in her congregation, Mose Gehman, stated at church that God told him someone from the congregation would go to foreign mission work in his lifetime. Mary looked around at her congregation, wondering who it could possibly be. Later the same minister, while shaking Mary's hand, asked her out of the blue if the Lord had called her to go. God had planted a seed that eventually grew into a decades-long ministry in Somalia.[38]

---

34. Omar Eby, interview by author, Harrisonburg, VA, April 6, 2013.
35. Sharp, "Voice of God."
36. Lind, interview.
37. Kraybill, Preface, 2.
38. Gehman, interview.

While studying at EMC, Carl Wesselhoeft met Paul Kraybill, who was visiting the area to interview people for missionwork. Kraybill told him they were looking for people to go to France or Somalia. It was 1955 and Wesselhoeft, who is German, thought to himself, "A German would never do well in France." But Somalia rang a bell and after studying linguistics in Oklahoma for the summer, he and his wife Leota began their service in Somalia.[39] On another recruitment visit to EMC, Paul Kraybill met Bertha Beachy. Her roommate, Fae Miller, was on furlough from Somalia, providing a sense of confirmation to Kraybill's suggestion that Beachy go to Somalia. Six people from her class traveled together to Africa, a testament to the success of Kraybill's recruitment efforts at EMC.[40]

Kraybill had a gift for matching people to mission assignments. In 1959 Paul Kraybill approached Ivan and Mary Ellen Leaman to ask them to consider a call to Somalia. As they prepared to go they read *God Led Us to Somalia* and Kenneth Cragg's *The Call of the Minaret*. Both Orie Miller and Paul Kraybill encouraged them to think of their ministry in Somalia in terms of presence rather than as overt evangelization, preparing them not to expect to see rapid or numerous confessions of faith in Christ.[41] Some years later in 1965 Kraybill and Harold Stauffer also recruited Elizabeth and Ken Nissley to teach in Somalia as Ken's alternative service during the Vietnam War.[42]

Eleven years after the work in Somalia began, Kraybill reminded Mennonites of Jesus' warning to look forward rather than back; remembering the past is an opportunity for thanksgiving, humility, and a fresh leading of the Spirit, as well as a fresh commitment to Jesus in the midst of changing contexts and strategies.[43] Kraybill's enduring exhortation for patience and willingness to adapt to a new context helped to sustain the early Mennonite work in Somalia.

The community loyalty of Mennonites informed their sense of calling to mission, but also allowed the deepest values and commitments of their tradition to be transmitted into a new cultural setting. Surely some of the strengths of the Mennonite ecclesiology, in which call and discernment was a communal phenomenon, are lost when calling is

---

39. Wesselhoeft, interview.
40. Beachy, interview.
41. Leaman, interview.
42. Elizabeth and Ken Nissley, interview by author, Lancaster, PA, March 19, 2013.
43. Kraybill, "Prologue," 11–12.

individualized. Is it possible in our present era for someone like Orie Miller, on behalf of a mission board or other body, authoritatively to connect the particular gifts of people with a particular need?

Women on the Margins

The work in Somalia did not render the Mennonites on the mission field immune from the issues on the forefront at home in North America. The changes within the Lancaster Conference impacted the mission policy abroad. One important shift, especially as it was experienced by the single missionary women, involved the patriarchal assumptions and practices both at home and abroad. Fae Miller recalls, "As the mission personnel grew, all the men were married and had to be ordained. And they were in charge of the stations, and the work. They wrote reports. They made the decisions. They often did not ask for or consider the needs and opinions of the single workers. Things did change as time went on."[44] Furthermore, in the case of married couples the assignment was given to the husband, and the wife ascertained her involvements along the way.[45]

One important vehicle of the patriarchal system was the fact that only men could serve on the mission council. The irony of this decision was that the women, especially the single women who had built the closest relationships with Somali neighbors, were frequently the ones with the most insight into a given situation. Says Bertha Beachy, "Because I was powerless, Somalis told me many things that they would never have told the men."[46] Miller observed that the Somalis saw a woman as less threatening than a man, and they would therefore come to their homes and share their views openly in ways they would not with the mission council. When Miller was later admitted onto the council, one of the Somalis members told her, "When we discuss things on this council, you always agree with the Somalis."[47]

Beachy insisted that she be included on the all-male council, even declaring that she would not return to Somalia if the change was not made. Eventually the EMM board voted for a change in the bylaws that permitted women to serve on the board and the mission council. Beachy

---

44. Miller, interview.
45. Nissley, interview.
46. Beachy, interview.
47. Miller, interview.

met with the council only once before the mission was expelled from the country, but change had come.[48] The patriarchy of the early period, however, did not disappear in the years that followed. Three decades later, Bonnie Bergey returned from her work in Somalia to discover that some churches were supportive of her quasi-pastoral role for the fellowship of Somali believers and risking her life as an MCC and EMM representative in a war zone, but were not receptive to her giving the sermon on a Sunday morning because she was a woman. There were many supportive congregations in the Lancaster Conference and elsewhere, but this made the experiences of exclusion no less incongruent and hurtful.[49]

The role of women was a disputed social norm imported from the Lancaster Conference in the early years of the mission's work in Somalia. At times the rigidity of the rules implemented by the home constituency made little sense or even hindered the witness of Mennonites in Somalia. Yet this is not a problem of a different era and place; it is a timeless challenge for those in mission to remove rather than place obstacles against encountering Jesus. And when that mission includes peacemaking, the challenge is no less: How can followers of Jesus present the deliverance and grace offered by the teachings of Jesus, an ethic to which they are not always faithful themselves, without inadvertently allowing their own cultural trappings to make peacemaking more difficult?

Core Convictions

One important factor in forming the character of individuals and communities is the convictions that are held as basic to their identity and calling in the world. The basic assumptions about the mission of the church, drawn from Scripture and shaped through Anabaptist history, were fundamental to the Mennonite work in Somalia. Within the dimension of basic convictions, two variables are particularly pertinent to a Mennonite theology of mission and peacemaking: convictions about how Christlikeness affects the way one views violence and forgiveness; and the path of discipleship as a costly commitment. The Mennonites found creative ways to live out these convictions in the difficult circumstances presented by life in Somalia. The transforming initiatives commanded by Jesus in the Sermon on the Mount brought positive outcomes and restored

48. Beachy, "My Pilgrimage," 210.
49. Bonnie Bergey, interview by author, Alexandria, VA, April 29, 2013.

relationships out of seemingly intractable problems. And the recognition that discipleship is a costly path gave meaning to the suffering endured by both Western and Somali Christians.

Chester K. Lehman, a professor at EMC who influenced and taught many early Mennonite missionaries, provides a good description of the basic Mennonite convictions regarding the mission of the church. Jesus continues to exercise lordship through all who follow him, are healed and redeemed like the Centurion, the Canaanite woman, and demoniac, and go on to tell others about him. The call to discipleship is dangerous, like sheep among wolves, and Jesus himself faced the cross as the path to a new covenant. It is also a narrow way, but surprising people like tax collectors and prostitutes enter. Jesus calls a church into being, and the apostolic task is to minister to it. The disciples relate to Jesus as stewards to a master, as personal responsibility is entrusted to us like the talents in the parable. The Great Commission is coupled with Jesus' lordship over a growing body of believers to build the church through the presence of the Holy Spirit, who leads to discernment in difficult situations. Lehman saw God's hand at work in calling the Mission Board of the Lancaster Conference to continue the work of mission started by Christ.[50]

Christ and Violence

The years in which Mennonites first established their work in Somalia, the 1950s and 1960s, were a relatively stable period. The democratically elected government experienced a successful transition of power. Tension and violence between clans was low. In this early period, therefore, conflict took different forms than the later violent outbreaks along clan and party lines. Nevertheless, the Mennonite missionaries were faced with the challenge of applying their convictions about violence, forged in the Reformation and in Europe and refined in the relative quiet of the New World, in a new context that did not share their Christian commitments or cultural assumptions. The conflicts of culture, religion, and even between and among mission organizations demanded a firm commitment to seeking a Christlike response in creative ways.

Although not articulated in those terms, much of the way in which the missionaries sought to emulate Jesus was modeled after the transforming initiatives of the Sermon on the Mount. Jesus' triadic teachings,

---

50. Lehman, "Jesus Christ," 13–22.

consisting of the traditional righteousness, the vicious cycles of sin, and initiatives that transform the situation, are concrete practices that emphasize not the negative prohibitions but the way of deliverance as a means of grace.[51]

One of the fundamental practices for Mennonites as guests in the Somali culture, in obedience to Jesus' exhortation in Matthew 7:5, is to be quick to acknowledge one's mistakes and to apologize, humbly seeking forgiveness. The result, in most cases, is that a potentially volatile and even litigious situation turns out to be a catalyst for greater cross-cultural understanding. Fae Miller relates one instance in which sincere apologies diffused a potentially disastrous situation. During a mission meeting with some Somali believers in Mogadishu, one young mission worker kicked off his flip flops and propped up his feet on the chair in front of him, where they touched a Somali man. The Somali was a Christian, but the incident was so deeply insulting that he was ready to fight, go to court, or take any necessary measures to rectify the injustice. Horrified, the young missionary was so profusely apologetic that his anguish was clear to his Somali brother, who realized that it was a mistake and that no disrespect was intended. Attempts to explain away or defend the insulting action could have caused a problem in Somali-Mission relationships. But sincere, profound apology diffused the situation and preserved dignity.[52]

Misunderstandings abound in a cross-cultural context. Ken Nissley found the night guard sleeping on the job on several occasions. One night Nissley nudged him with his foot to awaken him. The next morning the guard was at the door with his spear. Through a translator he declared that he was so offended that he and Nissley were going to fight to the death, right there in the street. Nissley apologized and tried to explain the cultural reasons behind his faux pas. After about half an hour of discussion, the man was satisfied and walked away. He continued as the night guard, and there was never any more trouble between them. In another incident, the windmill at the school was broken, so the Nissleys were forced to keep water in barrels for three months. The water became somewhat stale, so they boiled it before serving it to the students. The students were upset about the water, and a group of about forty approached the Nissleys' house with rocks in hand. When Ken learned what the problem was, he explained that the water was safe. When the students

---

51. Stassen and Gushee, *Kingdom Ethics*, 131–43.
52. Miller, interview.

insisted that they were being treated as second-class people, Ken took a cup, dipped it in the barrel, and drank it without boiling it. In both instances, the Nissleys realized that only a respectful, non-confrontational response could diffuse the situation. Elizabeth observes, "It didn't work to go head on head; you had to find another way through it. Sometimes there was no textbook answer, so we tried to demonstrate that we take them seriously, we're not putting them down, and we're not treating them as inferior. Injuring Somali pride is the unpardonable sin."[53]

When Carl Wesselhoeft discovered that some of the Somali teachers in the Mahaddei school were using the drug *qat* on the campus during their breaks, he told them that it was not allowed. The teachers were offended, and were even more incensed when some students heard about the incident. The teachers threatened to strike unless they received an apology in front of the students. Cultural worlds were colliding; the social significance of *qat* in Somali society met the Western value of a drug-free educational environment. So the next morning Wesselhoeft apologized in front of the students, but also made it clear that there could not be any *qat* on campus.[54] Once again an apology helped to diffuse a heated conflict.

The habits of cultural sensitivity and humility had to be learned and cultivated in order to take initiatives that could transform conflict. Adjacent to the Mahaddei school lay a series of graves, little mounds of earth covered with weeds. As the Mennonite teachers discussed how to improve the school grounds, someone suggested that they level the mounds discreetly during the night. Having learned about the Somali respect for graves, Wesselhoeft firmly objected to that idea. Instead they built a star out of stones over the graves, representing the Somali star, a respectful initiative that both beautified the school and was greatly appreciated by the Somalis.[55]

In other cases, even instances of false accusations could be transformed by an attitude of humility that seeks to make peace with the adversary while still on the way (in obedience to Jesus' words in Matthew 5:25). One such instance is the murder trial of Mennonite doctor Gerald Miller. Without admitting that Miller was at fault in the death of a patient, the mission agreed to pay compensation in the equivalent of

---

53. Nissley, interview.

54. Wesselhoeft, interview.

55. Ibid.

one hundred camels. As a result of this humble attitude and the relationships the mission had cultivated, the family of the deceased man chose to forego payment in favor of reconciliation.[56]

Fae Miller notes that one cannot be fully prepared for every situation that requires humility rather than retaliation in kind, but that the Holy Spirit provides the right words to say (Mark 13:11). Miller had one such experience when she was called into court in Mahaddei. The richest man in the town, whom she knew because his family would often come to the clinic for medicine, sat smugly in the courtroom, ready to bring a lawsuit against Mennonite Mission. Miller's rendition of the story is worth quoting at length:

> They said that the complaint of this man had just occurred the evening before. I knew what he was talking about. The herd-boys were just returning with all the village cows, and were delighted to see the compound gate open enough to allow the cows to enter. Then the boys would hide behind the "thorn-fence" surrounding our compound. They just loved to see us chasing the cows! But anyway they must have reported this. So this biggest fattest cow, I couldn't chase it, it was eating the flowers where we'd watered the grass and so on, and here was this big stick. Well, she moved. I didn't think I did any harm to her, but the man said that he's going to sue the Mennonite Mission because she has a little scratch and she might get blood poisoning and die. So what do you say, what do you do? Just off the cuff, I said, "No, the mission had nothing to do with this." I said, "I hit her, if you want to sue somebody, sue me." Ooh! That changed the story! These policemen then got after him, saying, "Here she is taking care of our people, and you're trying to make trouble for her." And they just piled in on him, and I didn't have to say another thing. I went back to the clinic. And of course he kept on bringing his family. Nothing happened to that old cow. But you see, I could have said something that would have brought the mission into it, and there would have been a long angry story. I often felt when faced with new or difficult situations, that at the moment I needed it, God's Spirit would give me unthought-of impromptu responses.[57]

The attempt to avoid litigation for the sake of making peace extended to cases in which accusations would have been possible. Bertha Beachy

56. Miller and Wagner, *Hundred Camels*.
57. Miller, interview.

notes that a significant way in which Mennonite convictions about peace were lived out was in the refusal to sue or demand punishment when they knew people were breaking into their houses and stealing things, both in Somalia and Kenya. Says Beachy, "We always believed doing things peacefully was the better way than to demand that people be punished according to what they had done."[58]

How did Somalis respond to the Mennonite convictions on peace? Mary Gehman recalls that the early days were much more politically peaceful than under Siad Barre. But interpersonal fights broke out at the boarding school from time to time, and the male teachers had to figure out how to deal with them. Gehman felt a certain level of freedom to incorporate peacemaking skills into the curriculum, especially when she was able to write her own syllabus for a government-initiated course on civic morality.[59]

The peace witness was even more powerful when it could be taught directly from Scripture. Young men like Ahmed Haile loved to come and discuss theology with the mission workers, asking them how peace applied to the current situation, the wars that were happening, and the actions of the United States. Wilbert Lind did his best to respond with practical peace teachings from the Gospels, and he became a much-loved Bible teacher.[60] One of Lind's students, who had become a Christian, worked on the police force. The police were commanded to evict squatters out of a certain area. The officer told them to open fire, and the young man refused. He later told Lind, "I couldn't do it, I just couldn't do it!" So he was held accountable for his insubordination, paying a price for his commitment to the peace of Christ.[61]

For the Somalis who came to faith in Christ, peace had both an internal and an external dimension. Glen Roth, who served as a history and English teacher at the school in Johar over the time it was nationalized, recalls a young man named Jama who approached him because he had a restless spirit. Compelled by Jesus' invitation "I am the gate" (John 10:7), Jama encountered Christ in a dream and finally found peace. When he got into a fight later, he was distressed because he knew this behavior did not match the peace he had found in Christ. Roth assured Jama that

58. Beachy, interview.
59. Gehman, interview.
60. Miller, interview.
61. Lind, interview.

discipleship is an ongoing journey in which his failures would not separate him from God. Faith is centered on Christ rather than bounded, but it is a centeredness that makes a difference whether one fights or not.[62]

The Mennonite commitment to peace, of which the Somalis were well aware, was one reason that some Somali believers who related to Sudan Interior Mission (SIM) chose to become Mennonites.[63] The two mission organizations sometimes diverged in their approaches, as when EMM decided to allow the teaching of Islam in their schools, while SIM closed theirs down. Good communication, humility, and willingness to work with people who had different perspectives and goals was vital, especially because the Somalis were observing the way in which missionaries related to one another. Fae Miller recounts that when disagreements within and between missions arose, she would hear from Somalis what others were saying or doing. She learned that the best thing she could do was simply to say, "There's no greater thing than to forgive each other."[64] Whether in conflicts involving Somalis or North American Mennonites, the willingness to seek peace, to forgive and to seek forgiveness, modeled after Jesus' transforming initiatives in the Sermon on the Mount, could turn destructive situations into opportunities to build Christlike character.

Most importantly, some Somalis testify that Mennonites were intentional in living out their convictions about following Jesus more than they were in describing them. Abdul-Cadir Wursame, one of the first Somali believers, recalls encountering Mennonite missionaries serving in Mogadishu in the early 1960s. "To him the Mennonites seemed to be a unique community of believers blessed with the virtues of humility, love, compassion, gentleness and meekness. In their humility and meekness, he saw Christ."[65]

At an international level Mennonites also brought a unique peacemaking gift to Somalia. The tension with neighboring Ethiopia would occasionally escalate into violence. Mennonites found themselves with a foot in both camps. As the Meserete Kristos Church, the Mennonite church in Ethiopia, moved toward autonomy from the Mennonite Mission, the question of military service arose. "No Ethiopian citizen dared

---

62. Glen Roth, interview by author, Lancaster, PA, February 4, 2013.
63. Wesselhoeft, interview.
64. Miller, interview.
65. Checole and Asefa, "Mennonite Churches," 199.

think in terms of not defending the motherland—with the Italian occupation still fresh in memories and the constant threat of Somalis to Ethiopia's eastern border."[66] The tension was particularly acute in the city of Dire Dawa, where many Somalis live, as war with Somalia approached in the late 1970s.[67] Mennonite Mission lived in both worlds, interacting with people at enmity with one another. They were uniquely placed to urge believers and others in both contexts to imitate God in loving all peoples.

Costly Discipleship

In Luke 14:25–35, Jesus warns his followers that becoming a disciple is costly, and may require the loss of relationships, comfort, and even one's life. The idea that the path of discipleship is a costly commitment became a stark reality for Mennonite missionaries in Somalia. Jesus' words are proven true to an even greater degree in the suffering and death of Somalis who came to faith, a number known only by God. Because so few Somali believers remain alive following the violence of persecution and civil war, their memory lives on in part within the missionaries who knew them.

From the beginning of Mennonite work in Somalia it was recognized as a harsh climate in a number of ways. Several missionaries suffered through the death of their children, and others through physical assault. A motorcycle accident killed the mission builder. The tension between the Islamic community and government and the Christian minority led to restrictions on religious activity, the loss of property, expulsion from the country, and the persecution of Somali Christians.[68]

As a decade of quiet work in health and education won the trust of Somalis, a small body of believers developed. In 1962 pressure mounted against Christians when several zealous young Somali believers distributed Christian literature in front of a mosque. Although this incident was unrelated to the work of the Mennonite Mission, the Somali government shut down most of the mission activities in March. When the schools reopened in July, Merlin Grove was fatally stabbed by a fanatical mullah while registering students. At the trial of the assassin, Omar Eby writes,

---

66. Hege, *Beyond Our Prayers*, 137.
67. Ibid., 177.
68. Eby, *Whisper in a Dry Land*, 173.

"Harold Stauffer explained that the mission would not press charges, but that even in this experience the mission wanted to express love and forgiveness. The surprised judge paused for a moment, swallowed, and then asked if Mrs. Grove had prepared any statements. Harold simply said that the attitude he had just expressed was hers as well as that of the whole mission."[69]

The martyrdom of Merlin Grove proved to be a watershed moment for the mission's relationship to Somalis. Where there had been suspicion, stirred up in part by Egyptian radicals and Somalis who were antagonistic toward any Christian presence, there was now condolence and sympathy expressed from all directions.[70] After Dorothy Grove and the mission took an attitude of forgiveness, many young men requested Bible studies, both in Mogadishu and in Jamama. Years later, some Somalis met with Dorothy in Toronto and asked her forgiveness for her husband's death, on behalf of the Somali people.[71]

Three years after the murder, Ivan and Mary Ellen Leaman were in the town of Galkayo in response to a famine in the area. The name of the town means "drive out the infidel," and sometimes they heard people there refer to them as *gal*. Ivan recalls, "Someone in Galkayo told me, 'The man who killed your missionary was from this town.' So they connected us to Mennonite Mission and wanted to remind me. But there was a strong invitation from the local people, 'Mission should come to Galkayo. We need you and we need your schools.'"[72]

The missionary community suffered other losses as well. Builder David Miller died when his motorcycle collided with a camel in June 1964. Leota and Carl Wesselhoeft lost their five-week old daughter Evelyn to illness in January 1958. In March 1960, Peter John Leaman, son of Ivan and Mary Ellen, died of illness at six months. The Leamans reflect that when they were planning to go to Somalia they chose 1 Peter 5:10 as a theme verse because they sensed that their journey might require suffering. Three and a half weeks after their arrival in Somalia, Peter John died in a Mogadishu hospital after a short illness. Ivan says, "It was quite a test of our faith and commitment. One wonders how we got through that

---

69. Eby, "Triumph in Suffering," 128–29.
70. Miller, interview.
71. Leaman, interview.
72. Ibid.

.... It was very very difficult."[73] The news of the death reached the United States just as a large missions conference was taking place. Both sets of grandparents were in attendance and were informed first. Then the entire conference was told the news, and the Leaman family was lifted up in many prayers. It was a difficult beginning, but they took some comfort in the fact their second child Deborah was born only ten months later in Shirati, Tanzania. Despite the hardship they did not think seriously of returning home. Mary Ellen came to see the loss as one way in which she could identify with Somali women, who lose many babies due to a combination of lack of access to medical care, remoteness from clinics, and the effects of the widespread practice of female genital mutilation (FGM). Ivan's work made them well aware of these issues, which often required spontaneity and trust. He says, "We sensed in many ways that God was with us during these difficult medical decisions, helping me in situations where I did not have full training."[74]

In addition to the suffering experienced by the missionary community, the cost for Somalis who came to profess faith in Christ was immense. This was increasingly the case as the political situation degenerated through the 1970s and 1980s, but was also true in the earlier period as well. The Italian Roman Catholics focused on caring for the Italian community, not on converts from Islam. In 1898 a Swedish mission was established and operated in the southern region until 1935, when Italy invaded Ethiopia and the missionaries were expelled. About three hundred church members affiliated with that mission mostly became nominal Muslims after the missionaries left. Wilbert Lind commented on the fact that little of the four decades of work could be seen when they arrived, "This is not necessarily a discredit to the Swedish mission, but rather indicates mostly the difficulty of winning converts to Christ in a Muslim community. They tenaciously hold to their Muslim beliefs not because they are soul satisfying, but for fear their community might ostracize or harm them."[75]

Following the 1963 constitutional statute that made it unlawful to spread any religion other than Islam, a Somali Christian named Musa was imprisoned for undermining the religion of his country. In a story reminiscent of the biblical Joseph, Musa earned the favor of his fellow

---

73. Ibid.
74. Ibid.
75. Smoker and Eshleman, *God Led Us*, 18–19.

prisoners, including a former official who paid Musa's fine so that he could be released. Musa discovered that he had more freedom in prison to share his faith in Jesus with fellow prisoners and government officials who visited him than he had before being incarcerated.[76]

When the mission was forced to choose between teaching Islam in the schools and shutting them down as SIM did, part of the reasoning involved was that Christian faith can stand the test of being placed alongside other religions. According to Rhoda Lind, the mission's decision to continue operations made Somalis think about faith in a way they did not before. God used the circumstances of faith meeting faith to speak to people in dreams. One of the students had a dream in which he was asked by an angel to choose between a Qur'an and a Bible on a table. Another woman who lived out in the bush had a dream in which she heard a voice repeating, "Follow the Jesus way." When her husband, who was the night watchman for the Mennonite Mission, returned to his home in the village after a long period away, she told him about the dream. He responded that he already knows this Jesus.[77]

Some of Wilbert Lind's students would talk to him about becoming Christians. In the last session of one class he was able to tell them that each one had become a Christian. They started a Friday night prayer meeting, for which each person had to sign a paper saying that they had asked for Bible studies. But even in the midst of growth and movement, the path was always costly for Somali believers. After one young man became a believer, Rhoda recalls how they watched him walk down the road and thought, "What a costly decision for him. Who knows what it will require."[78] As the ensuing decades revealed, for many Somalis following Jesus required no less than their lives.

Discipleship in a Somali context had a material cost as well. When the schools and hospitals were nationalized in 1972, the mission had their buildings apprehended by the government without compensation. The ten mission personnel were forced off the compound, leaving possessions behind, and moved to different housing.[79] Ken Nissley went to Mogadishu to talk with the Ministry of Education, and there he learned that one of the teachers in the middle school, Ahmed Gedi, had been

---

76. Hostetler, *They Loved Their Enemies*, 63–65.
77. Lind, interview.
78. Ibid.
79. Beachy, interview.

named principal of the former Mennonite school. Gedi was studying at Lafoole Teacher Training College at the time, so Nissley drove his scooter out to the college and told him the news. Gedi jumped on the back of the little Vespa and they drove back to Mogadishu.[80]

When the Italians were forced to turn over their schools, they emptied the buildings of materials, such as typewriters. In contrast, after nationalization Nissley approached Gedi to offer the assistance of the mission in any way that was helpful. The collaborative precedent had been set years before with the decision to teach Islam in the schools. In that sense the Mennonite workers were not simply improvising, but continuing in the same posture. The cooperative rather than resistant attitude paid off in the long run. Gedi served as a liaison between the mission and the government on educational matters, seeing the mission personnel as "his people."[81] He facilitated the registration of the mission with the government, based on his trust they had built. Gedi later became Director General in the Ministry of Education, and in that role he initiated the invitation of Mennonite Mission back to Somalia after their expulsion.[82] Thus the educational collaboration between Somalis and Mennonites was further strengthened despite a decision on the part of the government that threatened the relationship.

A Communal Way of Seeing

The Mennonite emphasis on community was instrumental in the calling of missionaries as well as in formulating basic convictions about mission. But the Mennonite communal worldview also impacted the way in which they interacted with Somali conceptions of community, including clans, traditional Somali peacemaking, and Somali authority systems. Discovering connections between Somalis' and Mennonites' vastly different but sometimes overlapping views of communal life laid the foundation for authentic peacemaking in a Somali context. An open and truthful approach with Somali political authorities, in obedience to Jesus' teaching on truth-telling, was a demanding path but resulted in a relationship of trust.

---

80. Nissley, interview.
81. Roth, interview.
82. Nissley, interview.

Mennonites, the Clan System, and Traditional Somali Peacemaking

The Mennonite relationship to the Somali clan system is informed by a number of different considerations that are often in tension with one another. First, Mennonites can identify with the Somali emphasis on genealogy, themselves coming from a background that values family history and interconnectedness. Second, Mennonites are therefore skeptical of the modern nation state's tendency to atomize and individualize citizens at the expense of communal authority. In this sense Mennonites are sympathetic to the importance of clan and sub-clan to Somali identity. Third and most important, however, the Mennonite response to clans is informed by the vision derived from Galatians 3:28, in which family, ethnicity, or any other identity can never be more than secondary in light of God's creation of a new human community.

The tension between viewing clans in Somalia as positive or negative can be seen in the mission's early interactions with the clan system. In practice Mennonites neither defended nor opposed the clan system, but treated it as a given in Somali society and sought to bring out the best qualities of clan identity and Somali political traditions. Somalis themselves perceived the clans to be an egalitarian system, in contrast with the racially divided United States. During the racial and social turbulence of the 1960s, Somalis asked Ivan Leaman why America has such racial discrimination, and why he would ever want to return to a dangerous place with such widespread violence.[83]

One place in which the mission had some influence related to clans was in the schools. They made it clear to the students, who came from different clans, that there would be no space for any antagonism along clan lines.[84] The approach seemed to have worked; clan differences never became an issue in the schools, and the students formed relationships across clans that to this day allow them to refer to themselves as "the Somali Mennonites."[85] Although their clan identity was surely not forgotten, in the schools neither the teachers nor the students saw it as significant. In the dorm the male teachers were also able to model peacemaking to solve the problems that arose among the boys.

---

83. Leaman, interview.
84. Wesselhoeft, interview.
85. Gehman, interview.

Yet even during that time there was a sense that in the wider political world the role of clans was changing. When the revolution came, clannism was ostensibly buried. Actual symbolic burial ceremonies were held, and Somalis were prohibited from talking about clans. Due in part to the violence and hypocrisy of the Barre regime, however, the effort to create an overriding nationalism backfired; the effect was not greater cohesion but the undermining of traditional Somali hospitality that reached across clan lines. Barre publicly executed clan leaders, instigating a cycle of retaliation from which Somalia has never recovered. Mary Gehman's students recalled that in the past one could travel from north to south, from Hargeisa to Kismayo, simply by walking along and receiving hospitality along the way with no regard to clan. The violence and repression of dictatorship greatly damaged the possibility of inter-clan hospitality, as well as some of the traditional peacemaking mechanisms.[86]

Bertha Beachy's approach to addressing the inter-clan tension that arose was to bring together women and girls from different clans in a variety of activities, including classes and special trips. Beachy notes, "I found it very important that women from different clans were together. Some were used to being more in leadership, and controlling, but my presence could help so that there was a more open discussion." Women play a vital role in the practice of talking through conflicts that affect the whole family or whole village, especially as mediators who can be trusted by both sides. Beachy was aware that clans were not the only differences; her students from lower social classes, as well as the Bantu people, were often mistreated. Other Somalis therefore noticed when the Mennonites visited them and interacted with them. Says Beachy, "We always had to walk a fine line, just to be there and aware of where we were, and who we were connecting with, and how it would impact."[87]

Mennonites approached Somali culture as a whole with much the same ambivalence with which they regarded clan. The missionaries began to make ethnographic observations as soon as they arrived, combining them with what they were able to read about Somalia secondhand. For example, the importance of livestock as payment for bride-prices and compensation for blood-feuds was well documented before Mennonites arrived. The 1956 book *God Led Us to Somalia* adds these observations: "This preoccupation with quantity inevitably leads to excessive cattle

---

86. Ibid.
87. Beachy, interview.

population, overgrazing, and intertribal conflicts over the use of lands. ... They are quick to use weapons, and stabbing with a knife is a common means of retaliation for some real or imagined injustice."[88]

Despite this early negative assessment, on the ground Mennonites developed a much more positive understanding of traditional Somali peacemaking. Fae Miller notes that peace is embedded in Somali culture, as in other cultures of the region, through its prominence in the practice of greeting. As in Hebrew and Arabic, peace is offered as the first words spoken. Fairness and dignity are of great importance to most Somalis, which makes peacemaking practices regarding compensation both necessary and effective.[89]

Bertha Beachy discovered that here Amish background was a gift in relating to Somalis. She observes, "I could easily share what I believed, but I felt no need constantly to give a word of witness. It was more important to me that I showed respect and was open to learning... Because I came from an oral background, I never tired of Somali storytelling, proverbs, poetry, and conversation."[90]

As a medical doctor, Ivan Leaman had a unique opportunity to interact with certain elements of traditional Somali peacemaking and justice practices. The notion of compensation for wrongdoing was specific enough that in some cases it required the determination of an expert. Leaman was approached by one woman seeking a medical statement because part of her earlobe had been bitten off by another woman in a fight. He was asked to measure how much of the lobe she had lost in order to determine compensation by the court. Leaman saw it as a type of peacemaking in that proper compensation prevented the conflict from escalating into retaliation.[91]

Openness and Truthfulness: Interactions with Somali Authorities

Somalia represented a new challenge for Mennonites in the mid-twentieth century. Despite the welcome extended at various times by some Italian administrators, the UN, and eventually the Somali government,

88. Smoker and Eshleman, *God Led Us*, 9.
89. Miller, interview.
90. Beachy, "My Pilgrimage," 211.
91. Leaman, interview.

from the beginning certain obstacles were in place (for example, the British discouraged them from working in Somaliland).[92] It was the first time that Mennonites established work in an African context that was nearly entirely Muslim. The influence of conservative Muslim elements within Somali society as well as external influence from neighbors like Egypt and Saudi Arabia made Somalia a context in which the propagation of any faith other than Islam was severely restricted.

To be consistent in obeying Jesus' teaching in the Sermon on the Mount means applying his words on truth-telling in Matthew 5:37. Does Jesus' admonition to let yes be yes and no be no leave any room for deceitfulness, even to those who might be antagonistic? Reflecting on the East African context, Nathan Hege articulated some other pressing questions. Should Mennonites agree not to teach the gospel in a Muslim context because there is opposition? Is the Christian life enough to communicate the gospel? Is it better to be driven out as Jesus was? Jesus and Paul, however, were driven out because they were understood. Can Christians leave a context where Muslims think they are polytheists? Hege concludes that we always communicate two messages—the one we speak and the impression we convey—and we cannot disguise one or the other.[93]

The mission chose to prioritize the long-term presence of its personnel in Somalia, which in its estimation required the tenuous policy of openness with Somali authorities at a local and federal level. This decision was both pragmatic and ideological. Taking cues both from their Anabaptist forebears and from the work of Kenneth Cragg,[94] Mennonites believed that the gospel is unobtrusive, seasoning a society like salt rather than through political leverage. The practical effect of these convictions was a remarkable amount of space to live and work, and open doors in sometimes unexpected places. On a pragmatic level, as Chantal Logan later discovered in her work in Djibouti, speaking an overt religious language was an "advantage in building trust and relationships."[95] In interfaith bridge building, especially in a Muslim context, to be a hypocrite is even worse than to be an infidel. Openness meant not disguising that

---

92. Smoker and Eshleman, *God Led Us*, 19.
93. Hege, "Communicating the Message," 88–93.
94. Cragg, *Call of the Minaret*; and Cragg, *Christian and Other Religion*.
95. Logan, "Reflections," 62.

Mennonites were there as Christian missionaries, even if that meant opposition from certain elements.

The Mennonite approach of openness took shape on two levels: with local authorities such as village elders, and with political authorities related to the Somali government. In both arenas the mission attempted to maintain positive and respectful relationships that would allow them the maximum amount of freedom to follow their convictions and best impulses.

At a local level, Wilbert Lind worked to establish good relationships with the elders at Mahaddei from the very beginning. He met frequently with them to discuss the plans of the mission and other local affairs. At one site he was negotiating with thirty elders, who all came to agreement that Mennonite Mission would be welcome.[96] The relationship was not always smooth; the first negotiations to establish a mission station at Mahaddei provoked the ire of the more radical local sheikhs. They told Lind that they would rather die than see one single Somali become a Christian, and one man stated that he would sooner have his own son starve than become a Christian. They stated that if any missionary would be hurt it would not be their fault, and said that the Mennonites should leave the country unless they agreed never to proselytize. Lind responded that Somalia supported the UN Charter that guaranteed religious freedom. He pointed out that Muslims could proselytize among Christians in the US. He recounted his experiences as a conscientious objector in World War II and told them, "Somalis may inflict injury on me, but I will never retaliate because I love them through God."[97] According to Lind, these words of love helped to break down the hostility, and the whole group felt embarrassment about the extreme statements of a few.

The relationship was not without obstacles, but a commitment to partnership on both sides made it workable, including some key friendships with influential elders. Carl Wesselhoeft recalls, "The chief with whom we dealt was an older man, and had a lot of wisdom. Sometimes when there was something between the village and our mission, he would say, 'The tongue and the teeth are close together, and sometimes the teeth nip the tongue, but that is no reason why they should separate.' I appreciated that attitude—we have to coexist and coexist amicably."[98]

96. Miller, interview.
97. Shenk, "Mennonite Presence," 136.
98. Wesselhoeft, interview.

The mission had a fair-minded advocate in this chief, who was gifted in settling disputes and could be trusted not to take advantage of them. A Somali peacemaker with social influence was an invaluable person for the Mennonites to know.

The establishment of a modern democracy in Somalia mostly bypassed the elders, who play an important role in Somali society. This was a serious mistake because the politicians, who were often young and inexperienced, lacked the social power of the elders. They therefore had to seek other kinds of power apart from the traditional authority. It is uncertain to what extent the role of elder has survived the political turmoil of the last decades, and whether there are still people who are respected not because they have political power but because they have wisdom and experience in settling disputes.[99] The chemistry between the role of the elders and the role of the politicians that has been fostered in Somaliland has been somewhat undermined in Somalia, paving the way for the emergence of warlords.

Although the mission had considerable freedom in the operation of its schools, the local community had a sense of ownership and a keen interest in what took place there. In the early days the mission felt the students at Mahaddei should join in tasks like cleaning the dorms and sweeping the classrooms. In Somalia, however, students were placed on a pedestal, at least before the attempts to promote equal physical labor during the revolution. The village elders discussed this policy and sent representatives to inform the mission that this was not work for students and that other people should be assigned to do it. The Mennonites conceded in the clash of cultures. Elders and parents of students were involved in other ways as well, forming a committee to discuss fees and the naming of scholarships for the students with the most need. According to Mary Gehman, "They came periodically to check on things. Certain rumors went around, rumors of baptizing a whole bunch of kids, different things like that. We always tried to have contact with parents, and with the Ministry of Education, so that what we did was known, so that we were not hiding anything. And the same way with the village elders where we lived."[100]

At the urging of the mission, Carl Wesselhoeft earned a Masters Degree in elementary administration in 1962 in order to act as a liaison

---

99. Ibid.

100. Gehman, interview.

between the Mennonite schools and the government schools. His relationship with the Ministry of Education was a good one. At the end of one term the teachers were enjoying the relief of an empty campus after the usual turmoil from a school full of students when a land rover pulled in with police and the educational director from the Ministry of Education. He announced, "In Mogadishu there is a rumor that you are going to baptize six boys. I've come to prevent you from doing this." Wesselhoeft assured him that they would not think of doing something like that to children, explaining, "I cannot make anybody a Christian. That has to come from God himself. I don't even want to make anybody a Christian, because that persuasion has to come from God. God puts that into your heart." The official drove away satisfied, and the good relationship continued. He later invited Wesselhoeft to his home along with the Speaker of the Parliament, where they all shared a platter of goat meat and rice.[101]

Although the mission would not engage in practices like baptizing children, without a doubt their hopes and intentions were that a fellowship of Somali believers would emerge. The Somali notion of adulthood at age fifteen, the age at which one becomes accountable for one's own decisions, became an important boundary line. Baptisms were not done at the school, but there were secondary school students who were baptized, as well as older adults, when school was not in session. Some of these baptisms were performed by Elisha, a Somali Christian from Jamama. At one point at least 10 percent of the students were believers.[102]

To what extent could Mennonites be open about this aspect of their work? Openness did not require offering exhaustive information about every relationship with individual Somalis. Yet even in this sense there was a general policy of openness and truthfulness. One step that the mission took was to ask Somalis who requested Bible studies to sign a paper declaring that this was something they had requested. In this manner the mission could be straightforward about their activities even as they plausibly denied that they were propagating a faith other than Islam, in accordance with the 1963 constitutional statute.

The attempts to be both truthful and evangelistic did not go unopposed. One day the district commissioner summoned David Shenk and angrily accused him of breaking the law, pointing to the fact that students were becoming Christians. The room was full of people, and Shenk was

---

101. Wesselhoeft, interview.
102. David Shenk, interview by author, Denver, PA, February 12, 2013.

fearful that it could get out of hand. He asked to speak to the commissioner with just one witness, to which he complied and dismissed all the others. Shenk recalls,

> I told him, "This is the problem: years ago when I believed in Jesus the Messiah, the Spirit of God filled me with joy and love and peace, and I cannot destroy that gift. The students come occasionally and say we know there is a gift within you, and it has to do with your faith. And we want the same, we want to get in touch with Christian faith. Well, what can I do? Can the government prevent someone from believing if he wanted to? Can you, when God made all people free?" He agreed that we are free. So I said, "Well, what shall I do?" He said, "You're doing very well. Continue as you're doing. No further investigation."[103]

During his role as director of the mission, Shenk approached a government official to tell him how they were functioning with regard to the restriction on propagating Christian faith. The official responded, "No, you don't need to tell me. In fact, I don't want you to tell me. We know what you're doing. But just don't make a mistake." The use of the word "mistake" was likely in reference to the closing of the mission following an incident in which energetic Somali Christians handed out tracts outside the mosques. Shenk observes, "When one functions unobtrusively, it was amazing how much space there was. The authorities were not interested in looking for trouble."[104]

In some ways the simple piety of Mennonites endeared them to Somalis. During that time Somalis held Americans in high esteem, but their regard for the Americans known as Mennonites was even higher. A man named Mohamed, who helped some of the missionaries with cooking, once told them, "You're not Americans. Americans swear and drink." Wilbert Lind describes the cocktail parties they sometimes attended at the American embassy in this way: the Americans at one end of the table with the beer, and the Somalis and Mennonites at the other end with the ginger ale and Coke.[105]

The attempts to maintain close connections with Somali authorities extended beyond the local leaders to the federal government. The mission worked closely with both the Minister of Health and the Minister of

---

103. Ibid.
104. Ibid.
105. Lind, interview.

Education, particularly so that the latter would approve and accredit the certificates granted by the secondary school. The Minister of Education always signed the eighth grade diplomas and report cards. The Somali government felt a sense of ownership in the education that was occurring in the Mennonite schools.[106] The children of government officials attended the Mennonite schools, including Siad Barre's daughter.

In addition to maintaining an open relationship with the Somali government, it was important for the mission not to be perceived as meddling in Somali politics. As mentioned above, clan identity was not discussed openly in the Mennonite schools. In Mahaddei the Somali Youth League was prominent, but the hired teachers and students came from many different clans, and in one election some of them voted for the opposition. The Somali Youth League accused Carl Wesselhoeft of being an instigator. He appealed to the teachers and students, who attested his claim that he had never talked to anyone about how to vote. Nevertheless, he was reported to Mogadishu and was forced to leave the country for a month. The party officials in Mogadishu went even further and sought to close down the school in an attempt to intimidate the parents and teachers. While the mission strove to avoid party politics, neither did it tolerate political bullying at the expense of its students and the parents who had entrusted them with their children. The decision to keep the school open led to some tension for a time, but nothing that lingered.[107] This would have been impossible without the trust and support of the local community, students, and parents.

The political climate under General Barre was such that any perceived opposition was not tolerated. Even after Somalis had long tired of his regime, he succeeded in suppressing the opposition. Mary Gehman recalls, "People were scared about who they talked to. And there were times too that people didn't associate with us much. There was sort of the fear of what could happen."[108] Massive demonstrations of military power masked the regime's constant fear that it could be deposed just as it had done to the previous administration in the 1969 coup. In such an atmosphere anything secret is suspicious, because a lot of information is transferred in clandestine ways. Furthermore, there was an incident in which a missionary in a neighboring country was discovered to be a

---

106. Gehman, interview.
107. Wesselhoeft, interview.
108. Ibid.

spy. It was therefore in part a pragmatic decision for the mission not to engage in secret activities, for the safety of both the missionaries and the Somalis with whom they interacted. The operating assumption was that Somalis would see through attempts to hide anything. The decision was not always easy. For instance, at one point there was some disagreement within the mission about whether bribes should be paid to continue the operation of the bookstore in Mogadishu.[109] But the policy of openness with the Somali government built the necessary trust for a relationship to continue.

A transparent approach with Somali political authorities, in obedience to Jesus' teaching on truth-telling, was a challenging path yet eventually bore the fruit of trust, as we shall see. Finding links between Somalis' and Mennonites' vastly different but sometimes overlapping views of communal life laid the foundation for authentic peacemaking in a Somali context, including the elicitive method later articulated by John Paul Lederach and put into practice by Somali and Mennonite peacemakers.

Taking the Long View: Patience as a Way of Reasoning

Mennonites entered Somalia prepared to build long-term relationships of mutuality and service with Somalis. Stassen and Gushee describe the principles and virtues that inform the way one makes ethical decisions as the *way of reasoning*.[110] One of the primary variables for the way in which Mennonites reasoned was patience, by which I mean the willingness to serve without seeing the kind of fruit that might be expected in some other contexts, such as explosive church growth or institutionalized religious freedom. But patience also means the investment in relationships over long periods of time through the establishment of hospitals and schools, and the building of friendships with Somali people.

After several exploratory trips, Mennonite leaders and missionaries entered Somalia with no illusions about the difficulty of the work there. Somalia was a new situation for them because it was nearly completely Muslim. The wisdom of such a huge investment was not evident to all. J. Paul Sauder voiced some of the questions as they considered Somalia: "Would it be advisable to throw in men and dollars and tears and perhaps

---

109. Miller, interview.
110. Stassen and Gushee, *Kingdom Ethics*, 59.

graves in so hostile a land where a seasoned Christian observer said, 'You will do well to see ten Christians in twenty-five years'?"[111]

It was clear from the beginning that Somalia required a long view, in which the fruit that was to be expected was the relationships that could be built. Nevertheless, the missionaries saw a chance to participate in the transformation of the country. They noted the tension between progressive movements within society such as the Somali Youth League on the one hand, and the more conservative elements on the other, observing, "So Somalia is on the move, and new ideas are pushing for recognition in this ancient land. No doubt God has great purposes in Somalia for such a time as this, and has given the missionaries the privilege of having a share with Him in His mission of love to a land which has known much violence and bloodshed." [112] The biggest challenge in this new context, however, was the "problem of patience in prayer and love."[113]

The emphasis on patient presence was cultivated by leaders like Orie Miller and Paul Kraybill. Mary Ellen Leaman recalls, "In Somalia that was the only way that we could serve. We had to go in through service institutions, and were not allowed to propagate, even though there was a freedom of religion clause in that initial ten-year period under the trusteeship with the Italians."[114] Overt evangelism was never an option in Somalia.

The missionary task was therefore to serve and to build friendships. Fae Miller saw this happening in her own life as she left on furlough in 1957. She sat crying on the Alitalia plane, and when the flight attendant asked if she was afraid to fly, he was shocked when she responded that she was crying because she was leaving Somalia. She had formed a strong bond with her Somali friends.[115] This sort of bond can only be established with a long view that truly values friendship.

Sometimes this bond was formed through God's direct intervention. Carl Wesselhoeft recounts that when they first moved to Mahaddei they had some trouble connecting with the community. About a month into their stay there was a knock on the door in the early morning. Three men they had never met stood at the door, one with a spear and two

---

111. Sauder, "Witness Grows," 62.
112. Smoker and Eshleman, *God Led Us*, 11.
113. Ibid., 15.
114. Leaman, interview.
115. Miller, interview.

with sticks, demanding a midwife. Leota was not a midwife, but had been present for home births in the US, and the Somalis insisted. So after a prayer Leota went with the men, while Carl stayed with the children. He anxiously looked out toward the village as the dawn approached, and several hours later he saw Leota returning with one Somali girl on each side, one carrying a basket of eggs and one carrying a chicken. She had successfully delivered the tenth child for a woman. The incident completely transformed the Wesselhoefts' relationship with the community. Carl recalls, "She delivered about a dozen other children. She went to the village every day to visit the mothers, and then the mothers would come to visit us. We couldn't have arranged that; the Lord arranged it for us."[116]

Language learning was an important way in which patience of long-term friendships played out. While Leota Wesselhoeft learned the Somali language from the women, Carl learned it by sitting out with the watchmen in the evenings. When Bertha Beachy moved to the town of Jamama, she did not have the same language resources as she had in Mogadishu. She therefore went into the village every day to visit any home—sometimes three in one morning—into which she was invited to drink tea. Beachy observes, "It was the best thing I could have done, because they knew me when I wanted to start the school, and they trusted me."[117]

Friendships were built in the homes of both Somalis and Mennonites. The home was a primary hub for hospitality, and if a home was open visitors would come frequently. During a brief stay in Galkayo the Leamans lived in a home just like all the others in the village, stone houses with rooms around a courtyard. Women passed by and stopped in to talk, sometimes bringing cakes. Ivan ponders, "As I reflected on that experience, I thought maybe the mission did miss an opportunity because there was an opening in Galkayo truly to live among the people. It was different than living in Johar."[118] Even if there was a missed opportunity for a longer-term presence in Galkayo, in other towns like Jamama, Johar, and Mahaddei the missionaries had many good relationships with neighbors.

Even though patient presence required willingness to serve without seeing much fruit beyond the blessing of friendships, there was still evidence that God was working through the missionaries. Several small fellowships of believers emerged and continued through the 1960s, despite

---

116. Wesselhoeft, interview.
117. Beachy, interview.
118. Leaman, interview.

the political agitation against the foreign Christian presence that came to a head in 1962.[119] David Shenk notes that from 1959 to 1962 "the questions had shifted from an emphasis on the how of evangelism to how to cope with success in evangelism; the stance had moved inexorably from aggressive witness to the witness of patience and suffering."[120] Kenneth Cragg expresses well the Mennonite way of reasoning in Somalia: "The Church that seeks to proclaim his ethic and to demonstrate his compassion may expect to see these make their way outside its membership. Moreover, we can never say at what point the human soul awakes to the knowledge of Christ. . . . If no Christians as such are gathered, this has not disarmed or immobilized the Gospel's criticism of human lives. . . . The leaven works silently and unseen. There is nothing barren about the Gospel wherever it is active."[121]

Shenk concludes that "the development of an embryonic church in Somalia has been remarkable. From a sociological perspective it would seem to have been an unlikely occurrence."[122] The Mennonite Mission, with reasoning informed by patience, took joy in these small developments even as they struggled in the challenging climate of Somalia. The Mennonite work was infused with a sense that only a long-term commitment would have any lasting impact among Somalis. Patience required building deep friendships, a foundation God could use to establish the church. The same patience required in sowing the seeds of the church is the chief characteristic of peacemaking. This is because to challenge the necessity of violence is to live with a different perception of time. In the words of Stanley Hauerwas, "The movement that Jesus begins is constituted by people who believe that they have all the time in the world, made possible by God's patience, to challenge the world's impatient violence by cross and resurrection."[123]

Mennonites in the 1950s and 1960s generally did not employ the language related to peacemaking that has gained greater currency in recent decades, such as nonviolent direct action, justice, and just peacemaking. They were more inclined to use the term nonresistance to describe the

---

119. Ibid.
120. Shenk, "Mennonite Presence," 174.
121. Cragg, *Call of the Minaret*, 323–24.
122. Shenk, "Mennonite Presence," 398.
123. Hauerwas, *Matthew*, 37.

Christian response to violence and injustice. Nonetheless, the peace witness of the Mennonite church profoundly informed their approach in Somalia. But Somalia was changing, and Mennonites were changing too. Would a constructive peacemaking vocation emerge?

2

Shifting Sand

*Religious, Political,
and Interfaith Changes,
1976–1990*

THE MENNONITE MISSIONARIES IN the 1950s and 1960s did not explicitly identify Christian mission with peacemaking. By 1987, however, the philosophy of mission of the Eastern Mennonite Board in Somalia begins: "We believe that as Christians we bear God's message of reconciliation. This includes a life of love, service, acts of justice, peacemaking, relieving of suffering, and verbal witness to the person of Jesus Christ."[1]

What made these developments in the direction of justice and peacemaking possible? The Mennonite mission in Somalia began with an emphasis on establishing Christian fellowships and service through education and medical work. In the decades following, however, the emphasis shifted to include justice and peacemaking. I posit that three factors facilitated this shift. First, broader theological patterns in the Mennonite church paid increased attention to activism over quietism and justice over nonresistance. Second, the changing political context in Somalia made questions of justice and peace more acute. Finally, the attitude toward and descriptions of Islam on the part of Mennonites became more positive as deeper interfaith relationships developed, setting the stage for a more elicitive approach to peacemaking.

---

1. "Statement of Eastern Mennonite Board," memorandum, July 19, 1987.

Religious Shift: Nonresistance to Peacemaking

The Mennonite history of pacifism lends itself to an approach that seeks to eliminate the use of and need for violent force. Recent developments in Anabaptist theology have also emphasized concern for justice that leads to wholeness rather than simply a lack of violent conflict. This approach takes a particular view of social change that confronts and rectifies injustice without resorting to violence. One of the basic claims of this view is that God has equipped each community with power to move toward wholeness, which provides the rationale for eliciting peacemaking resources from within rather than externally.

The nature of these changes within the Mennonite church has been labeled in various ways, including a move from sect to denomination, quietism to activism, separatism to engagement, apolitical church life to political involvement, premodern to postmodern, and conservative to liberal theology and politics.[2] Here I consider two aspects of this shift: the sociological move from quietism to activism, and the theological move from nonresistance to just peacemaking.

Sociological Changes: From Quietism to Activism

Ervin Stutzman analyzes the transformation in one hundred years of Mennonite peace rhetoric. Until the beginning of the nineteenth century Mennonites mostly maintained their historical anti-war attitude by closely guarding the boundaries around issues of nonconformity. In the last four decades Mennonites have changed drastically, moving toward the middle of society from the edges, and look more like the surrounding society than ever before.[3]

Sociologists Leo Driedger and Donald Kraybill trace the changes in Mennonite political involvement over the latter half of the twentieth century. Modernity's blend of rationalization, technological advances, and individualization chipped away at the traditional Mennonite emphasis on nonresistance. Five dimensions of change in the twentieth century contributed to this shift. First, Mennonites became more urban, diverse in their occupations, mobile, educated, and transitory in their social ties. Second, the Mennonite church moved from a sectarian to a

---

2. Stutzman, *Nonresistance to Justice*, 17.
3. Ibid., 45–46.

denominational model, relaxing congregational discipline and taking on a more bureaucratic mode. Third, psychological changes began to emphasize self-esteem, assertiveness, and global consciousness over self-denial, meekness, and local affairs. Fourth, a theological shift took attention from a two-kingdom theology to a posture of civic moral responsibility. And finally, Mennonites began to see themselves as citizens rather than simply subjects, fostering a more proactive stance on government and political involvement.[4]

World War II jolted Mennonites out of their rural shelters and into higher education, new professions, and service in different parts of the world. The political upheaval of the Civil Rights Movement, assassinations, and the Vietnam War helped to turn a mostly quietist people into activists. Martin Luther King Jr.'s movement was undeniably nonviolent but some Mennonites were wary of his impatience.[5] Much more attention was given to the concept of the Christian witness to the state as articulated by John Howard Yoder.[6] As Mennonites started to find a middle ground of cooperation, they "could now under the shadow of the lordship of Christ noisily implore the nation to repeal the laws of racial discrimination and to stop the bombing in Vietnam." Furthermore, although few Mennonites were directly involved in the Civil Rights Movement, it "cracked the credibility of nonresistance and led some to consider—even endorse—civil disobedience on behalf of *others* who were the victims of unjust laws."[7] Involvement in other parts of the world also contributed to the shift. For example, MCC volunteers in Palestine initially focused not on speaking out against injustice but on showing God's love through the binding up of wounds. In 1967, however, they initiated a reconciliation ministry that sought to "make a contribution to peace and reconciliation in some slightly more direct way than is simply done through our development and education programs."[8]

Despite the activist turn, a majority of Mennonites still cooperate with taxes and registering for selective service, and some have regarded the ideological turn toward activism as a mistake. The concern is that the influence of modern ways of thinking would signal the end of biblical

---

4. Driedger and Kraybill, *Mennonite Peacemaking*, 47.
5. Ibid., 14, 109–10.
6. Yoder, *Christian Witness to the State*.
7. Driedger and Kraybill, *Mennonite Peacemaking*, 123, 127.
8. Weaver and Weaver, *Salt & Sign*, 79–84.

peace commitments. Has this been the case? The evidence indicates that the answer is both yes and no.

Some elements of modernity, most significantly individualism and materialism, did have a negative impact on peace commitments, especially through the influences of fundamentalism and increased political participation. What happens to peace convictions as a group enters the cultural mainstream as Mennonites did in the latter half of the twentieth century? One effect, as Stutzman points out, is that "As Mennonites have assimilated with their society, they have also become more closely aligned with the nation's political polarities."[9] Identifying with either the right or the left in politics can distract from Christ and often deeply divides the church. There are also historical warning signs about the impact of cultural assimilation on peace commitments themselves. In Europe, Mennonites lost their pacifist beliefs as they gained social respectability. In the United States, the Church of the Brethren also lost once-strong peace convictions. According to Driedger and Kraybill, "The historical evidence is clear: peace convictions are fragile. Stubbornly held by one generation, even to the point of death, they can quickly shatter with the winds of nationalism and social success in the next."[10] A prime example of this transformation is the Assemblies of God, which was officially a pacifist denomination for the first fifty years of its existence but lost its peace commitments in favor of nationalism and political and economic success.[11]

On the other hand, some sociological forces related to modernity served to cultivate more activist peacemaking attitudes among Mennonites. These included denominational pressure, pastoral leadership in peacemaking, the reformulation of Mennonite identity and Anabaptist belief, and Mennonite college attendance.[12] David Weaver-Zercher notes, "The growing public-mindedness of Anabaptist scholars is evident at many turns, perhaps most impressively in the realm of peacebuilding

---

9. Stutzman, *Nonresistance to Justice*, 280.

10. Driedger and Kraybill, *Mennonite Peacemaking*, 37, 238.

11. Paul Alexander describes this change as a "growing identification with the evangelical church world and secular culture. Between 1941 and 1967, the Assemblies of God made great strides toward entrenching itself into the religious and political establishments. They also moved away from appealing to Christ's example alone for their model" (*Peace to War*, 240–41).

12. Driedger and Kraybill, *Mennonite Peacemaking*, 238.

and conflict transformation."[13] Weaver-Zercher cites the graduate program in conflict transformation at EMU and Victim-Offender Reconciliation Programs (VORP) as examples of Mennonite contributions to the broader academy. In this sense the structural forces of modernity, such as urbanization and education, did not erode but rather encouraged the peacemaking impulse.

The way in which peacemaking is practiced is diverse. Driedger and Kraybill identify six arenas for peacemaking in which Mennonites are involved: church communities, interpersonal networks, vocational opportunities, church agencies, voluntary organizations, and government agencies. Models for peacemaking engagement include the just peacemaking approach of Glen Stassen, Ted Koontz, and Duane Friesen, in which there is some overlap of goals between the church and the political community; activist nonviolence such as the Christian Peacemaker Teams; and political liberation approaches that emphasize delivering justice, such as that of Hugo Zorrilla.[14]

Jonathan Rudy, who worked with MCC in Hargeisa during the turbulent years of the late 1980s, suggests that activist peacemaking impulses were in the DNA of Mennonites before they had language to articulate it. The alternatives to war structures put in place by MCC, such as the PAX program, impacted the generation that followed. Rudy writes, "I joined MCC because of hearing the stories of the PAX generation and other missionaries, and found myself in a conflicted situation that my quietist upbringing did not service. I needed an activist spirituality from the likes of Thomas Merton and King to answer the questions Somalia threw at me."[15]

Rudy describes his first experiment with nonviolent direct action, before he was even aware of the concept. In direct contravention of international law, President Barre's army trucks rolled into the refugee camp near Hargeisa and began conscripting young men for the military at gunpoint. Young men were running away, jumping over and hiding behind the fence in front of Rudy's house. Rather than hunkering down until the chaos had passed, he went out in full view to observe the proceedings, hoping that his status as a Westerner might mitigate the situation and that he could give a firsthand report to UNHCR. Rudy notes, "The 1980s

---

13. Weaver-Zercher, "Scholarship in Anabaptist Tradition," 112.
14. Driedger and Kraybill, *Mennonite Peacemaking*, 249–61.
15. Jonathan Rudy, e-mail message to author, August 29, 2015.

was when all was this was forming in the Mennonite psyche. So I didn't think about it in terms of peacemaking. I did that nonviolent tactic, and it was twenty-five years later when I reflected on it and realize that it all fits. How did I know that that is something to be done? I'm not sure. I didn't know that you do that en masse and it really blunts violence."[16]

Theological Changes: From Nonresistance to Just Peacemaking

In the twentieth century certain modes of speech came in and out of fashion among Mennonites, including the doctrine of nonresistance, the principles of peace, biblical nonresistance, the way of love, witness to the state, nonviolent resistance, peace and justice, peacemaking, and peacebuilding.[17] In some cases the spectrum in Mennonite separatism and activism reflected the work of a particular scholar, such as Guy F. Hershberger's "nonresistance," Yoder's "witness to the state," J. Lawrence Burkholder's "social responsibility," and Gordon Kaufman's "radical love."[18]

The early Anabaptist writers affirmed that the office of government is ordained by God to order human society. The state is therefore an expression both of God's wrath and of God's grace. Since the necessity of civil order is consistently upheld, rebellion against the state is not an option in the minds of the early Anabaptist theologians.[19] In response to the necessity of the state, Anabaptists developed a two-kingdom theology that continued until the twentieth century.

The early twentieth century strained the Mennonite communal ethos through industrialization and new voices challenging traditional views, including theological liberalism and fundamentalism. Furthermore, premillenialist theology disputed the goal of peace itself, since it contended that the Kingdom of God must come through war. The traditional doctrine of biblical nonresistance challenged both theological liberals and fundamentalists, who marginalized the practical relevance of the Sermon on the Mount for different reasons. One influential theological broker during this period was Guy Hershberger, who guided Mennonites through the rift between historic nonresistance and activist

---

16. Jonathan Rudy, interview by author, Manheim, PA, April 15, 2013.
17. Driedger and Kraybill, *Mennonite Peacemaking*, 62.
18. Yoder et al., *Development to a Different Drummer*, 256.
19. Detweiler, *Mennonite Statements on Peace*, 12–13.

pacifism during World War II with his theological work in *War, Peace, and Nonresistance*. Hershberger argued for a "single moral law," undermining the two-kingdom theology and setting the stage for later theological developments.[20]

An important theological step for Mennonites was the "Anabaptist Vision" defined by Harold S. Bender. This vision moved from the earlier defensive stance of maintaining boundaries toward a positive calling to make disciples. It was not a set of doctrines but a mandate, bringing a new sense of identity and self-worth for Mennonites. In the 1950s Mennonites continued in keeping with two-kingdom theology, carefully limiting church member participation in the affairs of the state.[21]

Along with the sociological changes noted above, the theological rhetoric of nonresistance has been largely abandoned in favor of other peace-related terms like peacebuilding, and just peacemaking, with figures like King and Gandhi as positive models for transformation. Some resisted these changes, fearing that they were too closely aligned with liberal politics and would undermine the church's long-held stance on violence. On the other side, "Advocates for change argued that peacemaking through nonviolent resistance was a valid expression of the historic stance of the early Anabaptists, in keeping with the essence of being Mennonite."[22] Both agreed that peace was the goal, but not on how it should be defined or realized.

One of the most significant vehicles for institutional change was the formation of the Peace Section of MCC in 1942. There were also ecumenical influences at play, arising out of dialogues between the historic peace churches. New theological formulations framed Jesus politically, but also tied peacemaking with the Anabaptist past. The language of peace and justice came in vogue in the 1970s, with new entities like the Christian Peacemaker Teams and Mennonite Conciliation Services. The peace and justice mode of speech was attractive because it was activist, holistic, and systemic. It also fit the Mennonite consciousness because it was pluralistic and irenic in the sense of employing positive language rather than negative.[23]

---

20. Driedger and Kraybill, *Mennonite Peacemaking*, 71–79, 157.
21. Stutzman, *Nonresistance to Justice*, 101, 124.
22. Ibid., 47–48.
23. Driedger and Kraybill, *Mennonite Peacemaking*, 142–58.

The new approach in Mennonite ethics taken by people like Yoder, Hershberger, and Paul Peachey emphasized the lordship of Christ over all the powers, not just over the church. There was a new confidence that the church had something to say to the state, and a fresh application of Anabaptist history to a modern context. The era of the Vietnam War found Mennonites with unprecedented companions in the anti-war movement. In rubbing shoulders with campus protests amid a general questioning of government authority, Mennonites broadened their associations with a variety of pacifists. Stutzman writes, "Mennonites were engaged in a search for a comprehensive peace ideology that could legitimize a more activist stance than had been possible under two-kingdom theology. Along the way, Mennonites came upon social justice as a fitting 'middle axiom' that could serve as a foundation for peace ethics in both church and state."[24]

It is worthwhile to note two influential books that both reflected and contributed to the shift in Mennonite ethics. The first is Yoder's *The Politics of Jesus*,[25] which framed Jesus' ethic of nonviolence in political and social terms that could be translated to a modern context. Jesus' messianic ethic has implications for responding to economic questions, warfare, power and leadership, and other issues that in a modern context are called social justice. The church is a community that practices this messianic ethic of servanthood and nonviolence, which serves as a witness and a model for other political communities, as Yoder later developed further.[26] While Yoder failed profoundly to live up to the ethic he articulated, his reading of Jesus was deeply influential on Mennonites and others.

The second is Ronald Sider's *Rich Christians in an Age of Hunger*,[27] which developed a biblical case for economic and social justice. Challenging the tendency of wealthy Western Christians to focus only on individual salvation, Sider called for attention to systemic dimensions of sin and injustice, including economic disparity, poverty, and violence. The book's influence went well beyond Mennonite circles, selling 350,000 copies and earning a spot on *Christianity Today*'s list of the one hundred most influential books in religion in the twentieth century.

---

24. Stutzman, *Nonresistance to Justice*, 180–81.
25. Yoder, *Politics of Jesus*.
26. Yoder, *Body Politics*.
27. Sider, *Rich Christians*.

With the disappearance of many aspects of nonconformity, nonresistance had to become more active to fill the role of setting the church apart from society. In the search for a unique Mennonite identity, many were drawn to peacemaking as a distinctive. The formation of the Mennonite Church USA in 2002 produced a new confession of faith and a proliferation of peace-related documents.[28] The events of September 11, 2001 also served as a catalyst for Mennonites to seek alternatives to the War on Terrorism.

Alain Epp Weaver and Sonia Weaver observe that as Mennonites developed more activist peace theologies, "their interest increased in exporting Mennonite peace convictions to others. If Mennonites believed that the life of peace was central to the Gospel, progressives reasoned, then the church must seek to present and embody that peace."[29] These two underlying convictions—that peace is integral to the gospel and that peacemaking is compelling to those who do not necessarily share pacifist Christian commitments—contributed to the most recent turn toward language of peacemaking, peacebuilding, and just peacemaking.

Political Shift: Somalia's Failing Government

A second factor contributing to the shift in emphasis by the Mennonites in Somalia was the changing political situation. Despite a successful transition of power between the first and second presidents, Somalia's political problems became clear in the years following independence in 1960. A 1969 military coup brought General Siad Barre to power and left the future of the mission unclear. The new revolutionary government assured the Mennonite Mission that it was welcome to continue contributing to education, health, and development endeavors in Somalia. But in 1972 the government's move toward scientific socialism resulted in the nationalization of all the mission's schools and medical facilities. All mission workers and administrators were dismissed from the country by 1974, with the exception of eight teachers. When the remaining mission teachers were asked to leave in 1976, some relocated to Kenya to continue to work with Somalis there.[30]

---

28. Stutzman, *Nonresistance to Justice*, 238–39.
29. Weaver and Weaver, *Salt & Sign*, 77.
30. Wenger, *People in Mission*, 63–64.

Barre's war over the Ogaden region, with full-scale fighting from 1977 to 1980, displaced 1.3 million Somalis, placing 750,000 in refugee camps. MCC sent its first aid workers in 1980 in response to this crisis. The following year the Barre government performed an about-face on the presence of Westerners, asking Mennonite teachers to return to Somalia. In December 1981 the first EMM teachers returned to Mogadishu on government assignments. More teachers followed in 1983, and from 1986–89 EMM and MCC placed workers in Mogadishu, Merka, Kismayu, and South Juba in the areas of community development, agriculture, and nutrition.

The Ogaden War drained the economy and cost thousands of Somali lives, seriously damaging Barre's popularity. Barre's attempts to suppress internal resistance throughout the 1980s further alienated influential clans and solidified resistance parties. Supported by Ethiopia, in 1981 Somalis of the Isaaq clan in what was to become Somaliland formed the Somali National Movement (SNM) in order to oppose Barre. After losing control of the region, Barre ordered his air force to bomb the northern city of Hargeisa, massacring tens of thousands.

By 1989, the political situation had deteriorated into such extensive inter-clan violence that MCC withdrew all its workers from Somalia. MCC's International Conciliation Service joined a Somali peace committee to promote dialogue between the clans in September 1989. EMM continued to place teachers in Mogadishu, but withdrew all its workers in December 1990 after the civil war aimed at ousting President Barre reached Mogadishu. Barre was deposed in January 1991, and control of the capital fell along clan lines. EMM again sent two nurses to Mogadishu in the fall of 1992, but was forced to evacuate them the following summer due to the fighting in the city.

Another contributing factor in Somalia's changes over this period was the ecological transformation of the region. Somalis' commitment to the traditional nomadic lifestyle is strained by the overpopulation of recent decades, both of people and of animals. Harold Miller, MCC Administrator for East Africa in the 1980s, described the situation in this way following a visit to Somalia in 1991: "In 'good' years there is sufficient, if not plenty, for all. In 'normal' years there is the disaster of dying cattle, hungry people and strained politics.... Drawing impressions from the whole of the Sahelian zone it would seem that the pastoral way of life is entering a period of accelerated change."[31] The ecological crises Somalia faced in the 1980s were a precursor to the recurring famines following the collapse of the government, especially in 1992 and 2011.

A Changing Missionary Experience

The early Mennonite missionary experience was significantly different from the period beginning in the mid-1970s. Independence was a jubilant time for Somalia. Some of the missionaries were present in the central square of Mogadishu at midnight on July 1, 1960, as the country celebrated. The new national flag was raised and speeches were delivered from the balcony Mussolini had built a generation earlier in anticipation of winning World War II.[32] It was a time of heady optimism. Somalis came to the different NGOs to see what they had to offer them. They wanted to join the developments of the English-speaking world. There were plans to build airplanes, print money, and all sorts of endeavors.[33] Nationalist fervor transcended clan divisions, and Somalis seemed embarrassed to admit that clans even existed.[34] The missionaries shared the enthusiasm of the Somalis, attending the demonstrations and parades. Around the time of the lunar landings Carl Wesselhoeft helped the people in Mahaddei in the construction of a car shaped like a rocket, which was proudly driven around town. The Arabic sign the Somalis placed above a school in Mahaddei expressed well the sentiment of the time: "Knowledge builds a house, and ignorance breaks it down."[35]

According to Rhoda Lind, peacemaking was not prominent in the minds of the missionaries because there was little violent conflict in the country at the time. They talked about peace with God, but not in terms of reconciling parties in conflict. Problems were resolved by the chief men of the village, not through the clashing of the warlords who later rose to power. She observes that when missionaries who served in later decades talk about their Somalia experiences, it sounds strange to her. "I often wish that they would know how Somalia was," she says. "It was just nice.

---

31. Harold F. Miller to Mennonite Central Committee Nairobi, "Impressions from Somalia Visit," memorandum, November 1981.
32. Gehman, interview.
33. Lind, interview.
34. Eby, interview.
35. Wesselhoeft, interview.

We just loved it. The people were nice, and they loved Americans."[36] Fae Miller agrees that it was a good time to be in Somalia as US Americans, in part because of historical factors. Somalis knew that Americans did not participate in the widespread slave trade on the east coast of Africa. Just as importantly, they knew that the United States was not an overtly colonial power in Africa, as European countries had been. Miller says, "In my first term, the US embassy put out calendars that could be given to anybody, and each month stated, 'All Men are Brothers.' The Somalis loved this! They thought highly of America. We were blessed in that sense."[37]

The political situation varied somewhat by region. When Ivan Leaman worked further north in Galkayo he treated many more gunshot wounds from the fights between the clans. But in the Lower Juba area, where the Jamama hospital was located, there was little violence and there were few guns.[38] Those who lived in Mogadishu in the 1960s witnessed the rapid expansion of the city, from about 100,000 to half a million people in a few years. As a result of such expansive growth, massive slums developed on the outskirts of the city.[39]

Despite these massive demographic changes, the decade following independence was politically stable. The first president completed his seven-year term and there was a peaceful transition to a new president in 1967, the first such transition of its kind in Africa. But just two years later the second president was killed by his own bodyguard, and within days General Barre took power in a bloodless coup.

Barre's regime proved capable of impacting Somali society with little delay. For example, he changed the established driving side on the road in one day. He also implemented a successful campaign that gave Somalia one of the highest literacy rates in Africa.[40] But Barre's friendliness toward the West soon shifted toward the Soviet Union. The establishment of scientific socialism in the early 1970s changed the situation for the mission drastically, especially when their buildings were confiscated and their personnel were gradually dismissed from the country. The first to go were the missionaries with religious degrees. David Shenk asked the Ministry of Education to be transferred to teach English or history at

---

36. Lind, interview.
37. Miller, interview.
38. Leaman, interview.
39. Miller, interview.
40. Nissley, interview.

Lafoole College. He was told that a Marxist society has no use for a PhD in religious studies. Shenk considered "attempting to see the President himself—I think our mission had the stature at that time—and asking him, 'Are you sure this is God's will? Because I'm here by God's appointment, he called me to come here. And I'm not all sure this is God's will for me to go. Are you sure?' That's what I would have asked him." Instead, he asked Somali friends who were connected to the Ministry what they thought about asking for reconsideration. They consulted a friend who was in charge of security files and told Shenk, "We have looked over your file, and there is no point in asking for an extension. The files say that you are an Israeli agent, so just quietly move on." Shenk laughs as he speculates how something so absurd could appear in an official file.[41]

During the time of nationalization Ken Nissley had to register the Mennonite Mission with the government. Ahmed Gedi assisted with the paperwork and ensured that the registration was approved at the Ministry of Education. He confided in Nissley that Somali government officials were much more concerned about the increasing influence of conservative Islamic groups, such as the growing number of Saudi-funded Wahhabi schools, than they were about the Mennonites, whom they already knew.[42]

By the 1980s, when the mission was invited by the government to return, the country was rapidly deteriorating. There was more thievery and crime. People were put in prison or even executed if they opposed Barre.[43] For the missionaries the situation changed as government favor swung from the West to the Soviet Union and back again. For Somali Christians, there was no such pendulum swing, only an increase in persecution.[44] In the years following the mid-1970s the situation became steadily more perilous for Somali Christians. The 1980s was already a period in which confessing Christ usually meant social alienation, persecution, and even death. But the worst was still to come; in the lawlessness following the collapse of the government, many Somali believers lost their lives at the hands of militant Islamists.

When Barbara and Lamar Witmer arrived in Mogadishu in 1986, they expected that Barre would last only a matter of months. Mogadishu

---

41. Shenk, interview.
42. Nissley, interview.
43. Gehman, interview.
44. Nissley, interview.

had a police state atmosphere that was remarkably different from the open aura of Kenya. People did not dare to mention anything negative about Siad Barre, at the risk of being overheard. In the next few years the paranoia of the government became more pronounced. When the Witmers first arrived it was common for Barre to drive through the town in a long motorcade, with soldiers compelling people to line the streets and cheer for him as his car rushed past. By the time they left in 1988, no one was allowed to get within a block of where he was driving, for fear of an assassination attempt. When the war started in Hargeisa there was much more air traffic, but people were surreally hushed, as if nothing was happening. The only exception was one Somali Christian who visited the Witmers regularly, sitting as far away from the window as possible and talking quietly about the war.[45]

The Witmers named their son Isaac, which in Somali (Isaaq) happens to be the name of the majority clan in Somaliland. Some of their friends in Mogadishu would not say his name, and even gave him other names, not because they were necessarily opposed to Isaaq people but because clan politics were such a sensitive subject. The flow of information and news was heavily monitored by the Barre regime. At one point MCC worker Deb Luper sent a description of what was happening in the north through Barbara Witmer, who smuggled the report in her son's diaper bag.[46]

Ivan and Mary Ellen Leaman, after leaving Somalia in 1969, returned for a visit in 1987. They returned again in August 1990 with a team of medical personnel to develop a community health center in the Lower Juba area, but were forced to leave along with all the Mennonite workers at the end of that year as the country destabilized. According to Ivan, "Somalis were afraid of what was happening, because there was a general sense of the civil war which was coming closer to Mogadishu, and might reach Mogadishu. There was violence, vehicles were being stolen on the street by shooting the owner of the vehicle. It was a time of fear, it was a different Somalia. In 1990 it had changed completely."[47] Another change at that time was that the professional women in the hospitals were wearing more conservative Islamic dress. A Catholic Sister who worked closely with the mission's medical involvements observed the growing

45. Barbara and Lamar Witmer, interview by author, Lancaster, PA, March 9, 2013.

46. Ibid.

47. Leaman, interview.

influence of conservative Islam, which combined with the general sense of fear as a premonition of what was to come. Ivan adds, "I think I never experienced fear like I did then. My fear had to do a lot with if one of our missionaries was hurt, would I be capable of knowing what to do?"[48]

Mennonites who arrived in Somalia in the late 1980s were well aware that the Barre regime was on its way out. In July 1989 Marian Hostetler heard shots from her home; a mob had emerged from a Friday service and partially destroyed a mission building that had a cross in the window. Hostetler recalls, "Things went downhill from there."[49] Bonnie Bergey arrived in Mogadishu to teach English in summer 1990, knowing that the government could be overthrown at any time. She was there for only four months before she and the EMM team left for the annual retreat in Kenya, and never returned to Somalia as a team. During those four months, the atmosphere was tense. On the way to Friday church services at the cathedral, the missionaries faced taunting and rock-throwing, travelling in two vehicles in case one got held up. Bergey just missed a carjacking at a bread shop because she decided at the last minute to go home instead of stopping. Another time she was driving alone and was held up by a man seeking a bribe. These incidents were a foreshadowing of what was to come. At the same time, Bergey's short experience of Mogadishu with an element of normalcy helped her to picture an alternative to the chaos she later witnessed. Even during her trips to Somalia immediately following the collapse of the government in January 1991, she saw a somewhat functioning society and markets. People sometimes thanked her for not being afraid to walk on the street with Somalis.[50]

The stability that Mennonites had experienced in Somalia in earlier decades deteriorated in the late 1980s, impacting every area of life in Somalia. The reality that medical and educational work became difficult, and the situation for Christians more dangerous, demanded that Mennonites pay more attention to peacemaking work.

Mennonite Central Committee Involvement

One development in the Mennonite involvement in Somalia in the 1980s held promise both as a new partnership and as a source of methodological

48. Ibid.
49. Marian Hostetler, e-mail message to author, April 6, 2013.
50. Bergey, interview.

tension: the beginning of Mennonite Central Committee's work in Somalia.

MCC, a relief and development agency of the Mennonite and Brethren in Christ churches, was formed in 1920 for the purpose of providing material aid to fellow Mennonites in the Soviet Union. Today MCC works in about fifty countries around the world, placing personnel in education, relief, and development positions. Additionally, MCC's Peace Office provides a forum for Mennonite peace concerns, linking peacemaking practitioners with Mennonites working at a more academic theological level. The Peace Office focuses on both international and domestic conflict situations, such as the Somali group *Ergada* and victim/offender conciliation.[51]

Mennonite theology emphasizes ongoing community discernment for the task of discipleship. The mode of discipleship in the realm of political engagement, however, has found expression in a spectrum of Mennonite separatism and activism. The genius of MCC is that it represents Anabaptists (including Amish) on all points of the spectrum, drawing them together under the motto *In the name of Christ*. The point of connection for all these groups is the centrality of service to Christian discipleship.[52]

What practical shape did the commitment to Christian service take in response to the needs of Somalia? For the first twenty-seven years of Mennonite involvement in Somalia, the educational, medical, and church formation work of EMM had been the focus. The shifting political situation, however, gave fresh urgency to conciliation and relief efforts.

Barre's devastating attempt to reclaim the Ogaden region from Ethiopia beginning in 1977 displaced over a million Somalis. MCC sent its first aid workers in 1980 in response to this crisis. By June 1980 the Horn of Africa had 1.7 million displaced persons due to unresolved conflicts. MCC brought food, water, sanitation, medicine, and craft programs in an attempt to meet the needs created by these crises. In early 1982 MCC chartered an entire cargo ship for a delivery of corn during a food shortage, providing $400,000 to cover shipping and trucking costs to transport the mountains of grain to twenty-seven refugee camps.[53]

---

51. Miller, "Peace Church Experience."
52. Yoder et al, *Development to a Different Drummer*, 256, 307.
53. Eby, *Fifty Years, Fifty Stories*, 69–72.

Harold Miller, MCC Administrator for East Africa, visited Somalia in 1981 in order to evaluate the MCC presence in the camps and the possibilities for long-term involvement in the areas of peacebuilding and development. There he encountered enormous residual goodwill, built up from the decades of EMM service, around the name Mennonite, even as MCC operated under the legal umbrella of the UNHCR. Miller wrote, "Just how much potential for 'development' will be realized from that goodwill will depend to a great extent on the continuing stability of the situation in Somalia."[54]

The dominant post-pastoral development models were based on irrigation projects, which were often funded by relief agencies and launched in times of climatic stress. Miller relates that the MCC involvement in agricultural and irrigation projects in the refugee camps was met with some resistance from Somali officials, suggesting that support for new forms of agriculture in a traditionally nomadic society was a somewhat delicate political issue. MCC's shared concern with UNHCR, however, was to take a longer-term perspective in which Somalis could become more self-reliant rather than depending upon aid. This vision served as the basis for nurturing irrigation and farming projects as peacemaking endeavors. The MCC presence in the camps was therefore concerned with identifying what kind of combination of irrigation, animal husbandry, and forestry could sustain food security in Somalia. Miller links MCC's involvements in these considerations explicitly to the longer-term peace process: "Some portion of the violence experienced in Somalia today has to do with pressure of ecological degradation brought on by misplaced and unviable development models."[55]

Agricultural and irrigation projects were not the only areas of MCC involvement during this period. From 1986–89 MCC placed workers in Mogadishu, Merka, Kismayu, and South Juba in the areas of community development, agriculture, and nutrition. In Mogadishu, Ed Rissler supervised the preparation of booklets for Somali farmers, along with Somali colleagues.[56] Responding to the centrality of camels to the Somali way of life, and also as a window into Somali and Kenyan commonalities, MCC sponsored a camel-breeding project. MCC worker Peter Grill drew upon

---

54. Harold F. Miller to Mennonite Central Committee Nairobi, "Impressions from Somalia Visit," memorandum, November 1981.

55. Ibid.

56. Eby, *Fifty Years, Fifty Stories*, 74–75.

the camel-breeding expertise of Ahmed Haile's father.[57] Grill eventually published a book with the UN on camel care.[58]

By 1989, however, the political situation had deteriorated into such extensive inter-clan violence that MCC withdrew all its workers from Somalia. The chain of events stemming from the murder of the Catholic bishop of Mogadishu on July 9 triggered a backlash against Christians and expatriates generally. Barre reacted to widespread anti-government demonstrations with indiscriminate gunfire, killing several hundred Somalis. MCC workers reported seeing women and children among the dead. Increasing lawlessness, including car hijackings, further clarified the decision to withdraw MCC personnel.[59]

Eastleigh Fellowship Center

Following the Somali government's dismissal of the EMM personnel from the country in the mid-1970s, several of the staff moved to Nairobi in order to maintain relationships with Somali people living there. Thousands of Somalis reside in the neighborhood of Eastleigh, an area of Nairobi nicknamed "Little Mogadishu." In 1980 the Mennonite missionaries founded the Eastleigh Fellowship Center, whose purpose was to provide a Christian witness in the city and a venue for interfaith dialogue between the faith communities. The center offers a positive alternative to the tense relationship between Somalis and Kenyans, including recreation programs for low-income families. Roughly one thousand people pass through the doors of the Eastleigh Fellowship Center weekly. In this sense, although the temporary dismissal from Somalia caused the Mennonite missionaries to grieve deeply, the changing political situation opened up new opportunities for relationships with Somalis in the diaspora.

When David and Grace Shenk left Somalia in 1973 they requested to the mission board that they be allowed to continue in East Africa. They moved to Nairobi, where David got a teaching job at Kenyatta University.

---

57. Harold Miller, e-mail message to author, February 7, 2013.
58. Grill, *Introducing the Camel*.
59. Eric Olfert to Mennonite Central Committee Nairobi, "Trip Report with MCC Somalia Team in Nairobi," memorandum, July 30, 1989.

There he met Badru Kateregga, with whom he eventually wrote the influential book *A Muslim and a Christian in Dialogue*.[60]

Intent on continuing relationships with Somalis, the Shenks drove up and down the streets of Eastleigh. They found an apartment building with an adjacent vacant lot, both of which they were able to rent and eventually purchase in order to develop a full-blown community center. The Shenks then invited other believers to join them as a visible community of Christian faith, forming an interracial, international group that included Kenyans, North Americans, and Somali believers (including Ahmed Haile, who eventually gave leadership to the fellowship). The intention of the community center was to have an identity by which they were known by the local people, not just a collection of individuals serving but a concrete presence that could be identified as a Christian center in the midst of a Muslim neighborhood. They began to ask people in the neighborhood in what ways they could serve the community. The request they always received was for a quiet place to study, so on the roof of one of the apartments they constructed a makeshift reading room for students. The center held weekend events planned for youth in the community. So the Eastleigh Fellowship Center became known as a Christian center that ministered in specific ways: scholarships for low-income high school students, a reading room and library, and sports programs and weightlifting. The basketball team, the Menno-Knights, gained prominence in the Kenyan league.[61]

The center was also meant to be a community of reconciliation between Muslims and Christians. The leaders at the center and of the surrounding Muslim centers would invite each other to services, evening meals, and special religious celebrations in order to build relationships. Out of the center the Eastleigh team developed the *People of God* correspondence course for Muslims. Directly across the street from the center was a Sufi Qadiriyah mosque. The team took the course materials to the Muslim leadership for evaluation. David Shenk says, "We didn't want to do anything secretly, we wanted to function with integrity. We asked for counsel if we were saying anything in this course that was offensive, that wasn't true. And that was trust-building, just to critique and comment on it."[62] An Ahmadiyah sheikh who stood across the street and

---

60. Kateregga and Shenk, *Muslim and Christian in Dialogue*.
61. Shenk, interview.
62. Ibid.

preached against the Christian faith turned out to be the most helpful and constructive critic of all.

The Eastleigh team joined with Canadian Baptists and the African Christian Church and Schools, an independent church growth movement, to help to replicate the center in the Northeastern Province of Kenya. They cultivated a positive relationship with a Salihiyah center in that region, and the Salihiyah sheikh advised them in developing a Christian *tariqa* in the town of Garissa. The two centers, in Eastleigh and Garissa, were known as communities of peace and reconciliation. Emulating the spiritual leadership in the Sufi orders, Ron Ward led the Garissa *tariqa* and David Shenk was the spiritual leader of the Eastleigh community. Most importantly, the spiritual authority of the Christian *tariqa* stemmed from the founder, Jesus himself, and the fullness of the Holy Spirit. Spirituality served as a strong point of connection to the Sufi movement, including language of being filled with the Spirit and prayers for healing in the name of Jesus. The portrayal of Jesus in the book of Hebrews as the appointed intercessor to God and the source of abundant *baraka* (blessings) played a basic role in the theology of the Christian *tariqa*.[63]

The Eastleigh Fellowship Center functioned as an important way for Mennonites to continue relationships with Somalis when they could no longer live in Somalia. The social services offered by the center provided a natural environment for interaction.[64] The Christian fellowship there served as a model of a community of reconciliation in a Somali Muslim neighborhood.

Interfaith Shift: Islam as Peacemaking Partner

The attitude toward and descriptions of Islam on the part of Mennonites became more positive as deeper interfaith relationships developed. When Mennonites first arrived in Somalia, their account of Islam reflected the broader sentiments of Western Christians at the time. Few resources existed to prepare them to relate to Muslims. As the relationships with Somali Muslims grew in the schools, hospitals, and everyday interactions, so too did the awareness that a deeper engagement of Islam was required. Facilitated by increased global interaction with Muslims

---

63. Ibid.
64. Kamau, "Eastleigh Fellowship Center."

around the world, Mennonite scholarship responded to this challenge in fruitful ways.

The centrality of Islam to the identity of most Somalis was a reality with which Mennonites were forced to grapple from the very beginning. Somalis often present themselves as a homogeneous group with one language, culture, and religion, making Islam an assumed component of Somali identity. Many Somali Muslims claim their religious origins to be Saudi Arabian, but more likely Islam was introduced to Somalia from Ethiopia. The assertions of homogeneity are likewise exaggerated, as evidenced by the historic presence of a few Christian clans and the Bantu minority groups in the south.[65]

Early Attitudes toward Islam

Islam was mostly unfamiliar to many Christians in the West in mid-twentieth century. When they entered Somalia in 1953, therefore, Mennonites were not behind the times in knowing little about the religion of the people among whom they were living. The groundswell of literature on Islam and Christianity had not yet occurred, leaving mission workers with few options for learning about Islam apart from their interactions with Muslims in situ.

The lack of a precedent of positive interactions between Muslims and Christians left Lancaster County Mennonites with few resources for combating any negative messages about Islam they received. Hence the attitude of the mission toward Islam in the early years tended to be more critical and less nuanced than in subsequent years. For example, a 1953 newsletter describes Somali Muslims as "sheep having a false shepherd. With a false conception of God, they have no real conception of sin." They are "fanatical," and are quickly aroused to bloodshed by politics and any threat to their faith.[66] An editorial from the same year approvingly quotes veteran missionary to Muslims Samuel Zwemer (1867–1952) in asserting that the Bible is like dynamite that can "blast the rock of Islam to pieces."[67]

Another example is the portrayal of Islam in the 1956 Mennonite-produced booklet *God Led Us to Somalia*, which demonstrates some

65. Logan, "Reflections," 57–61.
66. "Glimpses of Somalia."
67. "Somalia Update."

significant knowledge about the faith but does not temper its harsh criticisms or nuance the historical accounts on the spread of Islam. The authors note the similarities between Islam and Christianity in the relationship of the names Allah and Elohim, the influence of Judaism and Christianity on Muhammad, and the shared content of the Qur'an and the Bible. The strong belief in God's transcendence, however, is not matched by Muslims' morality in life; followers of Islam spread their religion by looting, conquest, and bloody wars led by the Prophet against infidels. The authors state that Islam is one of the chief threats to the spread of Christianity in Africa, having spread rapidly over the last five centuries by slave traders and shopkeepers. Since the Qur'an is the only source of learning, the people are trapped in illiteracy, ignorance, and prejudice against education. Furthermore, "the ones who know least about it are the most fanatical Muslims."[68]

The authors strongly criticize the fatalism of Islam, linking the mantra *God wills it* to rampant divorce and polygamy, enslavement of women, and the moral corruption of children. They continue, "In Islam there are no duties of love to one's neighbor nor of honoring one's wife. A man is allowed to have four wives and as many concubines as he wants. Slavery is permitted. There is no racial discrimination within the Islam brotherhood, and this is very attractive to Africans, who often feel that there is discrimination by Christians. But Islam is an enemy of democracy because it cannot confer equal rights, religious liberty, equality, or fraternity to those who are not Muslims."[69]

The missionary problem in the lands of Islam, they conclude, is the problem of patience in prayer and love. Muslims are resistant to the gospel for three reasons: "the aggressive, militaristic nature of their religion," poor examples of Christian faith, and the lack of serious evangelistic undertaking in Muslim contexts.[70]

Any of these sweeping statements can and should be challenged by Christians who seek a respectful, honest, and sufficiently self-critical conversation with Muslims. Comparing the worst manifestations of Islam to the ideals of Christian faith is deeply unfair, especially in light of the ways Christian hegemony has been spread by violence as well.

---

68. Smoker and Eshleman, *God Led Us*, 13–14.
69. Ibid., 15.
70. Ibid., 15–17.

The adversarial tone of these passages, however, does not reflect the practices of the mission in the early period. This is especially clear in the mission's decision just ten years after their arrival, under counsel from the Somali believers and the permission of the Lancaster Conference Bishop Board, to allow the teaching of Islam in the mission schools. A more adversarial relationship to Islam would have caused the mission, like the other Protestant mission in the country, to shut down the schools instead.

From the earliest years, moreover, the Mennonite missionaries were beginning to sense the need for much deeper engagement. A young Omar Eby wrote as he departed for Somalia in 1957, "I was never in a Muslim mosque, nor have I knelt toward Mecca and listened to a Muslim pray, and I can't even quote passages from the Koran, but maybe I'll have to. Maybe I'll have to identify myself with the people in this way to understand them."[71] An attitude of humility and openness was beginning to challenge the preconceptions about Islam.

North American Mennonites in the 1950s and early 1960s were generally disconnected from both academic and grassroots association with Islam. The Mennonite Mission in Somalia was the first Mennonite initiative in a majority-Muslim context in Africa.[72] Little preparation was available for missionaries who were called out of their rural Mennonite communities to serve in Somalia. The Mennonite missionaries were therefore learning as they went, discovering the role that Islam played in the lives of their Somali friends.

The mission board told the first missionaries that they were looking for three qualities for workers in Somalia: overseas experience, linguistics training, and an Islamic studies background. Says Fae Miller, "Three of the four of us had experience overseas, but I was just graduating, so I was a novice. None of us had any training in Islam whatsoever; we were very naïve. And we didn't have linguistic training."[73] The ideals of the mission on paper for their personnel were lofty; in reality much of the missionaries' training happened on the ground.

Rhoda Lind recalls that the mission board did the best they could in preparing them, but that they were quite ignorant of Islam when they arrived. Wilbert had more familiarity with Islam and the Qur'an than

71. Eby, "Testimony."
72. Wesselhoeft, interview.
73. Miller, interview.

she did, and he had more discussions about faith with Somali men and his students than she did with Somali women.[74] The missionary women especially interacted with a more strictly popular form of Islam, because Somali women were less likely to be educated in relation to Islamic beliefs and the Qur'an.[75] Moreover, women did not go to the mosque with the men as they did in some other Muslim cultures. But even though the male missionaries could have gone to the mosque if they had wanted, this was not something in their consciousness.[76]

Mary Gehman agrees that there was little background training on Islam for the missionaries, in part because there was a much smaller pool of resources on the subject of Islam than in subsequent decades. She observed a more open and positive attitude toward Muslims as the mission developed relationships, especially around holidays like Ramadan and feast days, when the Mennonites would visit or be visited by Somalis. The mission board was ready to offer more direction; on one of her furloughs she attended a World Missions Institute at EMC, where she studied Islam. Gehman was also introduced to Kenneth Cragg's *Call of the Minaret* and the writings of Samuel Zwemer through her mission connections.[77]

Ivan and Mary Ellen Leaman were also encouraged to read some of the same materials on Islam, but were not offered any direct teaching about Islam before their arrival in Somalia in 1960. Cragg's description of the Christian role as the task of interpretation made an impact on the way the Leamans perceived the institutions of schools and hospitals as conduits for interpreting the life and person of Jesus Christ in a Muslim context. Even with minimal training in Islam there was sensitivity to Islamic sensibilities; when Ivan preached he refrained from referring to Jesus as the Son of God, finding other terms that would be better understood.[78]

Cragg himself addressed a conference on Christianity in the Middle East attended by some EMM missionaries in Eritrea, Ethiopia in April 1959. There Cragg exhorted them to begin with Muslim understandings and convictions rather than with external propositions. The paradigm

---

74. Lind, interview.
75. Beachy, interview.
76. Wesselhoeft, interview.
77. Gehman, interview.
78. Leaman, interview.

for engagement is Christ's incarnation, relating his message and work to human needs.[79]

One way in which the missionaries started to learn about Somali Islam was through the acquisition of Somali language. When Fae Miller began to teach a Bible class on Friday mornings for women from her English classes, she had a Somali friend help her translate *Marian's Big Book of Bible Stories* and a few songs. In pursuing the best translations of the simple stories and songs, she learned Somali religious language. Thirty years later, she met some of her students in Mogadishu; they now had government and university positions, and they still remembered the songs and stories from the 1950s Friday Bible studies.[80]

Elizabeth and Ken Nissley did not receive any training in Islam, beyond their own reading of I. M. Lewis, before serving with EMM.[81] Neither did Glen and Annabelle Roth before going to Somalia in 1972. In Glen's words, however, the Somali people were prepared, and the missionaries embraced the "mystery of unpreparedness." They did not criticize Islam or the Qur'an. When a student asked Glen whether he thought Mohammed was a prophet, Glen responded that Mohammed was "prophetic." This answer seemed to satisfy the student.[82]

Without much formal preparation to interact with Islam and little time for extracurricular activities, Mennonite missionaries discovered Somali Islam through their everyday interactions with Muslim colleagues, friends, and students in the schools and hospitals. They were therefore mostly interacting with the popular Islam of the people, not with the religious institutions and leaders.

The recommendation of the mission council to accept the teaching of Islam in the Mennonite schools was approved by the Lancaster Conference bishops. It was not an easy decision on the part of the missionaries and the mission board in the US. In the end the decision was both pragmatic and philosophical. Mary Gehman recalls, "We felt teaching Islam doesn't negate or diminish the power of the gospel. And having some service that permits Christian presence and witness, why should we jeopardize that? We discussed it with the Somali believing group too, and

---

79. Wenger, "Christian Faith and Islam," 3–4, 12.
80. Miller, interview.
81. Nissley, interview.
82. Roth, interview.

their feeling was too that it shouldn't be prevented. The mission board really worked to bend with the Somali Mission."[83]

Omar Eby had returned from Somalia and was working at the EMM Salunga office at the time. He was therefore present for the joint sessions with the Bishop Board in which these deliberations were occurring. There were questions about how a mission school could be characterized as such if it were not missional. Eby recalls that Paul Kraybill was a convincing mission diplomat and presented a compelling case for compliance with the Somali government. Kraybill and fellow bishop Raymond Charles managed to convince the board that the openly evangelistic activities that were happening in Tanganyika could not be replicated in a majority Muslim context like Somalia.[84]

Because of the decision to allow the teaching of Islam in the schools, the mission schools continued to have great influence in the country through the education of many Somali students. Furthermore, the decision communicated to Somalis in ways that mere words never could that the mission was respectful toward Muslims. This incident has had a long life in Somali collective memory.[85] Mark Logan recounts that decades later Somalis told him that they felt they could trust the Mennonites because they stayed, and they were not simply there to evangelize but sincerely cared about Somalis. The incident took on a life of its own; people sometimes pointed to schools that had not belonged to Mennonite Mission and told Logan, "That was a Mennonite school."[86]

There was a range of religiosity among the students at the Mennonite schools. Some had a strong sense of identity as Muslims and faithfully prayed at the little mosque that was built on campus of the secondary school at the request of students and parents. Others did not have an interest in religion, and did their best to skip as many religion classes as possible. The endeavor to teach Islam in the schools seems not to have increased student interest in the faith, and may have had the opposite effect. There was limited space to incorporate discussions about faith into the classroom, especially for elementary school students. While topics like the crucifixion and salvation through Christ were off limits, the Mennonite teachers found that they could freely talk about God as Creator

---

83. Gehman, interview.
84. Eby, interview.
85. Leaman, interview.
86. Chantal and Mark Logan, interview by author, Bridgewater, VA, April 7, 2013.

and the human responsibility to obey God, even more than they could have in some American schools. After the revolution, the state-approved curriculum included English stories that provided opportunities to discuss some Christian ideas without offending anyone. In one of Mary Gehman's classes, a poem by a Somali about striving in the right way led into a discussion about how God helps us to do what is right.[87]

Carl Wesselhoeft notes that it is easier in retrospect to observe potential points of contact with Muslim students and friends. For example, the ubiquitous term *bismillahi* ("in the name of God") could have been used to start the day in the Mennonite schools. The common names of students, such as Abdul-Qaddar (Servant of the Judge) and Abdullahi (Servant of God), were another point of contact that could have been made. At one point some students made a small mosque on the compound out of thorn bushes and had prayer. Says Wesselhoeft, "That made tension, but only tension because of our attitude. I could have said, 'You're praying, wonderful! No more lying, no more cheating in school.' But somehow we didn't think. Hindsight is twenty-twenty."[88]

Some Somalis were searching for a connection between the pieties of the two faiths. They did their prayers right in front of the missionary houses, and would come to them with dust on their foreheads, in order to demonstrate their piety. They perceived Christians as generally secular and infidels. After the death of Merlin Grove, who was more outspoken in his faith, a Somali man told Wesselhoeft, "He was more religious than you are." Looking to create more interfaith conversation, one Christmas the Wesselhoefts invited the leaders of the village of Mahaddei for tea and cake, and they viewed slides about the prophets Islam and Christianity had in common, from Adam to Jesus. The Somali men were quite interested but responded, "Just don't teach that to our children." Interference in the lives of young children would have been resented. Once the students moved on to secondary school in Johar, there was more social freedom to discuss matters of faith when the students raised questions.[89]

Sometimes the interactions with Islam occurred in the midst of everyday street life. While riding to Mogadishu with a busload of Somali teachers, Bertha Beachy happened to be on the same bus as the renowned Somali poet and intellectual Musa Haji Ismail Galaal, whom Beachy

---

87. Gehman, interview.
88. Wesselhoeft, interview.
89. Ibid.

knew well from her work in the bookstore. Galaal was reciting poetry, and when he came to the word *gal* (infidel), realizing that she was listening, he stopped short and explained, "That's not you, Miss Beachy, you believe in God," and then continued.[90]

The Mennonite missionaries likewise learned to navigate the Islamic faith of the Somalis in the realm of medicine. The hospital was a natural setting for conversation to take place. Some Somali hospital employees requested Bible studies. There were many obstacles to open sharing, however. One young man who worked in the lab, after having some discussions with Ivan Leaman, told him, "It's wrong for us to be talking about Christian faith."[91] Somewhere this young lab technician had been influenced to think that even a conversation on this topic was sinful.

The doctors and nurses tried to be sensitive to the traditional religious beliefs and practices. For example, if a person was unconscious from an illness like malaria, the Somalis sometimes requested to take the patient from the hospital in order to have special Islamic prayers to drive out the *jinn* (spirits). Ivan Leaman's response was, "You can pray here, and we will also pray." Generally the Somalis respected and trusted the medical work of the mission, but occasionally misunderstandings or accusations arose. Great care was required in order to explain things sufficiently. When patients died there was rarely any incrimination, as the Somalis tended to take a fatalistic view of the world.[92]

If a woman had a difficult labor and delivery, a mullah often was asked to recite an important verse of the Qur'an and spit in a cup of water, which the woman then drank. Pregnant women also placed a qur'anic verse as an amulet on the neck or arm. Fae Miller recalls, "I always encouraged them; if it helped the woman, fine. Sometimes the women surrounding the woman in labor spit on her stomach to help her. They saw me as a very powerful, educated person, and they wanted me to spit too. You didn't do a big glob, just a little saliva. I thought, 'Yes, Jesus did that, he spit in the eyes of the blind man.' And it helped the woman to relax."[93]

While they brought little formal preparation from the mission with them, the early Mennonite missionaries received an education in grassroots Somali Islam in the schools, clinics, and everyday life. These

---

90. Beachy, interview.
91. Leaman, interview.
92. Ibid.
93. Miller, interview.

interactions helped to challenge prior assumptions about Islam, paving the way for the development of a more collaborative approach.

Increased Scholarly and Global Engagement

During the second half of the twentieth century there was a sharp increase in global interactions between North American Mennonites and Muslims. This was certainly not the first intersection of the two faiths. John A. Lapp helpfully identifies several historical windows in Anabaptist/Muslim interaction. The spread of Islamic influence was prominently in the conscience of most Europeans during the formative period for the Anabaptist movement. As the Ottoman armies threatened Vienna, Michael Sattler insisted at his trial that Christians should not resist them, but should ask God for defense. Dutch Mennonites pioneered the modern mission model in Indonesia in the mid-nineteenth century, following Reformed and Catholic patterns. At the end of that century Russian Mennonites sent missionaries to Central Asia and northern India. The intentional engagement of Muslims by Mennonites in the twentieth century emerged out of MCC work with Palestinian refugees, Mennonite Board of Missions involvement in Algeria, and EMM work in Somalia; "Any interest in Islam per se appears to have followed experience and practice."[94]

MCC began service ministries in India, Bangladesh, Jordan/Palestine, Algeria, and Ethiopia. Mennonite agencies have also worked in Muslim contexts in Afghanistan, Turkey, Iran, North Africa and the Middle East, Albania, Kosovo, Central Asia, Indonesia, Burkina Faso, Senegal, and Djibouti. When North American Mennonites first arrived in Ethiopia, they intended to evangelize among Ethiopia's Muslim peoples. But their focus shifted rapidly to the Orthodox Christians, who offered them a willing reception.[95] In some cases Mennonites were invited to majority Muslim areas because of their previous relief work in other parts of the world.[96]

As these global interactions increased, one significant factor in the shift toward a more collaborative interfaith approach was an increased engagement of Islam on the part of Mennonites at a scholarly level.

94. Lapp, "Mennonite Engagement with Muslims," 100–103.
95. Kanagy et al, *Winds of the Spirit*, 43.
96. Lapp, "Mennonite Engagement with Muslims," 104.

Among Mennonites involved in Somalia, this engagement began in the 1960s and 1970s. Bertha Beachy and Fae Miller studied Islam, Arabic language and culture, and missions to Islam at Hartford Seminary during furloughs. Harold Reed studied Islam at Temple University. David Shenk completed a PhD in religious education at New York University. Before Elizabeth and Ken Nissley returned for their third term, they studied at the Islamic Training Institute at Hartford Seminary. Each of these individuals had significant experience in Somalia previous to their studies, enabling them to locate their work within a particular context. According to David Shenk, "Very quickly we began to sense a need for a much more intentional engagement. But we never felt it deeply enough to commission anyone to study Arabic. I think that would have been a huge asset, to have a Jon Hoover among us."[97]

Fae Miller's intellectual curiosity about Islam was sparked soon after her arrival in Somalia. When she went to Nairobi she bought any book she could find on Islam and Somalia. On her first furlough she did a degree at EMC. Then Don Jacobs of EMM connected her to Hartford Seminary on her second furlough. There Miller discovered the importance of language as a key to cultural understanding. Poetry plays a vital role in Somali communication, even in such trivial interactions as greetings. The Qur'an itself is written as poetry and must be understood as such. Hartford professor and missiologist Elmer Douglas made a statement in one of Miller's courses that had a lasting impact on her work in Somalia: "Mission boards need to move beyond sending only theologians; what we need is missionaries who know some anthropology and sociology."[98] The skills of careful listening and learning are intrinsic to the missionary task. Bonnie Bergey learned from Bertha Beachy the importance of going to Somalia in a learning posture. Bergey observes, "It ended up being crucial for working with Muslims, to be in a kind of posture that wasn't arrogant or condescending. I think it saved me on many occasions, to be a learner. And I not only wanted to be able to trust Somalis, I *had* to trust them

---

97. Shenk, interview. Jon Hoover is a Mennonite Associate Professor of Islamic Studies at University of Nottingham, UK.

98. Miller, interview. The discovery that anthropology and sociology were critical to the process of translation did not eliminate the challenges. For example, one of the Somali interpreters told the Mission that the term *Lamb of God* should never be used with Somalis.

with some of the places where I was, to trust that I was getting truthful information or that they would keep me from harm if possible."[99]

Miller felt that the ideas she received in her training at Hartford Seminary were somewhat novel for Mennonites in the early 1960s. For example, she emerged from that experience believing strongly that only after intense study and deliberate understanding could one appropriately make critical statements about Somali culture and religion. One must know the language and the people in an intimate way before deeming to speak about them. Likewise, one should be familiar with the Qur'an and Islam before saying anything negative about the Islamic faith, giving priority to Muslim descriptions of their own faith over second-hand accounts. After studying Islam at Hartford and building friendships with Somali Muslims, Miller began to feel that "Islam is a wonderful religion. . . . The only thing they don't have is a savior. Otherwise, I could accept much of it."[100]

Through their graduate programs and other connections, Mennonites were reading scholarship written by Christians meeting other faiths, particularly Kenneth Cragg and Lesslie Newbigin. These works demonstrated the possibilities for deeper engagement that was both confessional and respectful. Probably the most influential development in Mennonite/Muslim relationships at a scholarly level was the work of David Shenk, especially *A Muslim and a Christian in Dialogue*, co-written with Badru Kataregga and first published in 1980. The two men developed a friendship while teaching world religions together at Kenyatta University. The book presents Muslim and Christian views and responses on the topics of God, creation, the prophets, revelation, community, worship, and mission, among others. Shenk further developed the commonalities and divergences between the *umma* (Muslim community) and the church, as well as other points of contact between the faiths, in *Journeys of the Muslim Nation and the Christian Church*.[101] While finding considerable common ground, Kataregga and Shenk take care not to minimize the substantial differences between the faiths. They conclude, "On this we both agree: truth is the *Word* of authoritative revelation from God. That common starting point is both the point of convergence and the point of divergence between us. Is the Word of revelation preeminently a book

---

99. Bergey, interview.
100. Miller, interview.
101. Shenk, *Journeys*.

or supremely evident in a person? That issue cannot be resolved by argument; the very nature of the issue demands patience, listening, and witness by both communities of faith."[102]

The *Dialogue* has had a lasting impact in the decades since its writing. It models for both Christians and Muslims what it might mean to identify both common ground and differences without disparaging the other. The non-confrontational approach seeks to listen carefully in order to let people of faith speak for themselves. The book has been used in peacemaking efforts in countries where there have been conflicts between the Christian and Muslim communities, including Turkey and Indonesia. It is now printed in a dozen languages, including Arabic.

Yet another result of a deeper engagement of Islam is the attempt to develop and distribute Islamicized materials with culturally sensitive ways of presenting the Christian story.[103] One such example emerging in the context of the Eastleigh Fellowship Center is the *People of God* correspondence and radio program developed by a team of writers led by David Shenk. According to Shenk, the course indicates a "shift where we really looked at the Qur'an to find bridges and began to see Islam not as an anti-Christ movement but a movement that missed the centrality of Christ, but within which there are signs pointing. We tried to build upon those signs."[104] The project has been tremendously fruitful, reaching a thousand Muslim readers per year in East Africa. The course has been translated into forty-four languages around the globe, including Somali. *People of God* has become "a bridge building trust and respect between the Christian community and the Muslim society."[105]

Mark and Chantal Logan took the same approach in collaborative peacemaking with Muslims. Their own paradigm was faithfulness to the teachings of Jesus, rejecting force and loving enemies even to the point of risking one's life. But that was not the primary language they used when working with Muslim people. Mark explains, "I would start with how we are all created as children of Adam and Eve, and we should live together peacefully as brothers and sisters. So start by building bridges to a Muslim perspective, just as Muslims quote the Qur'an about being brothers."[106]

---

102. Kateregga and Shenk, *Muslim and Christian in Dialogue*, 206.
103. Lybarger, "Mennonite Engagement," 33.
104. Shenk, interview.
105. Schaup, "People of God," 392–93.
106. Logan, interview.

Such a bridge-building approach requires the kind of familiarity with Islamic faith that Mennonites learned to develop in various ways during these years.

Finding Footing

The Mennonite presence in Somalia from 1976 to 1990 took a decisive turn toward the language and practices of justice and peacemaking. Three kinds of changes—religious, political, and interfaith—made this development necessary and positive, but also ushered in potential hazards to a sustained Christian peacemaking presence.

1. *Greater attention to activist justice and peacemaking also requires an integration of grace.* The transformation to an activist mode that Mennonites have undergone in the last half century must be accompanied by an inner transformation as well.[107] Ervin Stutzman issues a reminder that we are stewards not only of God's justice and peace, but also God's grace. Our expression of gratitude for God's presence among us checks our tendency to overemphasize our role as humans in ushering in God's peace. Stutzman writes that Mennonites can fill a niche that "combines a centuries-old core of evangelical concern for spiritual salvation with equal concern for setting things right in the world. There is room for practice of nonresistance as well as just peacemaking. The world cries out for an integration of grace, justice, and peace."[108]

    A second caution is that the rapid assimilation of Mennonites into mainstream North American culture, which has helped to facilitate the move toward more activist justice and peacemaking, has presented new challenges for maintaining a distinctive theology. While it has opened up fresh possibilities for influencing society in positive ways toward social justice and conflict resolution, the influence is never a one-way street. Assimilation often means the loss of an exile identity, which can erode long-held convictions about violence, peacemaking, and the reign of God. Conrad Kanagy wonders "if we shouldn't be doing two things at once: connecting to the broader culture while at the same time spiritually discerning what

---

107. Driedger and Kraybill, *Mennonite Peacemaking*, 263.
108. Stutzman, *Nonresistance to Justice*, 280, 297–98.

distinguishes us from that culture."[109] The next chapter addresses how the breakdown of the traditional Anabaptist two-kingdom theology ushered in new questions of how Mennonites should respond to a situation that seems to require military intervention.

2. *The changing political context in Somalia, which rendered questions of justice and peace more acute, also makes a community centered on Christ more needed than ever.* As Somalia's golden decade of the 1960s gave way to the disasters of the following years, the violence, food shortages, and masses of displaced persons rightly focused the Mennonite work on caring for the material needs of the Somali people. The tension between providing material aid, peacemaking, and development services on one hand, and the establishment of fellowships on the other, need not be an unhealthy one. These goals are not exclusive, and Christians who emphasize one or the other must learn from and support one another in confronting ethnocentrism and abuse of power. While avoiding the kind of evangelism that imposes itself upon a culture, Christians must continue to commend Christ and the church in unobtrusive ways. The church is a bulwark against violence as it seeks God's grace and peace by establishing communities in which God's ideals for social justice are most fully realized.[110] A Somali church, more than any other institution, would be capable of drawing out the peacemaking impulses of Somali culture and transforming the violence the country has endured.

3. *Greater openness and understanding of Islam can never replace or supersede sustained relationships with Muslim people.* North American Mennonites have come a long way in developing more informed, sympathetic perspectives on Islam. This development must be applauded in no uncertain terms as a more faithful way of relating across faiths. What is important for Mennonites to remember, however, is that training in Islam is not about grasping concepts, but building relationships. Long-term EMM worker in Djibouti Mike Brislen writes, "We have learned that we are not witnesses to Islam. Our ministry is not to a religion, but among people."[111]

---

109. Kanagy, *Road Signs*, 174.
110. Stutzman, *Nonresistance to Justice*, 298.
111. Brislen, "Djibouti," 213.

In this sense, the early missionaries' learning on the ground was not better or worse than if they had received formal preparation in advance. Their understanding of Islam emerged from interactions with ordinary Muslims with real passions, commitments, and expressions of their faith. The dialogue that surfaces from a shared life is deeper than any academic engagement or intellectual understanding. For example, some Somali men approached Ivan Leaman to discuss the racial discrimination that was happening in the US. Leaman responded that Christians are taught a different way, and read Galatians 3:28 to demonstrate the radical equality of the gospel. His Somali friends appreciated that response, but asked him to read the Qur'an with an open mind, and not just accept what he had always heard.[112] In the Somali town of Galkayo a profound interfaith dialogue happened that day, of the kind that can never be replicated on a foreign university campus or over email. Fae Miller reflects, "I don't think that communicating with Somalis means that we introduce them to the American way of life. However, it is always important to welcome them into our homes—to visit, share a cup of tea, food, or other things that interest them, sitting on their mat around a large platter of spicy rice and goat meat."[113]

The shift to a more collaborative, engaged, and informed approach to Islam has been a necessary ingredient for long-term Mennonite commitment to Somali people. This does not mean that the central questions become any easier. Chantal Logan cautions that MCC, EMM, and other organizations must decide what they believe about conversion, because it will come up in a Somali context. Working out what it looks like to be a presence that is both unobtrusive and invitational is difficult and complex, but it must be done. The biggest risk, however, is that Somali-Mennonite relationship will not survive, because it is too challenging, dangerous, or produces too few results. Building bridges of trust takes time. It also involves risk, both in a physical sense (as in the case of Mennonites who continued to work in Somalia during the tumultuous 1990s) and because bridge-building can lead to uncharted theological territory.[114] In other words, faithful Christian witness leads to the borderlands between peoples and faiths.

112. Leaman, interview.
113. Miller, interview.
114. Logan, "Reflections," 64–65.

The borderlands where Jesus met the Samaritan woman, the Syro-Phoenician woman, and many more, is also where we can expect to meet Jesus and hear his voice in these ordinary encounters. Alain Epp Weaver writes, "Interfaith bridge building is not about adherents of different faiths relinquishing their truth claims, about finding a supposedly neutral space free of confessional bias, or about watering down religious convictions to a lowest common denominator. For Christians, interfaith bridge building is motivated by the confession that Jesus Christ is Lord over all of creation and history. Thus we should expect to meet Jesus in the borderlands, in our interactions with persons of other faiths."[115]

The significance of Christians mingling lives with Muslims, in Somali and elsewhere, cannot be overemphasized. We need both the informed academic engagement that has flourished in the last several decades and the sustained, intentional neighborliness at a grassroots level that is the legacy of the Mennonite presence in Somalia.

The mission experience in Somalia confronted and changed the Mennonite peace clan, even as they strove to present the good news of God's Reign. Their eyes were being opened to both personal and systemic challenges, both spiritual and material needs. The pressing necessity of radical peacemaking, whether in the US or in Somalia, could not be ignored, nor could the calling to a deeper understanding of their Muslim neighbors. But with this new consciousness came fresh challenges that threatened to divide the Mennonite witness, as we shall see in the next chapter.

---

115. Weaver, "Meeting Jesus," 11, 14.

— 3 —

Salt, Light, and Deeds

Tensions in Mennonite Involvement

As one of the most ancient cities in Africa south of the Sahara, Mogadiscio had known centuries of attrition: one army leaving death and destruction in its wake, to be replaced by another and another and yet another, all equally destructive: the Arabs arrived and got some purchase on the peninsula, and after they pushed their commerce and along with it the Islamic faith, they were replaced by the Italians, then the Russians, and more recently the Americans, nervous, trigger-happy, shooting before they were shot at. The city became awash with guns, and the presence of the gun-crazy Americans escalated the conflict to greater heights. Would Mogadiscio ever know peace? Would the city's inhabitants enjoy this commodity ever again?

— NURUDDIN FARAH, *LINKS*

IN A THESIS EXPLORING the Mennonite approach to working in Islamic contexts in East Africa, North Africa, and the Middle East, Loren Lybarger identifies several forces at work.[1] First, the Mennonite endeavors took place within the broader context of imperialism and colonialism. Second, Mennonites faced legal barriers and restrictions that led to the development of new theological descriptions for mission. Mennonite institutions have defined their goals in different ways, leading to a distinct differentia-

---

1. Lybarger, "Defining Presence."

tion in the approaches of MCC and Mennonite mission agencies.² Here I address these two tensions with regard to peacemaking endeavors, and propose that Jesus' calling to salt, light, and deeds in the Sermon on the Mount creates space for a variety of approaches.

The Colonialist Moment

Mennonites must recognize that they have interacted with Somalis at what Willie James Jennings calls the "colonialist moment." According to Jennings, Christianity in the Western world, including its mission endeavors, operates within a "diseased social imagination."³ What he means is that our theology lacks the ability to connect to the earth and to strangers because it has been shaped by and woven into the processes of colonial dominance. Colonialism created its own reality that established private property and racial segregation as normative. Capitalism and racism, when joined together, destroyed the possibility of identifying with the land and place. People could carry identity only on their bodies—blacks as property and Native Americans as resident foreigners, for example—rather than in the land to which they were historically tied. In colonial Africa, learning French and English was imagined as passing from blackness to whiteness/civilization, trapping Christian theology in the universalism of central literary power languages.⁴

Like many peoples in Africa, Somalis face challenges in part wrought by a long history of colonialism. The pan-Somali issue carries such importance for many Somalis because colonial powers divided the territory in the Horn of Africa not along linguistic or clan lines but rather based upon the particular interests of the European nations involved, or in some cases simply arbitrarily. The conflicts in the Ogaden region are a legacy of these policies, as are ongoing tensions between Somalia and Kenya (which includes regions that are primarily ethnically Somali). The colonial powers, especially the Italians in the south, sought to undermine the traditional clan-based systems of justice and law in favor of Western-style courts.

The colonial project has also impacted the way in which Somali history is written. For example, Douglas James Jardine's *The Mad Mullah of*

---

2. Lybarger, "Mennonite Engagement," 31–33.
3. Jennings, *Christian Imagination*, 6–9.
4. Ibid., 224–31.

Somaliland remains one of only two book-length accounts of Mohammed Abdullah Hassan (1856–1920), an important figure in Somali history. Originally published in 1923, this book is dedicated "with affection and respect to His Excellency Sir Geoffrey Francis Archer, K.C.M.G., His Majesty's representative in Somaliland from 1914 to 1922 to whom the downfall of dervishism and the re-establishment of British prestige in Somaliland is primarily due."[5] Jardine's account of the "Mad Mullah" of Somaliland, whom Somalis to this day regard as a hero, is condescending and prejudiced in the same way that leaders of oppressed peoples are always portrayed by those defending the interests of the powerful. Jardine has no qualms about the British colonial project of the "civilising of Somaliland" so that Somalis "might experience for the first time in their history the benefits of peace and plenty." Jardine rues the fact that suspicion and mistrust toward the British have misplaced the appropriate gratitude and loyalty that Somalis should feel toward their protectors; yet "the time must surely come when the Somali tribes will take their place as happy and prosperous members of the British Commonwealth." This, he notes, is the hope of many Englishmen "who have known Somaliland in its darkest days and have learnt to like and respect a very proud, intelligent, and virile native race."[6]

Modern scholarship and journalism is perhaps less prone to explicit defense of foreign economic and imperial interests in Somalia. Nevertheless, it is still commonplace to frame Somalia policy in terms of Western security, especially with reference to combating the militant Islamist group al-Shabaab and piracy, without regard for ways in which the perspectives of Somalis might differ. A more recent example is the use of the term *warlord* to describe leaders and leadership styles in Somalia. Anthropologist Vinodh Kutty points out that in Somalia, males who are aggressive, independent, and sophisticated are called *hal-karaan* or *belaayo*, and are admired because they exhibit traits to which many men in Somalia aspire.[7] A term like *warlord* can actually serve a political purpose rather than adequately capturing cultural meanings. For some Somali commentators, however, the term *warlord* adequately describes certain figures whose legitimacy rests only on control of militias, and whose participation should be utterly excluded by those seeking genuine peace.

5. Jardine, *Mad Mullah*, v.
6. Ibid., 318–19.
7. Kutty, "Tol, Xeer, and Somalinimo," 38.

Maxamed Afrax traces the negative view of Somalia that is propagated by most media to a lack of understanding of Somali culture; "A mature knowledge of Somali custom disproves recent arguments widely propagated by the Western media that violence and anarchy constitute the cornerstone of Somali culture, or that in Somali society political tolerance is anathema."[8] This description fits both Barre's regime and the warlords, but not Somali traditions.

The same tendencies are evident in approaches to state-building and peacekeeping in a Somali context. BBC correspondent Mary Harper points out several shortcomings and mistakes related to an imported Western approach to state-building in Somalia. First, the record of the nearly twenty peace conferences hosted by foreign entities, often outside Somalia, is dismal. The divide between Somali leaders who have talked about peace for two decades and the reality on the ground is stark. In fact, it has resulted in a cottage industry of professional Somali peacemakers who escape the conflict and enjoy luxurious hotel stays.[9] Second, the US and Ethiopia's misguided deposing of the Islamic Courts Union (ICU) in 2006, which was justified by equating Somalia's home-grown political Islam with international terror groups like al-Qaeda, was a self-fulfilling prophecy in that it led to the formation of al-Shabaab as a response. That the ICU actually brought more stability because it developed from the ground up, much like Hamas or the Muslim Brotherhood, adds to the irony that it was destroyed by outside intervention purportedly seeking peace. In contrast, Harper notes, Somaliland is the most stable region in the area in part because it was left alone the most by outside power interventions. She concludes that the United States should distance itself from Somalia, even though this is counter-intuitive; "The more successful experiments in Somalia have been 'home grown,' emerging from the grass roots of society, rather than being imposed form the outside."[10]

Jennings asks whether there is in the modern world a form of cultural joining and interaction that does not depend on the destructive global economies and cultures of the powerful. In order for that to happen, he avers, the diseased moral imagination must be traced back to its roots, the question of how the people of God are constituted. The colonial gospel saw whites as the bearers of a message that was entrusted into their

---

8. Afrax, "Mirror of Culture," 237.

9. Harper, *Getting Somalia Wrong?*, 8, 64.

10. Ibid., 5–13, 198.

hands, with no significant prior history. But Christian theology is unintelligible without the people Israel; Gentiles must remember that we are outside Israel and have been allowed to enter, to overhear and to be included. We cannot read Jesus as though we are his disciples before we are Gentiles. "Reading Israel's story is intended to be disruptive, especially for Gentile existence," Jennings writes. This means that disciples sense that Israel is being reborn in Jesus. Jesus' election is the inauguration of a new age for Israel, and one sign of this new age is speaking the languages of other peoples. In Jesus a new cultural politic is born, a new biracial humanity of Jew and Gentile that is the basis for peace. Christianity must return to the original relationship of Israel and Gentiles, which has been blocked by the advent of whiteness. The Christian imagination requires a radical remembering of place, story, and connection to land, disrupting the logic of displacement that is still at work in global capitalism.[11]

According to Jennings, the story of race is a story of place. Geography matters because of the connection between identity and land, which is difficult for Westerners to see because we have been formed otherwise. The bitter fruit of colonial forgetfulness is a disconnect between peoples and the land, a rendering of creation as private property, and a kind of Christianity that belongs to peoples without relating to Israel. Jennings states his purpose: "I want Christians to recognize the grotesque nature of a social performance of Christianity that imagines Christian identity floating above land, landscape, animals, place, and space, leaving such realities to the machinations of capitalistic calculations and the commodity chains of private property. Such Christian identity can only inevitably lodge itself in the materiality of racial existence."[12]

Jennings's incisive criticism is not without hope. He sees the redemptive grace of the gospel shining through at various instants in the colonial moment, which leaves him hopeful that a rightly remembering Christian faith can restart a conversation between people who live beside each other but remain isolated. He tells four stories about Christians attempting to live Christian lives at various times in the colonialist moment, two of whom—the royal intellectual Zurara and the Jesuit scholar Acosta—fail utterly to receive the gospel because their theological imaginations are trapped within a racial construct. But a third, the Anglican Bishop John Colenso, comes to see the lives of his African neighbors as bound to his

11. Jennings, *Christian Imagination*, 247–88.
12. Ibid., 289–94.

own flesh, becoming an advocate for Zulu lives through close friendship in the act of translating Scripture. Colenso came to feel pathos for those treated as nonhuman. "This, finally," Jennings writes, "is Christian translation. And such translation cost Bishop Colenso everything."[13] The lesson from the lives of Christians like Bishop Colenso and Bartolomé de las Casas is that seeing God at work in the world requires Christian bodies loving people concretely, participating in God's love.

Mennonites can learn several lessons from Jennings's account of the Christian imagination. First, stories are important; we must learn to tell ours in ways that highlight God's redemptive acts and downplay our own merit. The Mennonite connection to the Anabaptist story, fostered by our hymns, our martyrology, and our identity of nonconformity, is often portrayed as a strength. This is true only insofar as it allows us to participate with God by loving people concretely with our bodies, to use Jennings's phrase. The theological basis for work in health care, relief, development, and education is that in Christ we cannot imagine any other way of relating to our fellow humans. Second, Mennonites must be carefully intentional about how we interact with US American identity. Teaching English, for example, is a frequent request by Somalis to North American Mennonites. The recognition that English is a language representing economic and military power does not automatically disqualify this activity, especially at the behest of Somalis. What it does mean is that Mennonites must seek the kind of mutuality with Somalis that derives from a different sort of moral imagination; learning the language of one's neighbor is not simply a gesture of respect, but a radical testimony to the gospel that makes every language its home.

Jennings' argument is that the Christian imagination has been co-opted and corrupted by racial and colonial domination. This corruption impacts the way in which conflict is imagined as well. Conflicts that are perceived as intractable, such as the enduring violence in Somalia, require what John Paul Lederach calls the "moral imagination" to envision a web of relationships with one's enemies included. Violence betrays a lack of imagination in seeking a solution, which results in resorting to established cycles and patterns of revenge and further violence. The alternative, he argues, is to develop "Schools for Moral Imagination" that mix people of different backgrounds together.[14]

---

13. Ibid., 165–66.
14. Lederach, *Moral Imagination*, 29, 177.

Breaking vicious cycles is precisely the language Glen Stassen and David Gushee employ to describe Jesus' teachings in the Sermon on the Mount. They challenge the traditional reading of the Sermon as a series of dyads comparing the traditional teaching and Jesus' new ideal. Part of the problem with this reading, they argue, is that it facilitates a view of the "hard teachings," such as enemy love in Matthew 5:44, as impossible ideals that can be marginalized in light of the harsh reality of the world. On the contrary, Jesus' teachings are triadic, consisting of the traditional righteousness, the vicious cycles of sin, and what Stassen and Gushee call transforming initiatives—concrete practices that emphasize not the negative prohibitions but the way of deliverance as a means of grace.[15] Lederach also recognizes that people who articulate a vision are often called dreamers or idealists, separated from reality. But he argues that the inverse is true: "To escape the crisis in which they are trapped, people must imagine and articulate the kind of community they desire."[16]

Just peacemaking theory further extends the transforming initiatives taught by Jesus to the international system and to situations of protracted conflict. One of the ten practices of just peacemaking is to take independent initiatives to reduce threat. The purpose of this practice—grounded in Jesus' commands in Matthew 5:38 to go the second mile, turn the other cheek, and so on—is to decrease each side's distrust or threat perception regarding the other.[17] The hope that drives this practice, confirmed by countless historical examples, is that one's adversary will reciprocate, deescalating the conflict and reducing the hostility and sense of threat on both sides. In all cases, these independent initiatives will be driven by a moral imagination that is able, in the words of Lederach, to "find the narrative that gives meaning to life and ongoing relationships."[18]

Evangelism, Development, and Peacemaking

The arrival of MCC in Somalia in 1980 raised questions as to the nature and limits of Mennonite involvement. As the new Mennonite organization in the country, MCC had overlapping but divergent goals in joining

15. Stassen and Gushee, *Kingdom Ethics*, 131–43.
16. Lederach, *Building Peace*, 116.
17. Stassen, *Just Peacemaking*, 57.
18. Lederach, *Moral Imagination*, 148.

the established work of EMM. Are the goals of church formation, development, and peacemaking compatible? Can the respective missions of the agencies be integrated, or must they operate in separate spheres?

Sympathetic outside voices can reinforce the notion that attempts to integrate evangelism, peacemaking, and development activities are misguided and unhelpful. Marc Gopin, a Jewish peacemaking colleague of Mennonites, argues that the experience of persecution explains the historical separatism, meekness, and rejection of proselytizing that continues today among the old order Mennonite and Amish. The mission movement has deeply impacted Mennonites in the last century, but mission is difficult to define because of its varied interpretations among Mennonites: "Some are uncomfortable with proselytizing altogether, while others are committed to mission as a religious calling but are looking to define peace work as mission. This would make sense as a development of the Mennonite focus on the life of Jesus. They would see Jesus' principal endeavors as involving direct service, aid to and healing those in need, and the teaching of nonresistance, not the construction of an empire of followers."[19]

Modern Mennonite peacemakers are therefore caught in a bind, because peacemaking is an invasive process of entering someone else's culture and problems in order to seek peace and justice. Gopin writes, "They seem to know intuitively, based on their religious pacifist training and culturally embedded historical memory, how slippery a slope this engagement is and how dangerous is the power that one feels in changing other lives, especially when those Others are in a vulnerable position economically and emotionally."[20]

Gopin points out that Mennonite quietism that emphasizes learning over intervening has an undeserved negative reputation. Long-term relationship building, which Mennonites have historically done better than some others, is healthier than swooping in to do conflict resolution. But Gopin calls for an end to the expansive ambition of religions that is the driving force of evangelism: "It seems clear that conflict resolution work that is confused with or in any relation with proselytism is seriously flawed in principle and will have problematic effects in practice."[21] Each religious community should find fulfillment in the internal quality of its

---

19. Gopin, *Between Eden and Armageddon*, 146.
20. Ibid., 147.
21. Ibid., 158.

communal life and values, not in a need for a numerical victory over others.²²

My response to Gopin's criticism is that while some Christians might frame evangelism in terms of "winning" souls or territory, Mennonites who embrace verbal witness do so out of obedience to the mission initiated by Jesus Christ rather than territorial or numerical ambitions.²³ Furthermore, as Gopin points out, peacemaking itself is an endeavor that involves an element of intrusion. Culturally sensitive peacemaking, which Gopin endorses, puts Mennonites in the same "bind" as culturally sensitive church formation. Both involve the interface of traditional culture with foreign elements, whether they are foreign peacebuilding frameworks (such as those offered to Somali women over the course of EMU's program) or the proclamation and demonstration of the difference Jesus Christ makes.

One way in which Mennonites have responded to anti-mission laws in Islamic contexts is through the practical and theological concept of *presence*. Lybarger notes that presence is a flexible concept among Mennonite organizations but can be defined as "the point at which service and dialogue begin to be seen as distinct and legitimate alternatives to the missionary activities of teaching, preaching and planting new churches."²⁴ Some Mennonites have taken presence to mean that one's work as a teacher or doctor is just as legitimate a form of service to Christ as traditional missionary activities. This position can be radicalized to the point of regarding quiet service as the *only* legitimate form of Christian involvement among Muslims, in light of the history of violence, oppression, and enmity between Muslims and Christians over the centuries. This stance can be combined with the theological position that Muslims need not be converted to Christianity.²⁵

Lybarger is correct in pointing out the difference in the way MCC and EMM have used the language of presence in a majority Muslim context. He explains, "[T]hose with more traditional views on mission have interpreted presence as the minimal form of evangelism possible in the face of anti-proselytizing laws and hostile community response. For the sake of the authorities and hostile neighbors, one was a teacher or a nurse

22. Ibid., 206.
23. Shenk, *God's Call to Mission*.
24. Lybarger, "Mennonite Engagement," 32.
25. Ibid.

and indeed, one could be true to Christ through selfless service to others, but the great commission demanded more of the missionary. So one remained alive to the possibilities to share the gospel quietly to those who seemed most open and willing to listen."[26]

This depiction accurately reflects the way many EMM missionaries saw their interactions in a Somali context. They understood their faith as the reason for their presence in Somalia, and resisted the idea that one's encounter with God through Jesus should be relegated to just a private personal relationship. For example, when Ivan and Mary Ellen Leaman spent some months in Galkayo in 1965, the local people invited Mennonite Mission to come and work in their area, but told them not to bring their religion. Ivan responded, "I have a call from God to be a missionary, and that is why I am here. If I would come here without my religion, I would be leaving my heart behind."[27]

Ken Nissley recalls EMM struggling as a mission with the relationship between evangelism and service. There were questions about whether EMM should be more evangelical, like Sudan Interior Mission (SIM). During that time East Africa director Don Jacobs visited Somalia and engaged the team in some serious study, in which they worked at developing and articulating a biblical theology of presence. This framework helped to establish some acceptable protocol and boundaries. For example, the mission did not distribute Bibles, but a Somali asking for one would first sign a paper indicating the request. A theology of presence was a satisfactory framework for the Nissleys, and they saw their subsequent work in Somalia in terms of this calling. Although they did not articulate peacemaking in this way at the time, presence is also a theology of peacemaking in that there is intrinsic value in Muslims and Christians relating to each other and existing together. This is reason enough for some Christians to work and serve in a Muslim country, and the Nissleys hoped that their presence might challenge some of the notions that Somalis had about Christians. They sensed that the world needs more examples of peaceful, mutual sharing of life and faith between Muslims and Christians.[28]

Barbara and Lamar Witmer viewed their agricultural and educational work in terms of Jesus' calling in Matthew 25 to meet the needs of

---

26. Ibid., 32–33.
27. Leaman, interview.
28. Nissley, interview.

the hungry and thirsty. They saw this as an essential part of a ministry of presence. At a 1987 team meeting, the EMM personnel discussed and based their official policy on Calvin Shenk's paper *A Relevant Theology of Presence*. The Witmers recall that this was helpful in shaping the way they perceived their work both practically and theologically. They add, "And now we affirm that missiology so thoroughly that we can't imagine anything else anywhere else, even in a place where one could openly evangelize."[29]

First Peter 3:15 served as a paradigmatic passage for shaping missionaries' identity and responses. Mark and Chantal Logan went to Djibouti and Somalia because they wanted personal contact with Somali people. Mark says, "As Christians in a Muslim country, our goal was to always be prepared to give an answer to the hope that was in us. You have that answer ready, but you have to live in a way that makes people ask questions."[30] The mere fact that Chantal was a person of faith and was respectful toward religion, unlike some of the French people in Djibouti, caused Somali friends to see her as an ally. There were many natural openings for conversations to occur about practices like fasting and prayer during Ramadan. The Logans resolved never to argue, but to draw out what faith meant to their Somali friends through sincere questions, and when it seemed right to comment on their own Christian beliefs. They found that their Muslim friends were overwhelmingly open to conversations about faith when the atmosphere was congenial rather than argumentative.[31] Fae Miller adds that the approach of readiness to share one's faith if asked depends on the guidance of the Holy Spirit in particular situations.[32]

While acknowledging that a broad range of views coexist within any given institution, Lybarger proposes that a decisive functional and ideological rift had occurred between MCC and Mennonite mission agencies by end of the twentieth century on the question of evangelism. MCC developed a distinct institutional value structure, especially under the leadership of Urbane Peachey and Leroy Friesen, that characterized Christian mission in terms of service rather than verbal witness. Lybarger writes that MCC "continues to view its involvement in Muslim-Christian

---

29. Witmer, interview.
30. Logan, interview.
31. Ibid.
32. Miller, interview.

dialogue efforts in terms of the justice, service and reconciliation themes stressed by Peachey and Friesen in the early 70s and 80s. These terms explicitly exclude, I think, evangelization and the formation of communities of Muslim believers."[33]

What contributed to this ideological rift between EMM and MCC, which not long before had been administrated by the same person (Orie Miller)? In order to understand the dynamics and challenges of MCC's peace efforts in the latter half of the twentieth century, it is helpful to pay attention to its work in the neighboring region of Israel/Palestine. The experience in Palestine tested the limits of MCC's political involvement. The "quiet of the land" mindset cultivated by Mennonites over centuries in North America caused some of MCC's constituency to question the move from clothing the naked and feeding the hungry into the realm of politics. But the activist awakening brought about by the 1960s and 1970s made it impossible to ignore questions of hunger's source. Furthermore, even seemingly non-political activities, such as MCC's development projects, are inevitably seen as political within a wider political setting.[34]

The challenge of operating in a politically sensitive environment in which Christianity has little influence raised some of the same questions as working in Somalia. How can peace education, or any education for that matter, avoid paternalistic patterns in which the powerful Western agency is the donor and the local people simply the recipients of knowledge? Alain and Sonia Weaver observe, "Just as MCC became suspicious during the 1970s of development models which emphasized technology transfer over local organizing and problem-identification, so it usually avoided models of peace education which defined Mennonites as the knowledgeable outsiders educating Palestinians."[35] MCC workers became convinced of the need to work with Palestinian organizations when promoting peace, taking a quiet, behind-the-scenes approach to peace education. In this vein, MCC operated the Wi'am Conflict Resolution program in Bethlehem, which uses traditional Palestinian as well as Western models of conflict resolution to help solve disputes within

---

33. Lybarger, "Mennonite Engagement," 35.

34. Weaver and Weaver, *Salt & Sign*, 100. The authors note that with the political developments in Israel/Palestine in 1967 there was discussion of joining MCC's program to that of Mennonite Board of Missions, which "probably reflected Orie Miller's continuing desire to have MCC's program in the Middle East evolve in a missionary direction" (*Salt & Sign*, 103).

35. Ibid., 88.

Palestinian society. MCC also supported the work of the Center for Rapprochement between Peoples in Beit Sahour, networking with Israeli and Palestinian peacemakers.[36]

The increased sensitivity on the part of Mennonites toward local ways of addressing problems also had an impact on the way in which they perceived Christian witness. In light of the power imbalance between the West and the majority world, it was entirely appropriate to reconsider with a critical eye how and when Western agencies should transfer technology, education, and peacemaking strategies, and to assume that much more attention should be given to local practice. Did the same logic apply to matters of faith? In other words, did the requisite humility toward the host culture preclude actively fostering religious conversion? Mennonites found themselves answering this question differently. The question was not an abstract one; the way in which one answered it had a direct impact on whether Mennonite organizations spent resources on the task of church formation, what kinds of projects they would undertake, and the relationship between EMM and MCC.

In addition to concerns about cultural humility in light of historical power imbalances, the complexity of fostering Christian fellowships presented some practical challenges for some. In a context infused by foreign aid, the difficulty of establishing fraternal relationships rather than dependencies was immense. According to one MCC worker, at one point there was a fellowship of about a dozen Somali believers in Nairobi, and they were claimed by every mission organization in the city. A number of them had likely experienced a real transformation, but there were others who found it profitable to align themselves with the group for other reasons.[37] The same problems characterized the small Somali church in Mogadishu, which is why some MCC personnel distanced themselves from that aspect of Mennonite work. Jonathan Rudy notes that the objection of some MCC workers was also more philosophical, in that they regarded the endeavor of church planting as misguided and unsustainable. The decades of Mennonite and Swedish Lutheran church planting work yielded only a handful of converts, mostly young men. Rudy explains that in engaging Islam, "I tend to say, if I can help you become a better Muslim as you help me become a better Christian, I think the world is a

---

36. Ibid., 12, 89.
37. Janice Jenner, interview by author, Harrisonburg, VA, April 8, 2013.

better place. That's my higher goal, and I'm not interested in dialogue for convincing you of anything."[38]

On the question of the goal of establishing Somali Christian fellowships, Bonnie Bergey comments,

> In my view, you try to do credible work with the people that you are around, and that allows you to have conversation and you don't know what can develop down the road. But if you go thinking it needs to be a fellowship or a cohesive group of people, and start segmenting people into those who are Christians and those who are not, that's a dangerous thing to try to do. I don't think that most Christians know what a cost it would be within a culture to change religious practice. I wondered about that at times: was this person killed because of an association with me? And in spite of us, there were Somalis that somehow knew how to live Somali culture and be Christian, and have a different sense of following Jesus.[39]

Although differences existed, the tension between EMM and MCC on the ground in Somalia should not be overstated. Elizabeth Nissley recalls that the most vocal opposition to church planting efforts was from MCC leadership who visited Somalia, and that the MCC people in Mogadishu were supportive of the local church. EMM and MCC personnel mostly interacted as a team.[40] Rudy also recalls a strong sense of collegiality and mutual admiration; "I think that Somalia was out in the lead in terms of the two organizations working together. It was such a hard place to live and work, and we resorted to our clan nature out of necessity."[41]

R. Scott Appleby and Angela Lederach provide a helpful typology that sheds some light on the ideological differences between EMM and MCC during this period. They identify four distinct but overlapping modes of evangelizing in world Christianity. The first is the *conversion* mode, which sees pluralism as a threat to Christian faith and is driven by a burden to evangelize the lost. This view generally has a sense of urgency, relies heavily on pneumatological missiology, and emphasizes that the proclamation of one's faith in public is a fundamental human right. A second mode of evangelism is *witness*, which "attempts to integrate both personal conversion to Christ and transformation of unjust

38. Rudy, interview.
39. Bergey, interview.
40. Nissley, interview.
41. Rudy, interview.

socio-political and economic structures, thereby offering a more holistic evangelization paradigm."[42] This mode lacks urgency in that it sees God at work everywhere. A third mode is *solidarity*, which is uncomfortable with exclusive truth claims, literal readings of the Bible, evangelism, and the modern application of the Great Commission. It focuses rather on the humanity of Jesus and the imitation of his life. This approach gives priority to transforming the corrupt sociopolitical and economic systems that captivate suffering people. Finally, at the far end of the spectrum the mode of *dialogue* consists of Christians "who have so deeply internalized teachings on human dignity and the spiritual dynamism of all cultures that they find proselytism of any kind to be antithetical to their understanding of the gospel."[43] Their goal is not conversion but the creation of peaceful relationships in an interreligious world, in which reconciliation is a spirituality rather than a strategy.

I suggest that EMM operated in Somalia primarily in the second mode, *witness*. The twin goals of establishing a Somali fellowship of believers in Christ and providing medical care and education to meet the material needs of people were undertaken as an integrated whole. MCC, in contrast, operated mostly in the third mode, *solidarity*. Sensitivity to the power differential and unjust practices of the West caused some to perceive the pursuit of personal conversion from Islam to Christianity, which most Somalis rejected outright, as an extension of foreign imposition. Moreover, the glaring needs of Somali refugees for food, shelter, and medical care at the time of MCC's arrival lent a new urgency to the task of providing material aid. The demands of justice in imitation of Jesus drew attention to the transformation of corrupt systems and the healing of the wounds of war and poverty. The differences between EMM and MCC in Somalia, therefore, did not stem only from divergent understandings of Christian mission, but also from the political situation during which they entered the country.

---

42. Appleby and Lederach, "Conversion, Witness, Solidarity," 15.
43. Ibid., 17.

Salt, Light, and Deeds as Witness, Elicitation, and Service

I contend that Mennonite peacemaking work in Somalia follows the triadic commandment of Jesus in Matthew 5:13–16, in which he describes the mission of the community of his disciples as *salt*, *light*, and *deeds*. Each of these three metaphors corresponds to a term that Mennonites have used to describe their peacemaking presence in Somalia. Salt refers to the mandate to *witness* to Jesus Christ the Prince of Peace through communal practices that are different from the wisdom of the world. Light means pointing the nations toward God's saving work, *eliciting* the cultural treasures that can glorify God. Deeds are acts of *service* that glorify God by reflecting God's concern for the wellbeing of people.

The community shaped around the life and teachings of Jesus responds to the challenges of colonialism and evangelism by embodying a radically different way of life than the violence of the powers and authorities. In the Sermon on the Mount Jesus initiates a family whose means and ends are peace—in Somali terms, a *peace clan*. The peace clan does not replace previous loyalties to culture and kin, but rather transforms them in light of God's Reign. The peace clan is always invitational, seeking out those who are willing to have their own lives turned toward peacemaking and against enmity.

Salt as Nonviolent Communal Witness

In order to understand what Jesus meant by saltiness in Matthew 5:13, it is best to consider the parable with the Qumran community in mind. This community withdrew from the corruption of the world in order to live a monastic life of covenant fidelity beside the Dead Sea. In this sense, Jesus was commending their effort to be faithful to God's will by separating themselves from evil practices, thus maintaining their saltiness. Jesus' polemic in this verse opposes the loss of identity as God's people through the blurring of the distinction from the world, just as salt loses its taste by mixing with the tasteless sand on which people walk. The Greek word for becoming tasteless can also mean becoming foolish, and salt is associated with wisdom in some rabbinic texts. This passage therefore serves as a parallel to the end of the sermon (Matt 7:24–26), which states that the way one avoids becoming foolish is by obeying the words of Jesus.[44]

The Sermon on the Mount is not addressed to individuals but to the community gathered around Jesus. It is a description of the communal life of Jesus' disciples. The preceding verses assured the disciples that they would be persecuted just as the prophets had been. According to Stanley Hauerwas, this juxtaposition is intentional and significant; "The office of the prophet has now fallen on this new community, who has become salt and light for the world."[45] A salty community exhibits love and peacemaking practices that are different from those of the world because they are based on the reality that the Messiah has come.

Mennonites have long emphasized that discipleship requires community. The way of life made possible by Jesus is not just for individuals, but for his followers collectively. From the beginning of the Mennonite presence in Somalia, therefore, the formation of fellowships of believers gathered around Jesus has been an indispensable goal. Witness to Jesus the Messiah was inseparable from the work of service to the Somali people in education and medicine.

Moreover, the content of that witness precludes the possibility of engaging in violence, deceit, or retaliation. A thick communal identity and sense of calling allowed the Mennonite missionaries to transmit these values into a different cultural context, even as they were being shaped and changed by their new setting.

The goal of establishing Somali Christian fellowships met with some success at various times, but the decades of violence and chaos have decimated the church in Somalia. Nevertheless, the goal remains despite the lack of visible fruit. The persecution faced by Somali believers bears out Jesus' dictum that no prophets (or prophetic community) are welcomed in their own hometown (Luke 4:24).

Light as Eliciting Peacemaking Resources

I propose that the imagery of light to which Jesus refers in Matthew 5:14, drawn directly from Isaiah, serves as a theological basis for the elicitive approach to peacemaking. This foundational principle for peacemaking,

---

44. Stassen and Gushee, *Kingdom Ethics*, 468–70. See also Stassen, *Living the Sermon*, 60–61.

45. Hauerwas, *Matthew*, 61, 65.

articulated especially by John Paul Lederach, seeks to explore, engage, and prioritize traditional cultural forms of reconciliation. Lederach's framework relies on a web of local actors, whose approaches to peacemaking draw primarily from other sources besides the work of international theoreticians. Knowledge of and respect for tradition is more effective in creating trusting relationships because it engages local actors at a deeply personal level.

Lederach's theological rationale for an elicitive approach, however, is mostly limited to its compatibility with the nonviolent commitments of Anabaptists. It is dependent more on an *ethos* of noninvasiveness and the pragmatic goal of peacemaking than it is built upon an explicitly stated scriptural or theological basis. I believe that Jesus' teaching on light in the Sermon on the Mount provides the theological basis for the elicitive approach.

To understand what Jesus meant by *light*, it is again helpful to remember the context of the Qumran community. Jesus' words of commendation for the Qumran community are immediately followed by a strong criticism of their separatism. In order to be faithful disciples of Jesus, the church must be a visible community. According to Dietrich Bonhoeffer, for Jesus' followers, "to flee into invisibility is to deny the call. Any community of Jesus which wants to be invisible is no longer a community that follows him."[46] By *light*, therefore, Jesus indicates an ongoing witness and invitation that is extended beyond the community of his followers.

Stassen and Gushee have demonstrated convincingly that Jesus' perceptions of his own mission are best understood in light of the prophetic tradition of Isaiah, with which he identified.[47] While preaching in Galilee about the Kingdom of Heaven, Jesus quoted from Isaiah 9:1–2 to declare that a light has come to the Gentiles (Matt 4:15–16). In Matthew 5:14, Jesus is drawing on the Old Testament tradition of light in reference to the presence of God, especially Isaiah's call to walk in the "light of the Lord" (Isa 2:5) and for Israel to be the light of the nations (Isa 49:6). Thus Jesus disavows the separatism of the Qumran community; "Disciples are a 'city on a hill' in the Isaiah 2 sense only if we invite and draw people of

---

46. Bonhoeffer, *Discipleship*, 113. Cited in Hauerwas, *Matthew*, 62.
47. Stassen and Gushee, *Kingdom Ethics*, 19–31.

all nations 'up the hill' and through the gates into an experience of shared eschatological community."[48]

The insight of the centrality of Isaiah for Jesus yields a fuller understanding of what he means by light shining from a city on a hill. Isaiah's call to ascend the mountain of the Lord and to walk in the light of the Lord (Isa 2:5) is explained in terms of peacemaking and disarmament. It is a call for a "new world order, shared with the prophet Micah (4:1–5)," in which Zion is a gathering place for the nations, including Israel.[49] The nations come at their own initiative, with the anticipation that the Lord will teach them the essential practices of peacemaking. The goal is justice and peace between the nations, and the evidence that the nations are serious about walking in God's light is their willingness to disarm.

The important connection that Jesus is making between the prophetic tradition of Isaiah and his own ministry is that he is depicting his disciples' mission in terms traditionally used for the mission of Israel. Isaiah speaks of God's people as a light to the nations (42:6; 49:6). Indeed, Isaiah 42:6 and 49:6 are likely Jesus' primary source for his teaching in Matthew 5:14–16. He himself would fulfill the mission of Isaiah's Servant, but he expected his disciples to assume the same responsibility (Matt 20:26–28).[50]

Isaiah 2, 42, and 49 are not the only passages informing Jesus' reading of light from Isaiah. Isaiah 60 begins, "Arise, shine; for your light has come, and the glory of the Lord has risen upon you. . . . Nations shall come to your light, and kings to the brightness of your dawn" (60:1, 3). The prophet envisions an open city into which the nations bring their wealth and kings are led in procession, an image echoed explicitly in Revelation 21:24–26. The kings are not compelled, nor is Zion portrayed as the locus of a new nationalism, but rather as the nucleus of the Lord's light.[51]

Anabaptists can learn a deeper reading of this passage from the Reformed tradition, which recognizes the eschatological dimensions of the cultural mandate to fill the earth in Genesis 1:28. Reformed thought takes this to mean not simply having children, but filling the earth with the "general products and patterns of human culture: language, labeling

---

48. Ibid., 471.
49. Friesen, *Isaiah*, 38.
50. Keener, *Commentary on Matthew*, 174–75.
51. Friesen, *Isaiah*, 381.

systems, tools, schedules, works of art, family activities."[52] Richard Mouw asserts that our enjoyment of culture reflects God's own pleasure. Indeed, the future God intends for humanity includes culture—art, music, clothing, and all the treasures of civilizations—in the New Jerusalem, as a fulfillment of God's creative intentions.[53]

Two points from these passages in Isaiah 60 and Revelation 21 are noteworthy in relation to culture and peacemaking. The first is that the nations are not required to surrender the particularities of their nationality. The same God who created humans with the mandate to fill the earth with culture is now calling them to the peace of Zion *as cultured people*. Secondly, the nations bring their wealth and splendor to the New Jerusalem (Isa 60:11; Rev 21:24). In light of the rich variety of ways in which Scripture portrays true wealth, surely this means more than silver and gold. It refers to the treasures that each culture has to offer in the new age of peace, the practices, customs, and values that are precious to its people.

Elicitive peacemaking, therefore, draws upon the treasures of particular human cultures, the gifts that God has given to people groups. God is faithful to the creatures God has called to fill the earth, working alongside them to establish a peaceful and just global community.

Not all of human culture is a gift, however. Viewing culture as a conduit for peacemaking does not mean affirming every aspect of culture, especially elements that are oppressive or unjust. As John Howard Yoder argues in *Body Politics*, the church cannot choose between being in the world and against the world; to be present in the world is always to be both.[54] Yoder provides examples of what it means to be simultaneously for and against the world:

> Some elements of culture the church categorically rejects (pornography, tyranny, cultic idolatry). Other dimensions of culture it accepts within clear limits (economic production, commerce, the graphic arts, paying taxes for peacetime civil government). To still other dimensions of culture Christian faith gives a new motivation and coherence (agriculture, family life, literacy, conflict resolution, empowerment). Still others it strips of their claims to possess autonomous truth and value, and uses them as vehicles of communication (philosophy, language, Old Testament ritual, music). Still other forms of culture are created by

---

52. Mouw, *Calvinism*, 79.
53. Mouw, *When the Kings*.
54. Yoder, *Body Politics*, 78.

the Christian churches (hospitals, service of the poor, generalized education).[55]

The Christian response to culture is always both yes and no. Like the biblical "rulers and authorities" (Col 2:15; Eph 6:12), culture can be distorted in harmful and sinful ways. But culture, the shared social knowledge of a people, is neither the problem nor the salvation. It is rather a locus of God's gracious action in the world, because it provides a venue for neighbor love. If social conflict is an opportunity for God's grace because it is a search for shared meaning, as Lederach argues, then culture makes available the resources for that grace to break through in the mundane reality of human relationships.

The yes and no with which Christians respond to culture is exactly the point Jesus is making in Matthew 5:13–16. The call to be salt represents the *no* to elements of the culture that render one a useless disciple, no different from the surrounding corruption. But the call to be light is the emphatic *yes* to the nations that are being drawn to bring their wealth to the peace of Zion. Furthermore, the way in which the light is being flooded into the world is through the community of Jesus' disciples, the city on a hill.

The tension inherent in Jesus' teaching of salt and light, to be simultaneously different from and involved in the broader society, to be in but not of the world, is also present in Isaiah. The fact that the cultural wealth of the nations is valued in the New Jerusalem is the foundation for the elicitive approach to peacemaking. Yet Isaiah states firmly that the nations do not come to the mountain of the Lord to teach, but rather to learn the ways of the Lord. The practices and richness of human cultures are not enough; the nations must be taught by God how to use those gifts to turn swords into ploughshares and spears into pruning hooks, and never to study war again (Isa 2:4). The gleanings of the elicitive approach to peacemaking are not an end in themselves, but rather the prerequisite for learning how to make peace. For this task there is one truly authoritative teacher, the Prince of Peace himself.

Deeds as Service for God's Glory

Glen Stassen and David Gushee argue that the traditional emphasis on salt and light in this passage ignores a critical third aspect of Jesus' ethical

---

55. Yoder, "Critique of Christ and Culture," 69.

mission for the church: good deeds. Here, in the third member of the teaching, is where the imperative comes. Deeds are emphasized as the climax of the teaching, clarifying the content of salt and light as actions that show God's light to the world.[56] It forms a bookend or *inclusio* with the climax of the Sermon in Matthew 7:21 and 7:24.

John Lapp describes the emphasis of Mennonite work in Somalia as bearing witness, defined as presence that takes the form of "traditional Mennonite incarnational servanthood."[57] For their first several decades Mennonites engaged in various types of service to the Somali people and nation. They ran elementary and secondary schools and taught English and agriculture. They built clinics and a nurse station and training school, and sent doctors and nurses in response to community needs for vaccinations and health care. They worked in agriculture, irrigation and food storage, and sanitation. One Somali witness noted that Mennonites earned trust by learning the language, demonstrating that they valued the community and the relationships they were building, and transporting the sick to hospitals.[58]

Paradoxically, the deeds motivated by Christian commitments might be best understood in terms of secularization. According to David Shenk, Don Jacobs was persuasive in encouraging the missionaries to think of the mission's presence as a secularizing influence, understood as a commitment to holistic development. Jacobs was formed in that thinking by two significant books: Lesslie Newbigin's *Honest Religion for a Secular Man*[59] and Arend Theodoor van Leeuwen's *Christianity in World History*.[60] The parallel arguments of these books—that secularization never happens in a society until the gospel comes, and that secularization always occurs when the gospel comes—were seminal in helping some of the missionaries to define their work in a broader way than the formation of church fellowships. Shenk recounts,

> A student came to my office one evening and said, "I want to be a believer, and I want to be a secular man. Could it be that the Christian faith is the faith for me? I don't want to go down the Soviet atheistic track. But I see that Islam is not helpful for

---

56. Stassen and Gushee, *Kingdom Ethics*, 472.
57. Lapp, "Foreword," 8.
58. Eby, *Fifty Years, Fifty Stories*, 27.
59. Newbigin, *Honest Religion*.
60. Leeuwen, *Christianity in World History*.

a secular man, because Islam says memorize the Qur'an and become more religious. And I want to be committed to community development, and where do I get the spiritual foundations for that?" I said, "What makes you suspect that the Christian faith is the faith for you?" He said, "Because the mission, that's what you're doing. You're obviously people of piety and faith. But you are revolutionizing this country in secular development. You're starting schools, even schools for women and girls. You're involved in agricultural work, and all kinds of things, for the secular uplift of the country."[61]

A life of Christian service has taken many forms for Mennonites. Pax was an alternate service program beginning with the Korean War and ending after Vietnam.[62] Pax workers served in Somalia in "appropriate technology"—oxen plowing, irrigation and food storage.[63] The program demonstrates how Mennonites can potentially be involved in post-war reconstruction in Somalia, as they were in other parts of the world.

Mennonites have cultivated a sense of responsibility for the wellbeing of neighbors near and far. The community loyalty to all peoples and ultimate loyalty to Christ that first called Mennonites to work with Somalis has transformed into practiced loyalties that reinforce the former commitments. Mennonites and Somalis have built a relationship of mutual respect that buttresses all cooperative peacebuilding efforts. This vital component of peacemaking—respectful, compassionate service—has even caused other traditions to take note; Anglican Bishop John Gladwin observes: "The Mennonite record of compassionate work in the world for the victims of power and oppression will stand comparison with any other and leaves the work of more established churches far behind in radical *commitment*."[64]

Disciples of Jesus cannot be content to remain a light to the world in only a theoretical sense. Their good deeds must reflect who they are as salt and light. Jesus' teaching later in the Sermon, however, issues a stern warning that Mennonites must take seriously. Doing good works to be seen by others in order to receive glory for oneself (Matt 6:1) is

---

61. Shenk, interview.
62. Redekop, *Pax Story*, 22.
63. Eby, *Fifty Years, Fifty Stories*, 4.
64. Gardiner, "Getting Stuck In," 367.

as worthless as flavorless salt.⁶⁵ Jesus tells his disciples to do their good deeds publicly for God's honor, never their own.

Living in the Borderlands

A peace clan—those drawn together by a vision to transform enmity into trust—is a precarious identity because it relinquishes control of boundaries and bridges. This is no more evident than when we cannot agree on what exactly peacemaking is. Chris Huebner suggests that the very disagreements about Mennonite identity—whether the so-called conservative/liberal split or the fact that we have separate development and mission agencies—indicate acknowledgement that our witness is precarious.⁶⁶

Returning to Appleby and Lederach's typology, I posit that those who tend toward different modes of Christian mission need one another in order to follow the commandments of Jesus faithfully, in keeping the calling to salt, light, and deeds in Matthew 5:13–16. Those who emphasize *conversion* and *witness* need to be reminded that the lordship of Christ extends beyond the individual to every aspect of life, including unjust systems and relationships that must be challenged and transformed. The acceptance of the other stressed by those who embrace the modes of *solidarity* and *dialogue* requires openness to change, hope rather than fear, and deep humility about one's own culture and identity. Dwelling upon the idea that Mennonites are called to live in borderlands (like the biological designation *ecotone*), Peter Dula asks, "What if MCC chose to inhabit the borderlands not because it has joined the liberals and secularists in doubting the truth of Christ, but precisely because of its unshakable conviction in Christ's lordship? What if MCC chose to transform the threat of otherness into opportunity, refusing to be controlled by fear?"⁶⁷

Those who emphasize *solidarity* and *dialogue*, on the other hand, need the reminder of those who affirm *conversion* and *witness* that Christian mission is inseparable from the call to discipleship. Furthermore, following Jesus is a communal calling, and there has only ever been one community that proclaims the lordship of Christ over all of life: the church. While avoiding the kind of evangelism that imposes itself upon

---

65. Keener, *Commentary on Matthew*, 175.
66. Huebner, *Precarious Peace*, 37–38.
67. Dula, "Interfaith Bridge Building," 161.

a culture, Christians must continue to commend Christ and the church in unobtrusive ways.

Another way to state the mutual dependence of the different modes is that Mennonite witness must consist of not only justice and peace, but also grace, as Ervin Stutzman contends. Peace with God is personal and communal, and therefore peacemaking is theological, sociological, and political. The gift that Mennonites might offer is the demonstration that the two can and must go together. Stutzman suggests that Mennonites have an unprecedented opportunity to be peacemakers in a violent world. The trust that Mennonites have built during "decades of patient presence, particularly in Muslim settings, has opened doors of opportunity for witness to people of other faiths. Mennonites may well be able to fill a unique niche in leading interfaith discussions in an anxious and tension-filled world."[68]

With the collapse of the Somali government, however, the nonviolent commitments of modernized Mennonites were tested in new ways. What could it possibly mean to make peace in a context of chaos?

---

68. Stutzman, *Nonresistance to Justice*, 260.

4

Strength is Weakness

The Appeal and Failures of Intervention

How does a diverse peace clan respond to a human crisis like that facing Somalia in the early 1990s? The question of an adequate response confounded Somalis, political leaders, NGOs, and Mennonites alike. In the face of such comprehensive fragmentation, pacifists must determine how and to what extent to use religious language when the US and the international community are contemplating military operations. This is particularly true for Christians who categorically reject the notion that violence procures justice. Can pacifist Mennonites enter a discussion about military intervention if their primary concern is faithfulness rather than effectiveness? I propose that pacifists can and must judge the justifiability of military intervention based both on its effectiveness and on a commitment to understanding the perspectives of those most impacted by the intervention.

The US and UN engaged in several iterations of humanitarian intervention in the early 1990s. The success or failure of these endeavors is difficult to measure objectively, especially because the intervention included a wide and diverse range of activities. Criteria for assessing the success of humanitarian intervention can include the long-term effects on stability within the country, region, or world; loss of life and violation of human rights; ability to adhere to the timeline and stated goals of the operation; or popular opinion within and outside the context of intervention. Each of these criteria has some value in assessing whether intervention worked in Somalia. For example, the limited scope and goals of US-led Unified Task Force (UNITAF, also known in the US as Operation Restore Hope) have led some to label it a success in feeding starving people, since its stated objective was not state-building or wide-reaching security in the country. United Nations Operation in Somalia (UNOSOM) II is widely considered a failure because it fell short of establishing security or a functioning government at the point of its withdrawal in 1995.

I believe that pacifist Christians have three important tasks on the question of humanitarian intervention. First, we must a) maintain a rigorous first-order language grounded primarily in faithfulness to the way of Jesus (what I have been describing as *salt*). But we also can and must b) employ second-order language in the public sphere that engages the merits and drawbacks of various options for response to violence and injustice. Most importantly, Christians c) demonstrate that another way is possible that is both faithful and effective in a measurable way. Glen Stassen demonstrates that presenting alternatives to war is empirically critical to a convincing argument.[1] This third task is the focus of the next chapter. My concern here is the second task, evaluating intervention on the basis of its effectiveness and justifiability.

In order to employ a second-order language it is necessary to formulate compelling principles on which to build. I identify two axioms than can inform a faithful second-order approach to evaluating humanitarian intervention. The first is the effectiveness of actions in achieving the results they claim to be seeking. In *The War of the Lamb* John Howard Yoder advocates a multilingual method in Christian ethics. Christians learn from and converse with social science, anthropology, humanists, just war ethics, Christians of all stripes, experts in diverse religions, and people of other faiths.[2] Since God is Lord of the universe, it should not be surprising if obeying God's way as revealed in Christ is more effective in bringing about movements toward justice and peace. Yoder writes, "Suffering love is not right because it 'works' in any calculable short-run way (although it often does). It is right because it goes with the grain of the universe, and that is why in the long run nothing else will work."[3] Our primary ethical norm must be faithfulness to the way of Jesus. But rather than stunting our ability to evaluate the effectiveness of a given action, rejecting violence out of obedience to Christ allows us a deeper perspective of how the world actually works. These insights can be and

---

1. Stassen, "Just Peacemaking," 174–75.
2. Stassen, "Jesus Is No Sectarian," 12.
3. Yoder, *War of the Lamb*, 62.

are reinforced by empirical social science, such as the extensive evidence provided by Erica Chenoweth and Maria Stephan that nonviolent civil resistance is far more effective than war in challenging injustice and tyranny.[4]

The second axiom is what Miroslav Volf calls *double vision*: the practice of recognizing the other's sense of justice, experience, and point of view. For Christians, double vision is guided by the will to embrace, flowing out of a new life and identity. This is not to say that truth is entirely relative, but rather that the truth as empathetic understanding makes us free in the sense that it allows one to see from the other's point of view.[5] Liberation and post-colonial perspectives have given wide currency to the notion that power imbalances make Western military action suspect. Double vision, like the elicitive method of peacemaking, opposes measures that are imposed from outside the context at the expense of peacemaking practices from within. The axiom of double vision likewise is comprehensible and compelling to many outside of the Christian tradition. For example, Ahmed Samatar argues that security responsibility belongs to the Somali leaders and people. Full democratic participation is required, strengthening cultural and Islamic values conducive to the common welfare and properly placing primary agency for ending conflict on the Somali people.[6]

Guided by these two axioms—effectiveness and double vision—I argue that the best way to measure the success of intervention in Somalia is the extent to which positive outcomes were achieved and Somalis themselves welcomed the presence and activities of foreign entities. Of course, a wide variety of opinions exist in Somali society at any given time, and accurate polls of public opinion are impossible. Yet it is possible to understand—from the perspectives of Somali clan leaders, politicians, scholars, clergy, and ordinary citizens—the extent to which foreign activities were welcomed or not.

Several key principles derive from the axioms of effectiveness and double vision: sensitivity to local traditions and experiences, consulting with local leaders, concern for long-term security rather than only short-term problem solving, and careful understanding of the narratives

---

4. Chenoweth and Stephan, *Why Civil Resistance Works*.
5. Volf, *Exclusion and Embrace*, 215–29.
6. Samatar, *Somali Challenge*, 253–54.

behind different worldviews. These are the criteria by which we must measure the justifiability of intervention in Somalia.

The issues of intervention and appropriate response in late 1992 sorely troubled concerned Mennonites, along with others in the broader church and in Christian NGO circles. I explore the contours of these debates before turning to the military operations to argue that the decision-making in the period leading up to intervention, actions during operations, and the results of the operations all indicate grave failures with regard to effectiveness and double vision. Some of these failures are due to a lack of understanding of the Somali context. Others are intrinsic to the nature of military intervention.

Imagining Intervention

The UN Security Council determined that the civil strife in Somalia was a threat to international security. Yet the action focused on feeding Somalis, not returning the refugees from other nations.[7] Several justifications and perceptions of the threat were therefore in play at the same time.

In order to understand the rationale and the persuasiveness of the arguments for humanitarian intervention in Somalia, it is important to recognize the extent of the crisis. As Siad Barre's legitimacy fell among Somalis following the Ogaden War, the strength of the opposition to his regime increased. The United Somali Congress (USC) formed in the spring of 1989 as an alliance between two Hawiye clan leaders, General Mohamed Farah Aidid and Ali Mahdi. Together they drove Barre from the capital in January 1991. The temporary cooperation immediately divided along sub-clan lines and fighting engulfed the city by November 1991, killing an estimated 14,000 people and wounding 30,000. What proved to be even more devastating was the destruction of livestock and agricultural production, which combined with drought to cause a famine that killed over 300,000 people in 1992.[8] At its peak in September 1992, 1,700 people a week were dying in Baidoa, the geographical center of the famine.[9]

---

7. Holzgrefe and Keohane, *Humanitarian Intervention*, 19–20, 42.

8. Wheeler, *Saving Strangers*, 174. Drysdale estimates the number killed by the fighting in Mogadishu in late 1991 was as high as thirty thousand (*Whatever Happened to Somalia?*, 38).

9. Drysdale, *Whatever Happened to Somalia?*, 4.

The media in the US did not begin to cover the famine extensively until two months after its peak, when the number of daily deaths had already dropped significantly. As President Bush began to move toward a US military operation in late 1992, however, the coverage accelerated. *Newsweek* printed major stories about the invasion of Somalia in every issue during the month of December, including a cover story on December 14. *Time* featured Somalia as the cover story on both December 14 and 21.[10] As US Americans received graphic photos and accounts of the violence and starvation, public support for US military involvement was overwhelming.

The vision for intervening in Somalia was articulated in several different ways in the US. Christian NGOs and publications framed the argument in terms of compassion and neighbor love. The liberal argument focused on human rights and a newfound sense of capability and responsibility within the international community following the Cold War. Both these frameworks were characterized by a perception of clarity about the threat and optimism about the role of the US in confronting the challenges of places like Somalia, Haiti, and the Balkans. During the Cold War, the potential hegemony of the Soviet Union had to be met on all fronts, including the seemingly innocuous African nations of Somalia and Ethiopia. In 1991 humanitarian concerns became the threat as a crippling famine accompanied civil war. More recently the threat has been articulated in terms of terrorism as Somalia is described as a haven for extremist groups.

The imagination driving intervention was also informed by optimism about the US and UN role in promoting democracy around the world. This vision makes several assumptions about social change and power. First, Western-style democracy must be established and defended from the top down. Second, the US and UN are the appropriate powers and authorities to police the world and rectify situations like Somalia. Justice and realism play an important role in determining both the responsibility to intervene and the conviction that military strength is necessary to confront Somalia's problems.

---

10. "Somalia: The US to the Rescue," *Time*, December 14, 1992 cover, and "Restoring Hope: Clinton's First Foreign Challenge," *Time*, December 21, 1992 cover.

Christian NGO Arguments for Intervention

In late 1992 several prominent Christian publications expressed support for US military intervention in Somalia, both from an evangelical and from a mainline Protestant perspective. *Christian Century* reported in September 1992 that the relief agencies World Vision, Catholic Relief Services, Church World Service, and Lutheran World Relief were struggling to provide for the 4.5 million Somalis in risk of starvation due to the lack of government and security.[11] An October 1992 *Christianity Today* article on the famine included a sidebar stating, "Many have said the United Nations moved too slowly in sending food (and accompanying military forces) to Somalia."[12] In November a *Christian Century* article by a Brethren relief worker in Somalia detailed the hazardous situation and recommended a food-for-guns program to reduce weaponry.[13] Religious leaders and hunger specialists in the US urged a diplomatic approach leading up to UNITAF, even as they did not rule out the possibility of backing a military solution with a limited scope. Bread for the World, for example, stated that military intervention was "necessary to save lives now,"[14] but was only a band-aid for deeper problems that must be resolved diplomatically. The Baptist World Alliance cited the use of military troops in Somalia as a precedent, calling for similar peacekeeping forces in Liberia.[15]

NGOs were mostly supportive of limited military involvement for the purpose of providing security for the delivery of aid. By some accounts, most civilian workers in Somalia advocated using whatever force was necessary against gun-wielding militia and "technicals" (truck-mounted heavy artillery). Just weeks after UNITAF forces invaded Mogadishu, Margaret Wilde wrote in *Christian Century*, "The debate reversed the usual positions on appropriate force: the United Nations and relief agency workers, including some Somalis, were calling for more force than the military wanted to use."[16]

One year after UNITAF began, and following the casualties of October 1993, most aid groups continued to insist that the US and UN should

11. "Aiding Somalia," 803.
12. Brander, "Somalia: A Deadly, Dusty Hell," 79.
13. Royer, "Relief Work in Somalia," 1052–53.
14. "Relief and Diplomacy in Africa," 1182–83.
15. Ibid.
16. Wilde, "Getting the Guns Out of Somalia," 46.

stay the course in Somalia, arguing that withdrawal would jeopardize relief efforts. Bread for the World and World Vision explicitly opposed a retreat, but called for abandoning attempts to kill or arrest Aidid.[17] In a November 1993 interview, World Vision President Robert Seiple defended the humanitarian intervention against comparisons to Vietnam, the difference being that "In Somalia, U.S. motives are both clear and right." Seiple continued, "I sense in the U.S. an increasing mood of isolationism. From a Christian perspective, this [attitude] is antikingdom."[18] According to Seiple, the US had a responsibility to intervene militarily and to stay in Somalia, and staying the course for the sake of saving lives was in the national interest of the US. Seiple was up against a growing chorus of voices calling for withdrawal from Somalia. In the same month, an article in *Christian Century* called for reevaluation of the role of the US in the world, urging greater clarity and restraint as the lesson of Somalia and Haiti.[19] When the UN withdrew the last of its troops at the end of 1994, most relief agencies, including Food for the Hungry, World Vision, and World Concern, felt they could no longer continue in Somalia.[20]

Mennonites and the Necessity of Force

The debate among Christian NGOs and North American Christians focused on two problems: the pragmatic questions of whether humanitarian intervention was effective or not, and the issue of what role the US and UN should play in addressing crisis situations around the world. Within the peace church tradition, the debate focused more on what *means* Christians should support in addressing crises like the situation in Somalia in late 1992. A few Mennonite leaders who were committed to pacifism pondered publicly what justice and neighbor love might demand in this context.

A debate along these lines took shape in the Mennonite publication *Gospel Herald*. J.R. Burkholder and Ted Koontz wrote: "Perhaps it is time to think again about some kind of dualism. By this we would acknowledge the importance of restoring order and accept the apparent need for governments sometimes to act with force or the threat of force."

---

17. "Aid Groups Support US," 1081.
18. Seiple, "Should America Stay the Course in Somalia?," 48.
19. Wall, "Nation-Building Deferred," 1075–76.
20. Guthrie, "Somalia: Warlords Await UN Withdrawal," 50–51.

At the same time, Burkholder and Koontz reiterated the continued rejection of violence on the part of Mennonites, adding: "But we believe that as pacifist Christians, military action is not our calling. For Mennonites, this may be *a time for silence*. It may be a time to neither condemn nor advocate this particular use of military force."[21] They add, however, that it is also a *time for action*, such as positive peacemaking efforts, relief activities, and nonviolent interventions like Christian Peacemaker Teams.

Robert and Judy Zimmerman Herr, former MCC East Africa Associate Directors, note that the significant backlash to this letter indicates that many readers did not understand what Burkholder and Koontz were advocating. Their argument was not in favor of military force, but acknowledged rather that there are times when a pacifist has no realistic alternative to offer and should therefore be silent. The letter was articulating that "Christian pacifists do not need to feel responsible for situations when military forces basically screw things up so badly that what we have is a humanitarian crisis of major proportions."[22]

Nevertheless, the position sounded too much like a two kingdom argument for Mennonites who had become convinced of the political relevance of Christian pacifism. J. Denny Weaver responded by calling for a continued categorical rejection of just war thinking: "The most seductive of all American myths—guns and violence solve problems, provide security, and produce freedom—has tempted Mennonites as a peace church." Weaver pointed out on a particular level the slippery slope of a situation like Somalia: "With the absence of an overt military objective in Somalia, the supposedly humanitarian use of the army is more subtle and perhaps more dangerous to Mennonites. Some claim that the use of the U.S. Army to force the warlords into a cease fire creates more good than not using the army. If Mennonites are principled pacifists, they shouldn't fall into the use of justifiable war criteria to rationalize military action. Accepting an initial compromise to make limited use of a military presence is the beginning of a series of compromises, each one allowing yet more violence."[23]

Weaver's argument points to the deep pacifist contention against the dominant acceptance of justifiable violence. In the case of humanitarian intervention in a crisis, however, the thrust is even stronger than

---

21. Burkholder and Koontz, "When Armed Force is Used."
22. Robert and Judy Zimmerman Herr, e-mail message to author, May 14, 2013.
23. Weaver, "We Must Continue."

the notion of acceptability. For many, intervention falls into the category of responsibility, ostensibly placing the burden of proof on those who reject violence categorically. Pacifists rightly feel the pressure to respond to these important questions: Can nonviolent approaches appropriately address the need for public order in a place like Somalia? Are development, service, and other peacebuilding efforts adequate alternatives to military intervention? Mennonites were divided on the question, even as the broader Christian community overwhelmingly favored humanitarian intervention in the face of violence and starvation.

After much deliberation, MCC declined to sign a November 10, 1992 letter from an association of NGOs in Somalia to national security advisor Brent Snowcroft asking for military intervention. MCC Africa co-secretary Eric Olfert explained, "We recognize that the urgent and imperative humanitarian needs must be responded to, but the approach advocated [by the UN] seems to us to be fraught with danger, unlikely to succeed, and likely to have very unhelpful impact on the even more important task of encouraging and enabling Somalis to rebuild their society. We would plead for more creativity in seeking ways to respond to the humanitarian needs which do not close off the peace processes which bring hope for the longer term."[24]

MCC, along with the American Friends Service Committee, called a meeting of ten NGOs in Washington, DC, on December 18, 1992 to discuss the implications of the military operations. Hershey Leaman, MCC disaster response coordinator, expressed concern that military intervention confuses humanitarian and political issues. Leaman stated, "The military is an ill-prepared entity to do humanitarian service. Military personnel are trained to hate, define and defeat the enemy. This training is exactly the opposite the attitude of congeniality required in humanitarian relief operations and the open consensus-seeking required for peacemaking."[25]

Gospel Herald editor J. Lorne Peachey recognized the tension between pacifists and the broader Christian NGO community in a January 12, 1993 editorial entitled "Feeding the Hungry with Messy Theology." Peachey notes the uneasiness of the pacifist rejection of military options that would allow critical aid to reach starving people. Christians are to continue obeying Christ's call to feed the hungry, he writes, "even when

---

24. Olfert, "Somalia Report."
25. Sensenig, "Relief Agencies."

our theology makes us uncomfortable with the circumstances under which we must operate."[26]

The debate around humanitarian intervention in Somalia helped to spark an ongoing conversation that culminated after September 11, 2001 in a three-year Peace Theology Project sponsored by the MCC Peace Office. The book *At Peace and Unafraid: Public Order, Security, and the Wisdom of the Cross*, edited by Duane Friesen and Gerald Schlabach, was a product of Mennonites pondering the question of what kind of response Christian pacifists can offer in a crisis situation. Friesen maintained that pacifists must embrace the responsible participation, while avoiding lethal coercive force, in "societies' legitimate need to restrain those who insist in sponsoring socially disruptive behavior."[27]

The thrust of the argument by those who urged greater responsibility for containing violence was that any response to Somalia that takes seriously the real needs of the Somali people must deal with the need for secure aid during the region's intermittent food crises. The effects of the aid industry on conflict, as well as the significant percentage of aid that is diverted from its intended recipients, have been well documented.[28] Diversion of food aid in Somalia during the 1990s was unprecedented; estimates range from 20–80 percent and many saying roughly half of the food was stolen.[29] Mary Anderson warns, however, that "It is a moral and logical fallacy to conclude that because aid can do harm, a decision *not* to give aid would do no harm."[30] Aid has an even greater impact on the conflict in Somalia because there are few accessible natural resources. Although it is often diverted and can mostly benefit warlords (as it previously did Siad Barre), suspending aid would punish the most vulnerable and create more population movements and greater poverty.[31]

Advocates of nonviolent approaches certainly cannot be accused of neglecting aid. They must deal seriously, however, with criticisms presented by those who prefer a just war approach. Martin Cook insists that in a situation of humanitarian intervention, just peacemaking—understood

26. Peachey, "Feeding the Hungry."
27. Robert and Judy Zimmerman Herr, e-mail message to author, May 14, 2013.
28. Maren, *Road to Hell*.
29. Terry, *Condemned to Repeat?*, 40, 218. Simeon Ilesanmi, citing Rwanda and Liberia as examples, argues that this kind of corruption and instability will not change without good leadership ("So that Peace May Reign," 223).
30. Anderson, *Do No Harm*, 2.
31. Anglade, "Somalia," 41.

as rejecting the use of force—should not be given moral preference over just war but rather seen as another "toolbox" available to leaders.[32] Ronald Stone argues that just peacemaking needs more serious engagement with realism, especially the kind formed by Scripture.[33] Somalia seemed to be an instance in which the potential force of a military could provide the necessary checks on the power grabs of corrupt warlords.

A nonviolent methodology that rejects violence as an option for administering aid must deal with the challenge that critical aid to Somalia has been administered under armed protection. The pertinence of this criticism is heightened by the fact that even MCC and EMM workers moved under the protection of armed guards in some cases. The MCC board agonized over this reality in a February 1993 annual meeting. Just days before, Bonnie Bergey and Marvin Frey were saved by intervening villagers in Somalia from what they thought was a certain death at the hands of armed youth. The incident reaffirmed the conflict between providing food aid for starving people and the refusal to hire armed guards, causing one board member at the meeting to observe, "It's not often that we get into a position where two fundamental beliefs conflict." The board decided that hiring Somalis with weapons would seriously compromise their peace stance, and reaffirmed the executive decision made in December 1992 not to send food to Somalia while it was so highly militarized.[34]

Not all instances of armed protection are equal, however; it is possible to identify three different ways in which Mennonites operated under the protection of people who were not committed to nonviolence. The first is protection of property by hired guards. Even before the collapse of the government, Mennonite mission workers often hired Somali guards to watch their houses, especially at night. The guards were normally armed at most with a heavy stick. But the practice raised questions not only of what kinds of actions a hired guard might take in defense of the Mennonite workers, but also in what kind of danger a guard might find himself, particularly because some of the guards were somewhat elderly.[35] A second mode is traveling on civilian buses that are protected by

---

32. Cook, "Challenges of Humanitarian Intervention," 251.
33. Stone, "Realist Criticism," 266.
34. Reimer, "MCC Board Discusses Somalia."
35. Leaman, interview.

military convoys, which was sometimes the only option in northeastern Kenya, especially the roads surrounding Garissa and Wajir.[36]

A third way in which Mennonites operated under armed protection is perhaps best understood in terms of hospitality. An early example occurred around an election time in the 1960s, when some people affiliated with one of the political parties issued death threats to foreigners. The district commissioner in Johar sent two armed police officers to guard the home of the Wesselhoeft family in Mahaddei. The Mennonites normally felt so safe that they only hooked the screen door. The sergeant who was guarding the house, however, implored them to lock the doors as well. He told them that no one in Mahaddei would ever hurt them, but that he had no way of knowing who would come from outside the area.[37] The armed protection of the Mennonites during that period was as much for the peace of mind of their Somali hosts as it was for that of the guests.

After the collapse of the government the situation was considerably more dangerous. Yet the same principle of respect for the Somali hospitality and sense of responsibility for foreigners could apply. In some cases the security of people was not the only consideration. Bonnie Bergey notes that most rented vehicles came with "gunmen included," which she realized was more for the protection and preservation of the vehicle than about her safety. Bergey writes that she always felt safer when there were no guns with her.[38] She often did not have any say in whether guns were present in a vehicle, but adds, "I don't think I ever hired guns. To me that was important. I sometimes asked them not to point the gun at me, because some of the kids would treat it so casually and haphazardly. I was more fearful of the kids who were chewing *qat*, and who didn't really care about what was going on. So I trusted them less than I did elders, women, and aid workers for NGOs."[39]

These three modes of operating under the protection of others—hiring unarmed guards, traveling with armed convoys, and accepting armed protection as a kind of hospitality—demonstrate that armed security is not a simple yes or no question for Mennonites, but is best understood in the context of relationships. Guests should not refuse what may be a

---

36. Witmer, interview.
37. Wesselhoeft, interview.
38. Bergey, "'Bottom-Up' Alternative," 153.
39. Bergey, interview.

gesture of friendship, especially when the hosts feel a sense of responsibility for their wellbeing.

Nevertheless, the question remains: the notion that some people should be armed, but that pacifists do not need to be responsible for that task, risks falling into the dualism that many Mennonites have come to reject since the latter part of the twentieth century. An adequate response to this challenge must argue one of two things: that armed protection does not make aid workers safer, or that there are alternatives to armed security. Those committed to a nonviolent approach could make claims for both, especially in a Somali context.

The first claim—that armed protection does not actually make aid workers safer—can be sensed at an intuitive level by those on the ground, as noted above by Bergey. But on a broader scale, Ken Rutherford has argued that the security industry that built up around the intervention contributed to rather than alleviated the chaos in Somalia. Some UNITAF commanders feared that NGO security guards doubled as nighttime bandits.[40] John Drysdale describes how the owners of "technicals" (four wheel drive vehicles with mounted guns) made a profitable business offering security to NGOs who were delivering aid. Despite their ethical and practical reservations, most NGOs eventually caved to the pressure to hire technicals, which was sometimes compounded by blackmail.[41] Moreover, in a context of military intervention, the wielding of weapons can move an entity from the category of a purely humanitarian organization to a political presence, at least in the eyes of local people. Aid workers become targets rather than protected personnel. According to Marvin Frey, MCC Canada overseas director, the distribution of food did not improve after the military forces entered Somalia. Part of the reason is that Somalis perceived the intervention "only as political, not as food movement."[42]

The second claim in response to the challenge of security—that there are alternatives to armed security—is especially important for an elicitive, bottom-up approach. The increasing vision among Mennonites to "seek the welfare of the city" (Jer 29:7) entails thinking critically about how order and security are maintained.[43] At *Peace and Unafraid*

---

40. Rutherford, *Humanitarianism Under Fire*, 94–95.
41. Drysdale, *Whatever Happened to Somalia?*, 46–47.
42. Reimer, "MCC Board Discusses Somalia."
43. Schlabach, "Just Policing," 418.

is an important work in a field that must be further developed. Gerald Schlabach argues that the work of putting love into practice shows that security is an important issue. He proposes the concept of *just policing* as a response to the security question. As disciples, we should not be afraid to ask what works, what is actually effective in creating security. But the various meanings of the term "security" demonstrate that assumptions are shaped by theology, ideas, and worldview, and ultimately the way that we respond to insecurity.[44]

Just policing is a point of connection with just peacemaking; a grassroots peacemaking group might take the form of a just police force. According to Lederach, just policing must work within a framework of local conflicts rather than on an international level, keeping in focus the well-being of the local people.[45] That UN peacekeeping forces and police in general are trained not to open fire indicates that there are security options and protocol that rely on alternatives to violence, which suggests the possibility of a nonviolent police force.[46] Advocates of a nonviolent approach must continue to develop this area if they are to present a credible alternative to armed security.

The question of security is an ongoing obstacle to Mennonite involvement in Somalia. In the words of Harold Reed, "North American Mennonite response to Somali requests for teachers, including peacemakers from the Mennonite community seems hampered by fear and concern about serving under protection of 'technicals.'"[47] Somalia tests the limits of the Christian conviction that our security is ultimately dependent on God. Duane Friesen argues that in order to sustain this conviction, we must keep a "thick" picture and narrative of Jesus at the center. But we must also recognize that security is integral to biblical shalom. Friesen challenges the widely held assumption that public order is dependent on violent force, which is based on a reading of Romans 13 that he calls an "ontology of violence." It is vital to distinguish between violence and coercion in public order. Yet he also acknowledges that the wisdom of the cross is an ethic of risk: "Nonviolence requires the same kind of courage as warriors who are willing to die in battle."[48]

---

44. Schlabach, "Tracing the Grain," 24–31.
45. Lederach, "Doables," 190.
46. Gingerich, "Breaking Uneasy Silence," 389–403.
47. Reed, "Believers Fellowships," 404.
48. Friesen, "In Search of Security," 38–54.

Implementing the Vision

The eruption of the civil war in Mogadishu in late 1990 went largely unnoticed in the US since it was on the eve of the Gulf War. When the US-led Operation Restore Hope was launched in December 1992 it was less on Somalia's own merits than as a test case for a new way to build an international coalition, based on discussions of the UN Security Council.[49] UNOSOM I operated from April–November 1992 under the direction of the UN Secretary General's Special Envoy, Mohamed Sahnoun of Algeria. A skilled facilitator of aid, Sahnoun's effectiveness was cut short by the abrupt and divergent approach of UN Secretary General Butros Butros-Ghali and President George H.W. Bush. When Aidid openly defied the UN presence in Somalia, demanding that all troops leave the country, Butros-Ghali made the case before the UN Security Council that Somalia required greater military force than UNOSOM could offer. UNITAF was launched as a transitional body whose purpose was to restore order and security, so that the suspended UNOSOM operations could continue.

The transition from UNOSOM I to UNITAF granted the US unprecedented latitude in determining what actions were necessary to secure aid. According to Nicholas Wheeler, the US intervention in Somalia is historic because it represents "the first time that the Security Council authorized a Chapter VII intervention—without the consent of a sovereign government—for explicitly humanitarian reasons. If Somalia is the site where humanitarian intervention broke new boundaries, it also marked a turning of the tide against such endeavors."[50]

UNITAF was a success militarily and resulted in little loss of life, but the competing warlords blocked prospects for peace. The UN Security Council established UNOSOM II in March 1993 to take over from UNITAF. The operation faced some steep challenges from the beginning, particularly in countering Aidid's anti-UN rhetoric that was persuasive for many Somalis. There was also a lack of a Somali government as a partner for state-building.[51] When Aidid's militia massacred twenty-four Pakistani peacekeepers on June 5, the UN had to choose between passive response or reprisals for the sake of deterrence. UN Resolution 837 essentially declared war on Aidid's army, and the ensuing campaign led

---

49. Marchal, "Islamic Political Dynamics," 114.
50. Wheeler, *Saving Strangers*, 172.
51. Rutherford, *Humanitarianism Under Fire*, 142.

by Admiral Jonathan Howe to find Aidid increased the tension between the Somalis and the foreign troops. At a July 12 meeting of Somali National Alliance (SNA) leaders to discuss reconciliation with UNOSOM II, which Aideed was supposed to attend, UNOSOM helicopters killed seventy-three people.[52] On October 3, a tip about another meeting brought out the Blackhawks that were brought down, resulting in the deaths of eighteen US Americans and at least five hundred Somalis, and another five hundred injured.[53] President Clinton feared that the American public, which had supported the US military presence in Somalia, would quickly change its mind at the sight of US deaths in Mogadishu. "'Americans are basically isolationist,' he said. 'They understand at a basic gut level Henry Kissinger's vital interest argument. Right now the average American doesn't see our interest threatened to the point where we should sacrifice one American life.'"[54]

The UNOSOM II coalition began to crumble following Clinton's announcement as other countries announced rapid withdrawal. The US military that had appeared invincible following the victory over Saddam Hussein's army was diminished in the eyes of many Somalis. The attempt at nation-building in Somalia had failed because of lack of resources and unclear assignment of responsibilities for the US and UN. The international community had been burned after crossing the "Mogadishu Line,"[55] a term referring to the point at which peacekeeping becomes war. The result was reticence to intervene, first in Haiti and then in Rwanda.

After UN troops left in March 1995 without achieving the goals of security and state-building, attention to Somalia mostly disappeared in the Western media and diplomatic circles until a few years after the September 11, 2001, terrorist attacks. Osama bin Laden declared Somalia as the third front of the global war against the US, after Iraq and Afghanistan. Concern about al-Qaeda links to Somalia served to justify the deployment of nearly 2,000 US troops to Djibouti in 2003, and the support of the Ethiopian invasion of Somalia in 2006–07. Tony Snow, Press Secretary for President George W. Bush, defended keeping US forces in Iraq based on the Somali experience.[56]

52. Drysdale, *Whatever Happened to Somalia?*, 196–203.
53. Bowden, *Black Hawk Down*, 333.
54. Rutherford, *Humanitarianism Under Fire*, 162.
55. Ibid., 179–82.
56. Ibid., 167–68, 184.

Western-backed transitional governments in the years following the departure of the UN enjoyed little legitimacy among the Somali people. In June 2006 local Islamic courts organized the Islamic Courts Union (ICU) and took power in much of south-central Somalia. Relative peace was restored for about six months, until the US responded by backing an Ethiopian invasion and launched airstrikes against the Islamists, reinstating the (TFG) in Mogadishu in 2007. The brutal invasion resulted in increased anti-American sentiment.[57]

The African Union's Peace and Security Council created the African Union Mission in Somalia (AMISOM) in January 2007 with an initial six-month mandate approved by the UN Security Council, with subsequent extensions. During 2007 and 2008 new Islamic militant groups organized (including the extremist group al-Shabaab) and continued to fight against the TFG's Somali and Ethiopian official troops, gaining control of large portions of the south and center of the country. Ethiopian forces retreated in 2009, leaving only an enclave of Mogadishu under TFG control. The moderate Islamic Courts Union merged into the Transitional Federal Government, and in January 2009 moderate Islamist Sheikh Sharif Sheikh Ahmed was elected president at a Djibouti peace conference.[58]

In July 2011 the UN declared a famine in parts of south-central Somalia. Millions of people faced food shortages due to crop failure and political instability. In October 2011 Kenya invaded southern Somalia with the goal of clearing al-Shabaab from the region. Journalist Mary Harper states that Kenya's attack on al-Shabaab was seen by Somalis as a US project, and in many cases actually disrupted rather than facilitated humanitarian aid. The TFG was likewise regarded by many Somalis as a puppet for foreign purposes, a satellite government that lacks legitimacy.[59] In November 2011 the Kenyan forces were subsumed under the AMISOM general command, and dispelled al-Shabaab from their stronghold in the southern city of Kismayu in 2012.

---

57. Gettleman, "Most Dangerous Place," 65–66.
58. Harper, *Getting Somalia Wrong?*, xiii.
59. Ibid., 177–79.

Why Intervention Failed

The judgment of the West leading up to the decision to intervene in Somalia was seriously impaired. Additional problems plagued the military operations after they had begun. Furthermore, both at a national and regional level the effects of intervention have been disastrous. Any good-faith defense of intervention must take stock of these shortcomings, and judge whether they are particular to Somalia or inevitable within the humanitarian intervention framework.

Sowing Distrust: Problems before Intervention

1. *Lack of proper consultation led to errors in timing, location, and strategy.* The underlying assumption of intervention is that international actors know how to proceed and are capable of resolving the problem. Westerners generally have a vision of a famine as something apocalyptic, for which the solution is simply more food.[60] As the US presented itself as the rescuer of starving Somalis in December 1992, British correspondent Richard Dowden asked:

   > Why was the decision taken to go in three months after the peak of the famine? August 1992 was the worst month for deaths but the decision to move was not taken till late November. Why did the troops land in Mogadishu at all? The famine was a local one, restricted to a particular agricultural area west of the capital around the provincial towns of Badera and Baidoa. There was hunger in the capital but the International Committee of the Red Cross (ICRC) had it under control. The famine area could have been secured as a safety zone and supplied from Kenya. Why was it necessary to try and take over the whole country?[61]

   Relevant NGOs with expertise and knowledgeable Somali staff, particularly those who had remained in Somalia over the course of the conflict (even after the UN left) were not consulted for strategy.[62] This led to a wrong diagnosis of both the timing and location of the need. The famine was over by the time the debates

---

60. Moeller, *Compassion Fatigue*, 100.

61. Dowden, "Covering Somalia," 94. Quoted in Moeller, *Compassion Fatigue*, 144.

62. Seiple, *US Military/NGO Relationship*, 106–11.

about withdrawal were happening. John Drysdale writes, "It was absurd to suggest, as UN and US spokesmen did in October 1993, when the question of a withdrawal of American troops was being debated, that, on such a withdrawal, Somalia would return to a state of wretched starvation. History in this case was most unlikely to repeat itself."[63] The famine had ended, but international actors exacerbated the conflict by sending in food aid and getting involved in clan politics, excluding Somalis from decision-making.[64]

2. *Military intervention precluded respectful relationships with Somali culture and religion.* When the culturally sensitive leadership of UN Representative of the Secretary-General Mohamed Sahnoun was replaced by the heavy-handed leadership that followed him, the possibility of distributing aid virtually disappeared. Thanks to good relationships with Somali clan leaders, under Sahnoun's leadership the number of deaths from the famine dropped significantly. Then UN Special Representative Jonathan Howe, a retired US admiral and an evangelical Christian, turned UNOSOM from a humanitarian mission into a crusade against Aidid that was operated out of a massive fortress.[65] The respectful relationships with Somali elders cultivated by Sahnoun were neglected; it became clear to the clan elders that they were not included in the vision of the future of Somalia held by the US and UN leadership.

After Aidid's killing of the Pakistani peacekeepers, the UN Security Council made a fundamental mistake in cultural awareness. According to the departed Sahnoun, the UN should have persuaded clan leaders to cooperate with the UN in bringing Aidid to justice, because "Somali tradition itself requires stern measures for slaughter and places the highest priority on collective undertaking in the matter."[66] Sahnoun demonstrated a deep understanding of Somali culture and values, proving an adept elicitive peacemaker. In his absence, the provocative insults to Somalis by the foreign presence were compounded. For example, it was profoundly offensive for Somalis, in a society in which showing someone a shoe is an egregious

---

63. Drysdale, *Whatever Happened to Somalia?*, 43.
64. Walker and Maxwell, *Shaping the Humanitarian World*, 66.
65. Drysdale, *Whatever Happened to Somalia?*, 4–5, 12.
66. Sahnoun, "Prevention in Conflict Resolution," 13. Cited in Wheeler, *Saving Strangers*, 205–6.

insult, to see the boots of US soldiers facing down on them as the helicopters flew their low-level missions over the city streets.[67] The choice is clear: cultural sensitivity that builds on the peacemaking practices of local traditions, or military intervention that excludes traditional forms of authority and locates authority instead in those who wield the guns. In Somalia, the UN and US moved from the former to the latter.

For Christians, an equally stark choice exists: Christian mission or military intervention. Many Muslims are highly critical of attempts to support the overlap of Christian NGOs and Western military intervention. There is a mutual distrust between Western relief institutions and Islamic NGOs, because many Muslims fear the political, economic and cultural influence of Western organizations and their donors. The connections that lead to these suspicions are not hard to detect: "The US government's readiness to fund and promote American 'faith-based' NGOs, many of whom have strong Christian associations, gives rise to Muslim suspicions about what is the 'real' agenda of these agencies. And, especially, they note with alarm the readiness of many Western relief agencies to call for Western military intervention, and occasionally obtain it. Islamic agencies are quick to fasten upon any perceived double standards in their Western counterparts."[68]

Christians who desire to demonstrate that their faith is not spread by force must recognize the difficulty that cooperation between Christian NGOs and the US military presents to Muslims, especially those who are experiencing the violence. Military intervention and cultural and religious sensitivity are not two sides of the same humanitarian coin; they are fundamentally incompatible with one another.

3. *The media and popular opinion drive policy, making involvement fickle.* Both Ethiopia as the archetypal media famine in 1984–1985 and Somalia's famine of 1991–1992 demonstrate that media coverage cannot serve as an effective warning system because it only follows a crisis. US humanitarian intervention missed the worst point of the famine in Somalia by three months, and it took more than a year for it to register on the international media's radar.

67. Wheeler, *Saving Strangers*, 205–6.
68. De Waal, *Islamism and its Enemies*, 13–14.

Furthermore, because millions did not die in 1991 after a famine was predicted, the "crying wolf" syndrome squelched coverage for the disaster of 1992. When the US finally decided to send troops on Thanksgiving Day, money and attention began to flow into the cause and the eventual "beach-party landing" delivering the aid was heavily publicized. Had the famine been covered more consistently in 1991 and early 1992 it would have done much to make intervention more effective in preventing deaths.[69]

Coverage of crises is prone to inconsistency based on what is perceived to be compelling to a Western audience. Likewise, at certain points Somalia was hyped while nearby Sudan was simultaneously ignored because there were no Americans there.[70] The media attention given to Somali pirates in 2011, even as Somalia went through another famine that left millions in need of assistance, indicates that the media focuses primarily on events' impact on the economic interests of the West rather than on the welfare of the Somali people. Any system that relies on media coverage and popular opinion for its motivation to respond (as does military action) will inevitably lag behind the needs of the crisis.

The media was not the whole problem, but it did contribute in that it was driven by the preferred American narrative rather than by the crisis and its responders. The media plays an important role in shaping the narrative of intervention. Popular support for intervention is built on a powerful self-perception that *we are the heroes.* One important factor in this is the tendency of the US toward chronic short-sightedness with regard to the root causes of conflicts and their own involvement and culpability. The professional priorities of journalists often lead them to report on famines with a particular storyline, including villains and heroes. For example, extensive media coverage following a U.S. military airlift of food in September 1992 focused on foreign aid workers as the heroes rather than the Somalis who were making the greatest efforts.[71] Villains are also an

---

69. Moeller, *Compassion Fatigue*, 112–55.

70. Ibid., 111, 126. Noting this inconsistency, a spring 1993 editorial in the *Christian Century* urged treating Sudan and Liberia the same as Somalia ("Sudan—the Next Somalia?," 359–60).

71. Moeller, *Compassion Fatigue*, 104, 137–38.

important part of the media storyline, whether at a micro-level or framed in terms of an over-simplified "clash of civilizations."[72]

One reason that Black Hawk Down was so traumatic for US viewers (and prompted President Clinton to call for a rapid withdrawal of all troops) was because it did not match the dominant narrative of Somalia. US heroes bringing food to hungry, grateful Somalis while staving off evil warlords fit the story; a dead US soldier being dragged through the streets of Mogadishu or soldiers in house-to-house combat did not. The impact of the Black Hawk Down catastrophe was far-reaching, undermining US and UN credibility and diminishing the will of the international community to intervene in subsequent crisis situations, including Haiti, Rwanda, and Bosnia. Images of the crisis served as an impetus both for intervening and then for abandoning Somalia after the images of dead US Army Rangers; "Live cable television news as an instrument of policy-making had clearly arrived."[73]

Deepening Anger: Failures during Intervention

1. *The US and UN had divergent goals in Somalia.* The period following the end of the Cold War was a heady time for reimagining the role of the international community, including unprecedented cooperation between the US and the UN in peacekeeping. During George H.W. Bush's four years as president and Clinton's first term in office, the UN Security Council, supported by the US, authorized more peacekeeping missions—more than twenty new operations—than the UN had attempted in its first four decades. Bush believed that the US should lead the world in military intervention because it was the morally right thing to do.[74]

Boutros Boutros-Ghali became UN Secretary General in January 1992. He was determined to use Somalia to prove his new doctrine that the sovereignty of nations was second to the universal authority and responsibility of the UN to promote the rights of individuals. From the beginning, therefore, the interests of the US and the UN were not the same in Somalia. The US State Department's

---

72. Weaver, "Meeting Jesus," 12.
73. Walker and Maxwell, *Shaping the Humanitarian World*, 66–67.
74. Rutherford, *Humanitarianism Under Fire*, 177–79.

interests were to keep their foreign policy objectives paramount, while the UN's stated goal is neutrality. The result was tension that made it unclear, even one year after Operation Restore Hope, who was supposed to be running UNOSOM: the US or the UN.[75]

While Mohamed Sahnoun was attempting to build on civil society to facilitate the delivery of aid, Boutros-Ghali was impatient for quicker results using his new doctrine of coercive peacekeeping. He wanted to use Somalia as a testing ground and pushed the UN Security Council to issue Resolution 794 in December 1992, authorizing all means necessary to establish a secure environment for humanitarian relief operations. Central to that vision was a country-wide mission of disarmament and restoring order. Somalis reacted with dismay to the combination of disarmament and a massive foreign military presence with essentially no restrictions on engagement.[76] The ensuing chaos destroyed Boutros-Ghali's ambition to use Somalia as a test for the new international sovereignty.

2. *The US and UN picked favorites with politicians and warlords, which provoked rather than settled conflicts.* Reliance on top-down democracy building results in a lack of cohesive strategy and can lead to justifying ill-advised partnerships. Jeffrey Gettleman describes the US as "among the worst of the meddlers" and points to the results: "U.S. forces fought predacious warlords at the wrong time, backed some of the same predacious warlords at the wrong time, and consistently failed to appreciate the twin pulls of clan and religion. As a result, Somalia has become a graveyard of foreign policy blunders that have radicalized the population, deepened insecurity, and pushed millions to the brink of starvation."[77]

The roots of the Somali conflict stretched back into the years of the Barre regime, but so also did the potential for reconciliation and a relatively peaceful transition of power. In contrast to the dominant narrative of intractable conflict between warlords, it is important to note that before the international community was involved there were significant movements toward reconciliation and national unity.[78] Furthermore, Sahnoun built up diplomatic relationships

75. Drysdale, *Whatever Happened to Somalia?*, 1–3, 14.
76. Ibid., 104–6, 165.
77. Gettleman, "Most Dangerous Place," 62.
78. Drysdale, *Whatever Happened to Somalia?*, 21–27.

with all parties, including both Aidid and Mahdi, in addition to clan elders. But after Aidid forced Mahdi out of Mogadishu, the UN demonstrated that it had not learned the lesson that taking sides would break down any possibility for reconciliation. The UN recognized Mahdi as the head of a nonexistent government, in hopes of having a formal link between Somalia and the UN. It was a grave error to treat Mahdi differently than other recognized political leaders, because Aidid began to see the UN as an enemy.[79] In taking sides with Mahdi and marginalizing Aidid politically during the Addis Ababa peace process, the UN lost vital credibility as a neutral mediator.[80]

A top-down approach to democracy building requires a government to partner with the international community. The mistake of the UN was to pick such a partner without first allowing him to emerge as a legitimate representative of the people. Such favoritism only stokes the conflict rather than moves it toward reconciliation. The interference of the international community, rather than working toward lasting peace, only provided artificial legitimacy for the warlords, against the will of the majority of Somalis.

3. *The justification and goals of the Western involvement in Somalia shifted from humanitarian aid to full-fledged confrontations with warlords—a classic case of "mission creep."* A UNOSOM massacre of what was essentially a peace meeting between SNA leaders was heavily publicized in the Somali newspapers. It was a turning point in UNOSOM II; *Medecins Sans Frontieres* president Rony Brauman called the event a "humanitarian crime," lamenting that "For the first time in Somalia there has been killing under the flag of humanitarianism."[81] Somali opinion turned almost unanimously against the intervening forces. However much Somalis generally disliked Aidid personally, they were appalled by what they perceived as neocolonialism in the form of foreign military presence and regarded the UN actions as American-inspired.[82] By October 1993 the depth of anti-US sentiment among Somalis was shocking to US Americans; Rutherford writes about Blackhawk Down, "It is clear that the American-led forces were taken by surprise by the

---

79. Ibid., 39–42.
80. Makhubela, "Conflict Resolution in Somalia," 97.
81. Peterson, *Me Against My Brother*, 118–28.
82. Drysdale, *Whatever Happened to Somalia?*, 196–98.

audacity of the Somali fighters. Unlike the American experiences in other African countries, such as Liberia, the Somalis disregarded the firepower of US soldiers and fought while absorbing high casualties."[83] The bloodshed of that incident set in motion the withdrawal of US and eventually UN troops.

It is important to ask why mission creep occurs in the first place. I contend that it is inherent in military intervention for several reasons. First, military presence, more than NGOs or even foreign diplomats, creates a psychological barrier for the local population. This is especially true when a society has a collective memory of colonialism and imperialism, and when religious identity and distrust are in play. In that sense, no matter what foreign troops are doing or intend to do, most Somalis will oppose their presence. Secondly, military strength creates an inflated sense of capability in the minds of the intervening powers. The force of advanced weaponry and technology instills false confidence, when in reality even the most seemingly straightforward tasks are exceedingly complex in an unwelcoming environment. No doubt Boutros-Ghali and his US allies expected that subduing Somalia would require mere days or weeks. Howe assumed that capturing Aidid would be painless with the sort of military dominance that the US enjoyed. On both counts, the intervening powers were drastically wrong.

The ensuing years demonstrated that the US had not learned any lesson beyond an increased hesitance to be as directly involved. Supporting the Ethiopian overthrow of the ICU in 2006 was a further extension of mission creep in Somalia. So was shutting down Mogadishu's al-Barakat market during the "war on terror" because of suspicions about funding terrorist groups, a move that was economically devastating to thousands of ordinary Somalis. By any criteria of effectiveness or double vision, with these ever-changing goals and tactics the West has lost any credibility it once had in claiming to care primarily about the welfare of the Somali people.

Reaping Chaos: Results of Military Involvement

1. *Foreign military involvement has resulted in a flood of weapons in the country.* Siad Barre was adept at procuring armaments from both

---

83. Rutherford, *Humanitarianism Under Fire*, 159.

the Soviets and the US during the Cold War. The long-term problems stemming from the hyper-militarization of the Somali state were foreseeable even in the 1970s. One commentator, observing the massive Somali army equipped with the latest Soviet weaponry, tanks, and aircraft, wrote in 1978 that Somalia's militarism had built up "a 38,000-man army (in a nation with a population of 3.5 million) and a defense budget far in excess of the total nondefense spending. And Somalia has one of the lowest per-capita annual incomes in the world (about $70)."[84]

Militarization indeed proved to be the enemy of democracy and development in Somalia. During the Cold War, the North supplied the ideologies, weapons, and loans, while the South contributed environments, people and national economies. When the global community legitimizes the use of armed force for security and defense, weapons production remains a legitimate and lucrative business, increasing the availability of weapons in conflicts. In some African countries more money was spent on military expenditures than on health and education combined. It is therefore not difficult to understand why places like Somalia are saturated with weapons but have a fragile social infrastructure.[85] Many of these weapons, particularly the smaller arms, found their way into civilian hands and continue to be the weapons fueling militias today. As his situation became increasingly desperate, Barre distributed large numbers of weapons to his fellow Darod clan members.[86]

In addition to the massive amounts of arms and military aid from superpowers during the Cold War ($200 billion to Barre's regime from the US alone), regional powers like Ethiopia, Egypt, Eritrea, and Libya fed the conflict by supporting militias against one another.[87] The influx continued in recent years; the US sent $2 million and forty tons of arms and ammunition to the TFG in 2009.[88]

Such ready availability of weapons has been devastating on the traditional Somali political process, undermining traditional forms of authority, peacemaking, and balance of power. The flood

84. Murphy, "Somalia: Militarism vs. Democracy," 447.
85. Lederach, *Building Peace*, 6–12.
86. Makhubela, "Conflict Resolution in Somalia," 43.
87. Anglade, "Somalia," 37.
88. Parke, "Terrorizing Aid to Somalia."

of weapons as "gifts" in the decades under Barre has made relationships among politicians and elders bitterer than they otherwise would have been.[89] It has turned ownership of a gun into a perceived economic necessity for some, and raised countless Somali children in a lifestyle of violence.

2. *Military intervention radicalizes and spreads the conflict to other parts of the region.* As a weak government fights to maintain control, both it and the opposition groups use more and more extreme violence to subdue the population on the other side. Michael Ignatieff writes, "This slow process of fission—observable in Sudan, Somalia, and Sierra Leone—may spread beyond the borders of the state itself, as refugee populations flee across the borders and as insurgent groups use frontier zones for their base camps. A collapsing state thus has the capacity to metastasize and spread its problems through the region."[90]

The events of recent years most clearly demonstrate the radicalizing and widening effects of military action in Somalia. It was a major mistake for Ethiopia, supported by the US, to take out the Islamic Courts Union in 2006. The ICU was the only entity to establish authority in Mogadishu since 1991, because it built government from the bottom up in the areas it controlled. Furthermore, the ICU enjoyed legitimacy among Somalis, who are always united against external military intervention.[91] Seeking to regain control, the warlords presented the ICU as a breeding ground for terrorism, to which the US responded by backing the Ethiopian invasion. Al-Qaida and other extremist groups had faced similar challenges to the US in Somalia in that they were seen as foreigners and distrusted. As a result of the invasion, however, new militant groups like al-Shabaab and Hizbul Islam formed in the wake of the ICU's defeat, and thus the US and its allies created the enemy they claimed to be destroying. The TFG propped up by foreign powers was seen as a Western tool. Furthermore, the invasion resulted in a humanitarian crisis, with

---

89. Drysdale, *Whatever Happened to Somalia?*, 55.

90. Ignatieff, "State Failure," 302–3. Regional instability is not only across national borders; journalist Jay Bahadur argues that the rampant piracy off the Somali coast, which has declined in recent years, can be traced to the dissolution of the state as well as to environmental factors (*Pirates of Somalia*, 39–41).

91. Makhubela, "Conflict Resolution in Somalia," 98–100.

Mogadishu emptying and refugee camps filling in 2007–2008. Kenya's attack on al-Shabaab in October 2011 was seen by Somalis as a US project, and resulted in the disruption of humanitarian aid.[92]

One of the regional implications of intervention is that countries with troops on the ground in Somalia face retaliation by al-Shabaab, which publicly declared allegiance to al-Qaeda in 2010. Uganda sent more troops to Somalia than any other nation under AMISOM, which seems to have been a factor in the July 2010 suicide blasts in Kampala that killed seventy-four people watching World Cup soccer, for which al-Shabaab claimed credit. Ethiopia, as a constant enemy presence in Somalia, faces threats of militant terror attacks both from Somalia and neighboring Eritrea. Across the gulf, Yemen serves as a hotbed for cooperation between militant groups.

More than any other country, Kenya now faces the biggest threat of Somali-based Islamist attacks on its own soil. It hosts Dadaab, the largest refugee camp in the world, in which half a million Somalis live in a space meant for ninety thousand. Kenya has been unable to control the movement and recruitment activities across its lengthy borders. Kenyan security forces suspect the Nairobi neighborhood of Eastleigh of being a terrorist haven, which Somalis in Kenya deny. Somalis in Kenya face discrimination based on the history of enmity, prejudice, and a sense of competition for business between the two nationalities.[93] The 2011–12 incursions into Somalia by Kenyan troops have exacerbated the already heightened bitterness. Even the successful expulsion of al-Shabaab from Kismayu resulted in spreading rather than containing the conflict.[94] Al-Shabaab has cited the Kenyan military presence in Somalia as justification for deadly attacks at a Nairobi shopping mall in September 2013, on Nairobi buses in May 2014, and at Garissa University College in April 2015.

Militant groups like al-Shabaab rise and fall on their popularity with the local people. When their self-centered power-seeking is revealed to Somalis, their authority and influence will be significantly weakened. Foreign intervention only legitimizes the narrative that

---

92. Harper, *Getting Somalia Wrong?*, 85, 170–79.

93. Ibid., xiii, 184–94.

94. Daoud Hersi (pseudonym), interview by author, Lancaster, PA, February 8, 2013.

they are the true defenders of Somali society, and killing the top leaders only solidifies the movement. Regardless of how successful such actions may be in the short term, only Somalis themselves can deprive ideological militants of their power and build toward lasting peace.

Contesting Intervention

It is critical for Christians in a Western democracy to employ persuasive arguments that appeal to the values of the context. I have been arguing that the two primary questions to ask in the quest for a public ethic with regard to humanitarian intervention in Somalia are these: the long-term effectiveness of the action, and how the action is perceived by Somalis. The axioms of effectiveness and double vision demonstrate glaring errors in the decision-making leading up to intervention, actions during operations, and the results of the operations. Some of these failures are specific to a Somali context, but some are intrinsic to military action in any comparable situation.

In the instance of Somalia, the burden of proof to justify actions lies heavily with those who advocate military intervention. Can it be demonstrated that what is being accomplished is enough to justify the destruction, loss of life, and further fragmentation and political enmity that it has caused? In light of the above critiques, the assumptions and variables on which this approach is built must be examined seriously by those who remain supportive of this type of response.

Has intervention performed positive functions in Somalia? There are many ways to answer this question, but one possible way is by comparing the outcomes of a mission with its stated goals. For example, the limited scope and goals of UNITAF have led some to label it a success in feeding starving people, since its stated objective was not state-building or wide-reaching security in the country. By some accounts, as a humanitarian mission the intervention in Somalia was initially successful in saving some lives, even as it turned out to be a political failure.[95] John Drysdale concludes of Operation Restore Hope: "As a mission of mercy it was a great success, though it could have been equally well achieved, and with greater alacrity, with a far smaller number of troops."[96] After

---

95. Rutherford, *Humanitarianism Under Fire*, 186.
96. Drysdale, *Whatever Happened to Somalia?*, 6.

reviewing the profound shortcomings of a military approach in Somalia, Christian pacifists might well ask if Drysdale's conclusion does not reach far enough: Might it actually be the case that missions of mercy, if they are truly such, are best achieved when there is *no* foreign military presence at all?

What About When Intervention "Works"?

Those who reject violent intervention must take seriously the challenge that seemingly positive outcomes can result from military action. The clearest example in the case of Somalia is the 2012 operations by Kenyan and African Union troops in southern areas of the country, which have succeeded in weakening the influence of the militant Islamist group al-Shabaab in particular areas. Many Somalis celebrated the waning of the organization's destructive presence, particularly in Kismayu.[97] The Somali women in EMU's Center for Justice and Peacebuilding who come from all regions of the country also welcome the decline of al-Shabaab.[98]

How does one committed to nonviolence respond to the challenge that military intervention can "work"? It is appropriate to respond on three levels: historical, theoretical, and theological. Historically, military operations that are justified in the short term as restraining evil, establishing security, and defending the weak often have the opposite effect in the long term. Military intervention in Somalia, especially the UN and US involvement from 1992 to 1995, has failed to stabilize the country, restrain warlords, or defend the innocent. Foreign diplomats, even those seeking to play the role of peacemaker, legitimized and abetted warlords rather than weakened their influence. In 2006–2007 the US-backed actions of Ethiopia actually destabilized the country, which under the Islamic Courts Union was experiencing its most peaceful months since the collapse of the government. That endeavor led to the radicalization of Somali groups and facilitated the formation of al-Shabaab. In light of this history, the assertion that further military action is the solution to the problem of extremism is absurd. The effects of the most recent incursions by Kenyan and AU troops are already indicating that although al-Shabaab can be ousted from its strongholds, as it was from Mogadishu

---

97. Hersi, interview.
98. Gloria Rhodes, interview by author, Harrisonburg, VA, April 7, 2013.

and Kismayu, militant groups can continue to kill in retaliation, as they have in Garissa, Nairobi, and Mogadishu in 2013.

Douglas Ansel argues that al-Shabaab's power and legitimacy among Somali civilians derive both from genuine benefits to the population and from coercion. Foreign military actions to weaken al-Shabaab, including designating it a terrorist organization, can have the opposite effect. Ansel writes, "Until harsh military reprisals against al-Shabaab locations end, which often harm more civilians than militia, al- Shabaab will continue to remain a viable source of security. Likewise, if Ethiopian troops and their proxies re-enter the country, their presence will provide a nationalistic rallying point for support of al-Shabaab. In a paradoxical situation, strengthening the TFG [Transitional Federal Government] militarily may be responsible for weakening its roots in society, undercutting any hopes it has to govern effectively in the long run."[99]

On a theoretical level, it is fallacious to assume that because military action yields some intended outcome in the short term, only force would have been effective in that situation. By some accounts, the relative success of the Kenyan and AU troops was due in part to the fact that al-Shabaab had already lost favor among Somalis, severely restricting how it could operate.[100] Furthermore, the assumption that violent strategies are more effective than nonviolent ones has been challenged, if not altogether disproven, by evidence from all over the world that civil resistance is far more effective than war in challenging injustice and tyranny.[101]

Even if it can be proved that a military action performs some particular good, like dispel or mitigate al-Shabaab, it is not necessary to conclude that Christians must condone the violent manner in which it is done. It is even possible to understand such actions as a part of God's providential plan without concluding that Christians should participate in them. In fact, understanding God's use of evil actions for good can actually strengthen the case against Christian participation in killing. In the words of John Howard Yoder, "There is a nonreversible relationship between our deeds, which may be evil, and God's use of them for ultimate good. God's sovereignty, which includes wrath, can integrate the works of human rebellion without rendering those actions morally good." Yoder continues, "That God reserves vengeance to himself and may then

---

99. Ansel, "Civilian Support," 32.

100. Ahmed Ali and Mohamed Farah (pseudonyms), interview by author, Columbus, OH, January 2, 2013.

101. Chenoweth and Stephan, *Why Civil Resistance Works*, 220–26.

'delegate' that vengeance to Cyrus or to Caesar (Rom 13:2, 4 and Isa 45) is grounds for his people to renounce human vengeance (Rom 12:19 but also Deut. 32:35) rather than claiming to be his instruments."[102]

Isaiah 45 employs striking language to describe the pagan Assyrian king, Cyrus. Just before calling Assyria "the rod of my anger" and condemning its arrogance and destructive deeds toward other nations, Isaiah labels Cyrus God's "Messiah" (anointed one). Just because God uses a pagan army for divine purposes does not mean that the deeds they do are good works, or that God's people are called to participate in them.[103] Isaiah's point is rather that the Suffering Servant presents a concrete civil alternative to the claims of Cyrus or Caesar,[104] and that God is at the center of history rather than Cyrus.[105] I have argued at length that military intervention in Somalia has accomplished much less long-term good than the killing, destruction, and chaos it has fostered. But even if some good outcomes emerge from military actions, it is because God's providence has brought good out of evil, which may happen despite the violence rather than because of it.

What Have We Learned?

Granting that some good can come of military intervention, it remains the case that whatever success can be celebrated in Somalia is overshadowed by profound failures. UNOSOM II is widely considered a failure because it fell short of establishing security or a functioning government at the point of its withdrawal in 1995. Many foreign policy scholars agree at some level on some of the basic "lessons" of Western involvement in Somalia, although there are differences in emphasis. Ken Rutherford writes that the UN should be careful to conduct peace enforcement missions in states with internal strife only with clear and narrow goals, that forced disarmament without a national agreement is unachievable, and that the US military must develop the ability to work with other nations rather than unilaterally.[106] For Michael Ignatieff, the first lesson from Somalia is that while democracy is good in the long run, in the short

---

102. Yoder, *For the Nations*, 244–45.
103. Sider, *Scandal of Evangelical Politics*, 96.
104. Yoder, *For the Nations*, 86.
105. Friesen, *Isaiah*, 277.
106. Rutherford, *Humanitarianism Under Fire*, 185–86.

term attempts to establish democracy in a society with ethnic stress can have explosive consequences. He asks whether failed states *should* be put back together with the same borders and populations, suggesting that in Somalia's case the answer is no.[107] Somaliland is prospering, Puntland is surviving, but only in southern Somalia does the conflict continue "in part because there is a capital for warlords to fight over and some dribbles of aid and other external sources of income. Reconstituting a central state would certainly require a long-term colonial occupation by some foreign power. It is not clear that this is either possible or desirable."[108] Somalia has cultivated strong sentiments about Western interference, causing some to question the value of imposing foreign solutions.[109]

Nicholas Wheeler sees the lesson of Somalia as the necessity of long-term commitment to social reconstruction and conflict resolution, not just the end to immediate suffering. The lack of commitment to Somalia in the US is symptomatic of liberal societies, which generally pay attention only when human rights violations are so gross that they are seen as affecting humanity everywhere. The ideological bias toward intervention only for a catastrophe obscures the slow death-dealing effects of poverty and malnutrition, because addressing these problems would require changes in lifestyle and consumptive practices. Wheeler concludes that governments are unreliable as rescuers, but that no one else can fill the void. Since only states have the capacity to fly troops around the world, what we need is a moral consciousness that holds our leaders accountable for not saving strangers in need.[110]

At one level these are all worthy responses in that they recognize the need for humility and creative thinking and action. Focusing on "lessons learned," however, can obscure the fact that Somalia has been used as a testing ground for the ambitions and worldviews of the global powers, at the expense of thousands of Somali lives. What needs to be questioned is not how to make intervention more efficient and less costly for the West, but the underlying logic that intervention can ever build toward a sustainable peace. Before the West purports to learn any lessons from Somalia, we must face the depth of the shame of UNOSOM. One moment in particular brings this shame into focus: the massacre by UNOSOM

---

107. Ignatieff, "State Failure," 300, 306.
108. Ibid., 311.
109. Menkhaus, *Somalia: State Collapse*.
110. Wheeler, *Saving Strangers*, 306–10.

helicopters of Somali clan leaders in a peace meeting. This incident alone is enough to shatter the myth that the US and UN were noble peacekeepers in Somalia rather than obstacles to peace.

I am not convinced that the Western powers learned anything new from Somalia, making scholarly conclusions of "lessons learned" ring hollow. Somalia caused the pendulum of justification for military intervention to swing from multilateralism to unilateralism, from global solidarity to isolationism, and from paternalistic ambitions of saving Somalis from themselves to rhetoric about how only Somalis can save themselves, even as the West continues to back military interventions by other African nations and prop up federal governments that are not necessarily perceived as legitimate by the Somali people.

What Christians must question at a more foundational level is the assumption that there is a need to decide between the dichotomy of intervention and isolation. For cruciform Christians neither one is an option. Our neighbors around the world are of no less value than those nearby. The sentiments that were stated as the impetus for intervention in Somalia, therefore, are ones that Christians must absolutely affirm. We are responsible for the wellbeing of our Somali neighbors. But—and this is the deep failure of intervention—we are required by our faith to treat them as neighbors, recognizing when we are guests.

The perception of pacifists as socially irresponsible in letting evil win out—an influential accusation of Reinhold Niebuhr's[111]—assumes that responsibility can only take a narrow governmental or military form. When the question of civic duty is given more adequate definition, however, the reality is that peace churches have responded to the needy in many significant ways without relying on a particular nation for legitimacy.[112] Those who reject both military intervention and isolationism are not left without alternatives to the dominant bias toward military intervention. Nonviolent practices, even in a fragmented context like Somalia, are both more attentive to the value of human life and more effective in bringing about lasting social change. We turn now to consider how Mennonites joined Somalis in imagining a peacebuilding alternative to military intervention.

---

111. Niebuhr, "Why the Christian Church is Not Pacifist," 301–13.
112. Driediger and Kraybill, *Mennonite Peacemaking*, 269–70.

5

A Salt and Light Alternative

Mennonites and Somali Peacemaking Practices During the Civil Conflict

When we share the *mayida* [common meal], there can be no bad blood.
— NURUDDIN FARAH, *LINKS*

CHRIS HUEBNER OBSERVES THAT the church, like the military, is always on the move into new territories, making claims to new ground. Both the church and the military speak of a desire for peace. But the peace they seek is of a radically different kind. A military understanding of peace is that it is something secured as part of a calculated chain of events and actions. It seeks to tame the world's chaos and bring balance and security. The military operates by extending its control over new areas. "The peace of the church, however, is a vulnerable exchange of gifts. It is not safe, but dangerous. . . . It moves as if from below, from the underground. Its vision consisting of glimpses and brief snatches, never putting itself above the realities it encounters."[1]

Having examined the failures of military intervention either to understand relationships to Somalis as a gift or to establish balance and security, here I develop what it might mean for Mennonites to be *salt* and *light* in a Somali context, particularly in the circumstances following the collapse of the government in 1991. Based on Matthew 5:13, I take *salt* to mean the task of the community of Christ to maintain distinct practices

---

1. Huebner, *Precarious Peace*, 19–20.

in contrast to the powers and authorities of the world, particularly the entrenched myth of redemptive violence and its derivative practices. The Mennonite presence in the preceding decades laid a foundation for an alternative response to the dominant mode of intervention in the face of Somalia's crises.

Light in Matthew 5:14–16 refers to the role of the Christian community in pointing people of all cultures to the city on the hill, where peacemaking practices are strengthened and practices of war are abolished (Isa 2:1–5). The elicitive approach builds on the conviction that the tools for peacemaking are not manufactured externally but emerge from within a culture. Somali culture has a wealth of resources for peacemaking that can strengthen security as well as provide for the needs of everyone. Kinship performs both the positive social function of ensuring that all have their needs met and the positive political function of resolving conflict through the traditional channels of authority, the elders. The traditional social contract *xeer* is a vital tool in moving conflict from the vicious cycles of retaliation toward restitution and even reconciliation.

Centering peacemaking on reconciliation rather than simply coexistence, Mennonites engaged these Somali traditions in a number of ways during this period. MCC and EMM supported ground-up peace initiatives led by Somalis, such as the peace group *Ergada* and the successful Borama Peace Process, rather than assuming the necessity of a highly centralized government at the expense of traditional forms of governance.

Even as the political situation deteriorated and inter-clan violence escalated in the late 1980s, EMM resolved to maintain a presence in Somalia. Motivated by the conviction that "a Christian presence and witness is necessary in times like these,"[2] EMM strengthened the team to nine people working in education and health ministries in Mogadishu by the end of 1990. By December, however, they recognized that returning to Somalia following a retreat in Kenya would be impossible. Within two months EMM's Northeast Africa Director called the timing of the retreat "providential,"[3] because EMM workers were already out of the country when full-scale civil war erupted in Mogadishu in January, forcing all remaining expatriates to be evacuated by US helicopters. EMM and MCC determined to remain present with the Somali people, opening an office

2. David W. Shenk to Pastors, Former Missionaries, and Families of EMBMC Missionary Team in Somalia, memorandum, January 15, 1991.

3. Harold Reed to EMBMC, memorandum, February 19, 1991.

in Kenya to stay connected to refugees and believers, as well as to issues of education, development, and peace.[4] Several personnel remained on standby in the hopes that the situation would settle enough for them to return to Somalia. Representing EMM and MCC, Bonnie Bergey made frequent trips into Somalia from Kenya, arranging for nurses to come during ceasefires, and along with John Paul Lederach attending meetings of clan elders, women, and others who were reaching across clan lines to discuss peace.[5] The relief and development work continued with great care to provide equal aid to various groups, so as not to aggravate inter-clan tension or conflict.[6] Mennonite service to Somalis extended even to the diaspora, helping with immigration, settlement, and advocacy in North America.[7]

Not until 2000 did EMM again assign workers to live in the country, this time for a brief period in Somaliland. Leon and Elaine Good, who had formerly worked in Somalia, taught biology and English at Amoud University starting in January 2000. Beginning in 1990 EMM sent teachers to neighboring Djibouti, a presence that continued until 2009. Work with Somalis in Kenya also continued throughout the period of civil war. In September 1992 the Canadian Somali Friendship Association for Peace and Development was formed in Toronto. MCC's peacemaking efforts during this time included financially supporting a five-month convention of clan elders to resolve conflicts in fall 1993, funding several peace conferences for women in 1997–98, and holding a workshop on AIDS in Mogadishu in January 2002.[8]

The Elicitive Method

One of the greatest challenges of peacemaking is developing an approach that builds on local culture and traditions rather than imports models based on foreign assumptions and practices. The leading pioneer of the theory and practices of this approach is John Paul Lederach, who teaches in the Kroc Institute for International Peace Studies at the University

---

4. Beachy, "Somali Journey," 238.
5. Eby, *Fifty Years, Fifty Stories*, 86, 92.
6. Lederach, "Mennonite Central Committee Efforts," 141–42.
7. Schwartzentruber, "Canada," 195–96.
8. Eby, *Fifty Years, Fifty Stories*, 128–29.

of Notre Dame and in the Conflict Transformation Program at Eastern Mennonite University.

Lederach challenges the assumptions that the model we use in one setting can be used in all others with some adjustments, and that culture is an aspect of conflict resolution that can be reduced to technique. On the contrary, conflict resolution itself is a socially constructed, educational phenomenon. Social conflict is a natural experience present in all cultures and relationships, and does not simply "happen" but is created by people. Conflict centers around the search for shared meaning, which occurs as people locate themselves within the accumulated knowledge of the culture. Lederach sees peacebuilding as a "profound adventure of digging" into this shared cultural knowledge that is at the root of meaning and therefore of social conflict. Rather than the static, foundationalist view that seeks to define conflict for all times and places, he prefers the dynamic, constructionist view that people act on the basis of the meaning that things have for them. Lederach concludes, "Understanding conflict and developing appropriate models of handling it will necessarily be rooted in, and must respect and draw from, the cultural knowledge of a people."[9]

Drawing from the *emic* approach articulated by Clifford Geertz, Lederach constructs what he calls an *integrated framework*—consisting of the three parts of popular education, appropriate technology, and ethnography—that relies on people's own interpretations of conflicts as a key resource. Empowerment to address conflict then emerges from the process of understanding and describing the problem. What needs to change in our approach is that "Metaphorically, we tend to translate our materials into another language, rather than create them in situ."[10]

An Ethiopian friend once told me, with evident concern for his Somali neighbors, that the problem with Somali people is their culture. This attitude is sometimes reflected in anthropologies that note the fierce independence and warlike nomadic history of Somalis. At the heart of Lederach's argument, however, is the assumption that culture is not an obstacle or a challenge to be overcome but a conduit for peacemaking, based on the shared social knowledge. In Somalia, this social knowledge includes proverbs and storytelling,[11] among other elements.

---

9. Lederach, *Preparing for Peace*, 5–10.
10. Ibid., 25–33.
11. Ibid., 78, 120.

Lederach contrasts the elicitive model with the dominant prescriptive approach. In the prescriptive model, the trainer knows what the participants need. This approach is built on the premises of transferability and universality. The elicitive model, on the other hand, assumes that training consists mostly of the discovery, evaluation, and adaptation of resources already present; "The elicitive-oriented approach is built on drawing out and using what people bring you, even when it is not understood by them as a resource." According to Lederach, however, these approaches are not mutually exclusive. Both have strengths and weaknesses; the prescriptive is often more expeditious, but runs the risk of attempting to be universal and not transferring well. We need both in any given context, but generally there is more need to move toward the elicitive side, which means not a change in techniques as much as a change in relationship between the trainer and the participant.[12] Lederach calls this a "nested paradigm" because it focuses on building relationships with people already embedded in the community rather than on top-down strategies.[13]

An elicitive approach is particularly important for deeply religious societies such as Somalia, because it can facilitate listening to the other, bring self-awareness of how one is viewing the other, and foster the realization that there are multiple paths to peace, not just one. Marc Gopin observes, "Most religious advocates of violence whom I have encountered do so reluctantly, feeling compelled by religious authority, by threatening circumstances, and by prevailing hermeneutic readings of their tradition. A slow and steady process of exposing them to the humanity of their enemies combined carefully with exploring alternative hermeneutic religious paths often creates a quiet revolution in religious thinking, both individually and collectively."[14]

If the tools for conflict transformation are found within a culture rather than imported from without, what role can an outsider possibly play in building peace? Lederach's answer is that the elicitive model relies on trainers, who can be from within or outside the cultural context. Training is the process of working together with a group to discover language for describing the conflict, and to develop a model of mediation. One guiding principle for such training is that the leader assumes the

---

12. Ibid., 48–70, 83.
13. Appleby, *Ambivalence of the Sacred*, 18.
14. Gopin, *Between Eden and Armageddon*, 63.

posture of a facilitator rather than an expert. Trainers must do two things throughout this process: first, do their homework about what cultural assumptions are implicit in the models they bring; and second, seek participants' knowledge as the basis for making peace. Because training is not an event but the development of a sustainable community, it becomes part of the broader peace-building framework. As such the relationship between the trainer and the participant is of utmost importance.[15] Lederach cautions about focusing on numbers rather than the quality of relationships. Critical mass is a popular concept in social movements and is often assumed to be the heart of social change. But the inverse is actually true; "Focus on quantity distract[s] from focus on quality and on the space needed to generate and sustain change." What is needed in places like Somalia is not critical mass, but critical yeast consisting of the right people in the right places.[16]

Just as Lederach identifies the roles and characteristics of trainers across cultures, Gopin emphasizes connecting cultures to create a bond that is able to withstand some insults and misunderstandings for the sake of the relationship. He claims that he learned from Mennonites the importance of evoking the peacemakers in each culture. The best peacemakers have internal qualities of peace, patience, and not too strong a connection with immediate outcomes, that is, no need to "win" arguments. Once peacemakers have been identified, a multitude of possibilities for cultural connection exist. Shared mourning is one way in which the common humanity of each party can be seen in new ways. Greeting and the face are another important symbol of both kindness and hardness in the Middle East across faiths. Compassionate, active listening can spark spontaneous outbursts of powerful reconciliation, putting a new face on the enemy. Compassionate actions that demonstrate awareness of pain on the other side communicate recognition of common humanity. A display of gratitude is yet another symbolic act that is central to tradition. It helps one see things in a new way and shocks one out of impaired vision. Gopin relates how his African students responded positively to having their cultures honored; he marvels that symbolic transformation and cultural methods of reconciliation are a natural resource all over the world, waiting for people to discover and employ them.[17]

---

15. Lederach, *Preparing for Peace*, 99–121.
16. Lederach, *Moral Imagination*, 90–91.
17. Gopin, *Holy War, Holy Peace*, 121–26, 163–85.

Gopin repeatedly evokes the power of symbol, for both good and ill. Attacks or aid during times of fasting or feasting are only amplified in significance. This is because symbol plays such a central role in the imaginations of people involved in the conflict. The possibilities for transforming symbols into peacemaking initiatives are everywhere: apologies and joint mourning over the dead, repentance and forgiveness through such symbolic gestures as planting trees, honoring homes instead of invading them, using public places to honor the dead rather than for terrorist acts, joint chanting and prayer, giving gifts at holy places rather than defiling them, civility and kindness at the borders, turning prisons into trauma centers; all of these evoke each culture's highest values and turn violence on its head by mirroring it positively. Gopin suggests that the Islamic practice of *sulh* (a form of contract designed to break the cycle of revenge and preserve the good name of the families involved) is a powerful, dramatic, and effective framework in which to imagine peacemaking initiatives. He asserts that these initiatives are not simply fantasy but are already happening, just not yet on large scale. Initiatives like these are not always embraced, but seep into the collective consciousness by displaying a kind of weakness that is actually powerful. They can also help to nurture a core group of people who trust one another and can weather the storms of conflict.[18]

Mohammed Abu-Nimer also emphasizes the importance of local actors. He advises that the study of Islamic peacemaking must integrate both *emic* and *etic* approaches to Islam, keeping in mind that the faith is not monolithic but comprises widely divergent approaches to conflict resolution. Islam is not uniformly distributed among members of a community but has many identities within that community. Peacemaking is best done through a "local Muslim actor" lens, always keeping in mind the complexity of the context. The main assumption Abu-Nimer advocates is that peacemaking is always more effective when carried out by the involved parties themselves.[19]

To put the notion of elicitive peacemaking in terms of my central image, a peace clan consists of both outsiders and local peacemakers who act as yeast in a divided society. Lederach, Gopin, Abu-Nimer all agree that local peacemakers, drawing from traditional forms of conflict resolution, are most likely to succeed in peacemaking because they will most

---

18. Ibid., 180–83, 205–12.
19. Abu-Nimer, *Nonviolence and Peace Building in Islam*, 6–10.

readily spark the moral imagination of their neighbors, both friends and enemies. Lederach summarizes this point well: "The general tendency is to think of peacebuilding as being initiated with outside resources, whether money or personnel. But the inverse is probably true. The greatest resource for sustaining peace in the long term is always rooted in the local people and their culture."[20] People are partners, not recipients, in peacemaking endeavors.

Both Western and Somali commentators have identified the two main pillars of Somali social organization as kinship and social contract—*tol* and *xeer*.[21] These are often portrayed negatively, either as a cause for the Somali conflict or as shattered beyond repair. An example of the latter view is that of Jama Mohamed: "In short, since the colonial period and especially since independence, Somali politics has been hobbling about with one very weak leg (kinship) as the other leg (social contract) withered under the assault of colonial rule and post-colonial hypocrisy."[22] The troubled history of clan relations and politics makes it easy to see how Mohamed draws such a conclusion. Conflicts have often formed along clan lines because family is so intrinsic to Somali identity. Yet when clans are abolished, as President Barre attempted to do, the effort is neither effective nor sincere; the hypocrisy to which Mohamed refers is no more evident than in Barre's active preference for his own clan, the Darod, even as he touted the end of clan identity in the new era of scientific socialism. Barre outlawed clan identification but continued to concentrate political power in his own Marehan sub-clan, his maternal Ogaden sub-clan, and the Dolbahunte sub-clan of his son-in-law. Siad Barre created a military and clan dictatorship in which political and economic power resided mainly in the hands of these three clans at the exclusion of others.[23] According to Richard Dowden, the numerous political parties and movements were "never anything more than political packaging for the clans. Mere fig leaves covering clan armies." He describes the relationship between clans as "a great wheel that brings one clan to power and then brings it down again. For a while Siad Barre froze

---

20. Lederach, *Building Peace*, 93–94.

21. Kutty, "Tol, Xeer, and Somalinimo," 15.

22. Mohamed, "Kinship and Contract," 247. Quoted in Kutty, "Tol, Xeer, and Somalinimo," 224.

23. Makhubela, "Conflict Resolution in Somalia," 39–42.

the wheel with his clan, the Marehan, at the top."[24] When he was ousted, the wheel began to spin again and soon tore the country apart.

The elicitive approach builds upon a much more positive view of the potential for traditional Somali social organization in the process of building peace. It is important to keep in mind Lederach's reminder that it takes as long to emerge from a conflict as it does to get into it.[25] But the tools for peacemaking, as we have seen above, are not manufactured externally but emerge from within a culture. As resources for peacemaking within Somali society, I identify *tol* (kinship), clan, and *xeer* (social contract).

Kinship and Clan

The term "civil war" expresses a paradox in human conflict. It describes violence that occurs between people who share a common culture, history, or lineage. The paradox is that those who are perceived to be allies in the struggle for communal survival turn upon one another. Yet in familial history, this phenomenon is as old as conflict itself; the first recorded act of violence in the Abrahamic traditions is between brothers, Cain and Abel. Much of what follows in the Hebrew Bible recounts violence between members of the same family, tribe, or people group. Marc Gopin notes that Islam, Judaism, and Christianity compete over the status of favored son, setting the stage for "mythically based conflict."[26] The family motif can be injurious when it is tied to land possession, exclusion, and revenge on enemies. But the power of the family metaphor can also be cultivated as part of the peacemaking process because of the recognition of relatedness. In this sense, the family motif contributes to good outcomes as much as do universalist mythic constructs. We cannot tamper with primordial identities, but we can use metaphors to imagine a new future. Commenting on the paradox of conflict and the intimacy of family identity, Gopin writes, "Often, one of the more bitter ironies of enemy systems is that one's enemy is in the best position to provide comfort because he knows exactly how you are feeling. For this reason, sometimes enemy systems and reconciliation systems are a hairbreadth

---

24. Dowden, *Africa*, 98–99.
25. Lederach, *Building Peace*, 78.
26. Gopin, *Holy War, Holy Peace*, 12.

away from each other, if only the relationships can be built."[27] Closeness becomes both a tantalizing goal and a source of frustration for those near both sides of a conflict.

In his novel *Links*, Nuruddin Farah observes the paradox of civil war and intimacy in Somali society. The main character, Jeebleh, has this exchange with Af-Laawe, the leader of a militia:

> "In a civil war, death is an intimate," Af-Laawe said. "You're killed by a person with whom you've shared intimacies, and who will kill you, believing that he will benefit from your death. And when you think seriously about an entire country going up in civil war flames, then you'll agree that 'intimacy' is more complicated."
>
> "I hadn't thought of intimacy in that sense," Jeebleh admitted.
>
> "Do you know the Somali term for 'civil war'?"
>
> "*Dagaalka sokeeye*."
>
> "Precisely," Af-Laawe asserted.
>
> In his mind, Jeebleh couldn't decide how to render the Somali expression in English, in the end preferring the notion "killing an intimate" to "warring against an intimate." Maybe the latter described better what was happening in Somalia."[28]

In the context of Somalia the clan system represents the sharp irony that Gopin has articulated: the deeply felt sense of kinship, reinforced by genealogy and mythic origins, is not enough to preserve the fabric of society in the face of political turmoil. Are Somalia's ongoing problems rooted in the political traditions of the culture?

Clans in Somalia are a complicated issue; some seek to ignore the system altogether, while others insist that they are the most important part of the culture to understand. Scholars like I. M. Lewis emphasize kinship as fundamental;[29] others, including Somalis, criticize this view as reductionist and neglectful of other factors. Nevertheless, the prevailing scholarly view concerning kinship (*tol*) is articulated well by Mark Bradbury: "The kinship system remains an important feature of Somali social, political, and economic life, despite more than forty years of

---

27. Ibid., 30–36, 90.
28. Farah, *Links*, 137–38.
29. Lewis, *Peoples of the Horn of Africa*.

state-building, urbanization, industrialization, civil war and international migration."[30]

The issue is complicated further by the fact that clans are split into sub-clans almost infinitely. In practice, Somalis seem to have a highly pragmatic relationship with clan identity. On the one hand, clan identity is fixed and ubiquitous; male lineage acts as a kind of passport in an oral culture, and attempts to make clans disappear, as Barre's attempt, fail. On the other hand, clan loyalty is flexible depending on the situation; the Hawiye first opposed Barre, then split and fought each other following the fall of his regime.[31]

Disagreement also exists about the contributions of clan identity either to conflict or to peace. Afyare Elmi writes "Clan identity in itself is not the cause of the conflict; it's a mobilization instrument."[32] Ahmed Samatar agrees, arguing that identifying the clan system as the root of the problem is simplistic and misleading.[33]

Yet it is certainly the case that clan identity contributes to conflict and injustice. Somalis see themselves as distinct from Africans, justifying the marginalization and segregation of minority people groups such as the Bantu (sometimes called Mushunguli).[34] Somalis form one of the largest ethnic blocs in Africa, much larger than the national borders. But the dream of a "greater Somalia" that has never existed has led to such conflicts as the 1977 Ogaden War.[35] And as noted above, clan politics has played a significant role in the disintegration of Somali society following the fall of Barre. The vacuum left in the political space by the collapse of Barre's regime is ripe for political opportunism, which often forms along clan lines. This helps explain why state-building that ignores clan dynamics actually adds to the intractability of the conflict as clans compete for scarce resources and political power.[36]

More recently, the power vacuum left by the expulsion of al-Shabaab reopens the possibility for politics along clan lines. Politicians use the rhetoric that clan interests are in the past to disguise continued

---

30. Bradbury, *Becoming Somaliland*, 14–15.
31. Harper, *Getting Somalia Wrong?*, 36–42.
32. Elmi, *Understanding the Somalia Conflagration*, 34.
33. Samatar, *Somali Challenge*, 6.
34. Kutty, "Tol, Xeer, and Somalinimo." See also Van Lehman and Eno, *Somali Bantu*, 4.
35. Harper, *Getting Somalia Wrong?*, 14–16, 31–33.
36. Makhubela, "Conflict Resolution in Somalia," 94–96.

corruption and potential for violence. This rhetoric is only effective when the situation improves, as it appears to be in Mogadishu, because politicians can appeal to previous times when the clan divisions were much worse. In the mid-2000s, for example, anyone not from the Hawiye clan who dared to set foot in Mogadishu was at grave risk of being killed. Now it is possible for people from the Darod and other clans to live in Mogadishu. The increased mobility of Somali society, however, can flood economically valuable areas with newcomers, exacerbating conflicts over resources like ports, roads, and airports.[37]

Positive Social Role of Clans: Mutual Care

It is possible to acknowledge that clan identity has contributed to violent conflict and to view it at the same time as a resource for peace. From this perspective, working with traditional systems gives peace a stronger foundation among Somalis.[38] This approach in both theory and in practice opens up a wealth of resources for peacemaking within Muslim Somali culture, including the clan system.

According to political philosopher Michael Walzer, conscience and resistance are shaped in individuals by groups, and are more likely to form in smaller circles than the nation state. Because people are never completely free of social relationships, they are never free of obligations; they are always bound or coerced by something.[39] In a Somali context, kinship identity fosters a sense of obligation to care for the needy that is deeper than national identity. It facilitates relationships of mutual care.

Anthropologists have emphasized the importance of geography in shaping Somali culture. Somalia's landscape is a mixture of grasslands and desert that has long been host to nomadic people and their livestock, leading I. M. Lewis to designate Somalia a "nation of pastoralists."[40] Centuries of nomadic lifestyle have formed Somali traditions in significant ways. One effect is a strong sense of independence; in the words of Richard Dowden, "Somalis know who they are; they are born with self-respect. The nomadic life engenders self-sufficiency."[41] Another direct

37. Hersi, interview.
38. Bergey, "'Bottom-Up' Alternative," 150–56.
39. Walzer, *Obligations*, xii–xvi.
40. Lewis, *Peoples of the Horn of Africa*, 4.
41. Dowden, *Africa*, 94.

result of the history of herding and transience is social and economic dependence on the camel. Camels feature prominently in Somali lore and poetry, and even bear some religious significance. Even after the transitions through colonization and independence, the nomad lifestyle is still central and remains connected even to urban areas through strong family ties and kinship responsibilities. Notions of hierarchy and national borders, so intrinsic to the Western political imagination, are foreign to that of Somalia. Loyalty is instead driven by the connections of kinship and lineage. In addition, the rigors of nomadic life make skill in warfare essential in order to protect access to natural resources. These combat skills are often available to the highest bidder, regardless of ideology, nationality, or notions of authority. Understanding these cultural forces serves in part to explain the resistance on the part of many Somalis to a centralized government. Mary Harper argues that a highly centralized Mogadishu-focused government is not the answer, and has never worked in Somalia. It is better to take a two-track approach that supports both successful regions and a federal government in Mogadishu.[42]

The independence and aggression that can be assets in a traditional nomadic society are not left unchecked, however. On the contrary, in traditional Somali culture genealogies give one a place in the social system, and a kind of political contract serves as an inter-clan police system. Certain religious leaders have a distinct non-warrior identity. When the colonial powers enforced a more individualized judicial system in the 1950s, the traditional system was weakened.[43] The Iise clan had a system for settling disputes that was ignored by the Western framers of the Somali constitution.[44] Journalist Scott Peterson writes: "Surprising as it sounds, in light of what has afflicted Somalia for the past decade, Somalis for centuries had developed peace making as an art form almost on par with war making. Some argue that these traditional restrictions could be considered a Somali version of the Geneva Conventions."[45] Peterson adds that Somali society traditionally offered men a choice between two roles: that of warrior (*waranle*, literally 'spear-bearer') or man of God (*wadaad*), whose task was not only to mediate between humans and God, but also between people in conflict for the sake of peace. But this

---

42. Harper, *Getting Somalia Wrong?*, 18–23, 43.
43. Lewis, *Modern History of Somalia*, 10–15, 156.
44. Metz, *Somalia*, xxiv.
45. Peterson, *Me Against My Brother*, 8.

careful balance toward peace that was achieved in the past has broken down during the modern age of the gun, as the old distinctions between the weak and the strong disappeared.[46] A *qat*-chewing teenager with an assault rifle redefines power and undermines the authority traditionally granted to elders.

Mike Brislen identifies the separation of religion and politics—the fact that clerics are above clan politics—as a factor for peace in Somali culture in Djibouti. Peacemaking on the part of clerics is driven by an identity of openness and a peaceful interpretation of Islam.[47] Clan leaders are a source of deterrence and traditional conflict management for clans. They provide protection and support during periods of crisis, acting as a moderating force for reconciliation and cooperation. Kutty, quoting Somali research partners, describes the clan as an "insurance policy and social security system to all Somalis."[48] Bruce Bradshaw, who served in Somalia in the early 1990s as a regional liaison officer for the US Agency for International Development, observed that "existing clan structures continued to function to help people meet their basic daily needs, even when states failed."[49]

The traditional clan system, along with the special roles of elders and clerics, provides a social safety net for Somalis that is able to care for needs when government structures are not in place.[50] Despite its limitations and possibilities for promoting rather than resolving conflict, in its most open forms the clan system provides a rationale and a structure for preventing and managing conflict.

Elders and Conflict Resolution

In addition to the social structures provided by the clan system for the purpose of security and survival, when the political infrastructure crumbled Somalis came to rely directly on clan and sub-clan structures to distribute power and to deal with disputes. Here I address the positive political and peacemaking role of clans and their elders, by which I mean

---

46. Ibid., 8–9.
47. Brislen, "Pacifism Among Muslims," 269.
48. M. Jibrell and H. Diriye, personal communication, February 2010 with Kutty ("Tol, Xeer, and Somalinimo," 195–96).
49. Friesen, "In Search of Security," 62.
50. Drysdale, *Whatever Happened to Somalia?*, 97.

not simply the involvement in government but in a general sense of making decisions, assigning roles, and distributing power.[51]

In Somali pastoral society governance is traditionally decentralized and based on consensus. Clan elders (*odayaasha*) assemble in councils (*shir*) to exercise authority on matters affecting the clan, such as the declaration of war or the payment of *diya* (addressed below). The *shir* have not been permanent institutions historically, but more often ad hoc gatherings formed in response to particular needs. These meetings might last for a few hours or for days or even weeks.[52]

Clan elders play a special role in addressing conflict, both among the clans in Somalia and in the Somali Diaspora. Elders are not primarily chosen based on hereditary status but on "a lifetime of earned reputation as effective negotiators, trusted mediators, moving orators, or wise and pious men."[53] When a conflict arises a special committee of elders, called a *guurti*, may be formed to facilitate its resolution. The *guurti* play a central role in the peace process, which "harnesses the services of the sacred authority of the religious leaders and persuasive power of the distinguished poets."[54] The elders act as brokers not only between parties in conflict but also between clans and the government. When an impending conflict involving two clans is perceived, suitable elders from clans not implicated in the conflict travel to the site. Religious leaders as bearers of moral authority may also be present for the process.[55] In this way a level of objectivity and fairness is maintained in the deliberations. The negotiation process is informal, consisting of representatives of the rival clans talking with the peacemaking elders in a suitable environment, traditionally under a negotiation tree.[56]

One possible outcome of these deliberations is the imposition of sanctions on those who oppose the peace process either by violating the peace or by refusing to engage in dialogue. The *guurti* can level a fine against such individuals or groups. They may also collect and pay *diya* from their clan members if there has been cross-clan killing, and also

---

51. Yoder, *Body Politics*, ix.
52. Bradbury, *Becoming Somaliland*, 16.
53. Kutty, "Tol, Xeer, and Somalinimo," 199.
54. Ibid., 198.
55. Ibid., 199.
56. Iye, *Le Verdict de L'Arbre*.

receive *diya* from another clan on behalf of their clan.[57] The question of who is obligated to pay and how much is owed depends on the relationship between the killer and the victim.[58] In this way, the "righteous majority" of the kin group, with the leadership of the elders, has been able throughout Somali history to control the violence of extremists. The collective will of the community was effective enough to deter the triumph of violence and other evil actions.[59]

What authority do clan elders actually exercise on the ground, in the midst of ongoing widespread conflict? The political effectiveness of the traditional power of elders can be seen at various moments since 1991. The Borama Peace Conference, which established a lasting peace in Somaliland, is a primary example. Another example is the October 1992 ceasefire and peace agreement between the Isaaq sub-clans, the Habar Yunis and the Ise Muse, after a six-month civil war in Somaliland. The groups agreed to share the port of Berbera, return some assets to the original owners, and encourage twenty-five inter-clan marriages.[60] The effectiveness of traditional authority was not confined to the north; during the invasion of the Ethiopian regular army in early 2007, the clan elders managed to persuade the Union of Islamic Courts not to make Mogadishu a battleground in the face of a superior military.[61]

John Prendergast notes that outside groups like Life and Peace Institute were somewhat effective in establishing district council training centers throughout Somalia, pairing international trainers with Somali counterparts. The goal was to bring together people from different communities, including at least one woman on each district council. The challenge is that in some places the Somalis owned these externally originated councils, but elsewhere the councils were marginalized as foreign entities. By far the most effective incentive to be involved in peace processes is loyalty to clan. Prendergast writes, "Clan affinity is the primary mobilizing factor. In fact, where district councils do remain, they are being reoriented and reconstituted by the local authority structure. Elders continue to be the primary agents of conflict prevention and

---

57. Kutty, "Tol, Xeer, and Somalinimo," 199.
58. Lewis, *Peoples of the Horn of Africa*, 108.
59. Afrax, "Mirror of Culture," 236–37.
60. Ibid., 72–73.
61. Makhubela, "Conflict Resolution in Somalia," 98.

management."[62] Peacemaking practices in Somalia must draw from the traditional social capital of the clan system, especially the corporate peacemaking roles of the elders.

Xeer Tradition: Restitution over Retaliation

Threads of peace can be found in Somali traditional law called *xeer* (alternately spelled *heer* or *hir*). The law's goal is to limit conflict among clans by ensuring that no one is above the law. Compensation for violence comes from the entire community, holding retaliation in check. The system has proven effective in maintaining peace in Somaliland and Djibouti.[63]

Clan identity has a remarkable degree of flexibility; attachments to those of other clans or sub-clans may ebb and flow over time. But the most binding and frequently mobilized group loyalty is to a unit known as the "*diya*-paying group." This contractual alliance of close kinspersons can consist of a few hundred to a few thousand men. The terms of the contract revolve around the obligation to pay and receive compensation for blood that is shed (the Arabic word *diya*). The underlying assumption of the system is that harm done by or to any member of the group implicates all those who are a party to the contract.[64] Different aspects of *xeer* apply to different situations, from interpersonal violence to war. Codes of war (*xeerka biri-ma-geydada*) are enforced through a sense of honor and compensation,[65] in what can be construed as a Somali version of the just war theory. *Diya* compensation is not limited to bloodshed but can be extended to other acknowledged offenses such as rape, kidnapping or abduction, and adultery.[66]

Livestock is the typical *diya* payment in the case of homicide, traditionally one hundred camels for a man and fifty for a woman. A combination of Islamic legal arrangements and traditional Somali regulations normally determine how much money or livestock must be paid for homicide, wounding, or assault.[67] An unlikely encounter between Mennonites and the tradition of blood compensation is recounted in the

---

62. Prendergast, "Applying Concepts," 178–80.
63. Brislen, "Pacifism Among Muslims," 266–70.
64. Lewis, *Modern History of Somalia*, 10–11.
65. Bradbury, *Becoming Somaliland*, 18.
66. Kutty, "Tol, Xeer, and Somalinimo," 197.
67. Laitin and Samatar, *Somalia*, 41–42.

book *A Hundred Camels*.[68] Just prior to the expulsion of all foreigners, Mennonite doctor Gerald Miller was tried for murder following the death of one of his patients. The mission, while admitting no wrongdoing on the part of Miller, agreed to pay the equivalent of one hundred camels as compensation as required by the court. The moving conclusion of the story is that the family of the deceased man chose to forego payment in an act of solidarity and reconciliation.

According to Ahmed Samatar, *xeer* is a critical social norm because it counterbalances the separatist, centrifugal tendencies of *tol* (kinship). These two elements of a functional society—*xeer* and *tol*—are held together in the figure of the elder, who along with the sheikh are the two pillars of indigenous political authority. *Xeer* as an unwritten legal and social practice stipulates the reciprocal duties and rights of individuals and groups, and administers criminal justice by defining legal and illegal acts and regulating feuds. Samatar writes that *xeer* and Islam "gave the stateless Somalis a rightful political center of gravity capable of controlling capriciousness, managing intersubjectivity, and offering order and continuity."[69] In this sense, precolonial Somalis did not see themselves as a nation but they did have a moral commonwealth, framed in terms of an *umma*.

It remains to be seen to what extent *xeer* can be adapted to fit a modern state. Hussein Adam avers that the traditional institutions for handling grazing and agricultural systems, conflict mediation, and legal adjudication have been effectively integrated into the government of Somaliland. The National Assembly includes two houses, one of which is the *Guurti* (House of Elders), comprising traditional clan and religious elders. *Xeer* is now widely practiced in both rural and urban areas.[70]

The effects of recent Somali history on the tradition of *xeer* are multifaceted. *Xeer* was undermined by the Barre regime long before the civil war broke out. Regarding the blood feuds between clans as a danger to national solidarity, Barre introduced the death penalty as a replacement for the tradition of *diya* between groups.[71] During the civil war, *xeer* was further eroded as war crimes with no precedence were committed. Moreover, armed militia groups rejected clan authority, making it impossible

68. Miller and Wagner, *Hundred Camels*.
69. Samatar, "Curse of Allah," 109–11.
70. Adam, "Somalia," 276.
71. Lewis, *Modern History of Somalia*, 208.

to implement *xeer*. By other accounts, however, the collapse of the state reinvigorated *xeer* as a way of filling in the gap in authority.[72]

According to one recent immigrant to the US from the city of Kismayu, the tradition of *xeer* has essentially vanished in the southern areas of Somalia. Part of the reason it does not survive is that a flood of newcomers are vying for access to the valuable port of Kismayu. Since the new leaders come from as far away as the Gedo and Ogaden regions, they have no kinship ties to the area that would promote concern for the local people or allow for traditional forms of peacemaking to occur. Their power rests on the strength of the militia they control. The new situation established by the presence of the Kenyan troops and the diminished presence of al-Shabaab has not stabilized but rather increased the number of politicians competing for power, including aspirations of an independent state and a new movement among the Bantu farmers to arm themselves in order to ensure economic access.[73]

Maxamed Afrax sees the preservation of *xeer* as integral not only to the political but also to the cultural renewal of Somalia. He writes, "It is my firm belief that a systematic cultural renewal is as urgently needed as any plan for political and economic rebuilding. Preservation of what is left of the nation's cultural heritage is a monumental task, but such culture can do miracles in Somalia; it can restore sanity and hope, reintroduce democratic thinking, and help formulate a new vision of local community and national reconstruction. But to come to the aid of their country, poets, artists, and other traditional intellectuals must be helped to pick up the pieces of their own shattered lives and regroup."[74]

One way in which the renewal of Somalia can begin is for Somalis to rediscover and reaffirm their cultural traditions that preserve communal solidarity. *Xeer* plays a critical role in the preservation of society through the promotion of restitution for wrongdoing rather than retaliation. The tradition is flawed—as is any tradition—by inequalities at a practical level, especially with regard to the exclusion of women. Nevertheless, *xeer* serves as a constant reminder of peacemaking possibilities in the face of violent acts.

---

72. Bradbury, *Becoming Somaliland*, 19.
73. Hersi, interview.
74. Afrax, "Mirror of Culture," 250.

Egalitarian Foundation and Democratic Resources

Somalia's troubled modern history has seen only one decade of democratic government. The years between independence in 1960 and the military takeover of Siad Barre in 1969 saw some corruption and a dependency on foreign powers, but also the stability of a functioning government and peaceful democratic transitions. In the years that followed, however, these gains were lost. The problem is not that Somali society is incompatible with a state as such or in the abstract, but rather that the tyranny of the Barre regime made Somalia into what Hussein M. Adam describes as "the perfect illustration of the state-civil society contradiction and its implosion, precisely because the Cold War had imposed an exceedingly heavy military state on a decentralized, relatively democratic civil society that was able to survive on meager resources."[75]

The record of the superpowers in the politics of Africa is often reprehensible. African rulers who failed to be sufficiently agile became the victims of military coups assisted by the East or West. Western states and businesses propped up or disposed of their preferred regimes in Africa at will. Countries like Somalia that played a crucial role in Cold War strategy were shamelessly courted. Both Somalia's value and its vulnerability during the struggle between East and West lay in the fact that it sits across the Red Sea from Saudi Arabia, making it a prime target both for military bases and for attempted coups. Siad Barre, unlike some other African dictators, proved remarkably adept at surviving even as he switched allegiances. But the result was that when the civil war began in the late 1980s there were more guns than people in the country. When the Islamic Courts Union turned into a popular uprising in the mid 2000s, it was in effect the first movement to unite Somalis across clan lines since 1991. Yet even the success of the ICU in earning overwhelming support from Somalis was not sufficient to overcome the stubbornness of the populace on the issues of dress, watching television, and other Islamist challenges to Somali freedoms. Dowden concludes, "If there is one lesson from Somalia since independence in 1960 it is that Somalis will be governed only by consent."[76]

---

75. Adam, "Somalia," 256–57.

76. Dowden, *Africa*, 85, 124. Drysdale notes that Somalis do not respect passive qualities in men, and demonstrate the same aggression toward foreign troops as they do toward unjust or overbearing Somali governors (*Whatever Happened to Somalia?*, 67).

Somalia has its own democratic transitions as a pastoral society with decentralized authority and decision-making by consensus. Authority is centered not in a monarchy or centralized government, but in the elders of the clans and sub-clans, who deliberate on matters pertinent to the needs of the clan. Somali culture supports a tradition of anarchy, not in the sense of disorder but in the lack of institutionalized authority roles. Even those elected by assemblies as a sultan (*suldaan*) or religious leader (*wadaad*) may be given deference in the assembly (*shir*), neither title ensures special powers. While inequalities still exist—most obviously in the exclusion of some minority groups and women—the ethos of traditional Somali society is distinctly egalitarian. In theory, all male members of a *shir* are entitled to participate in its deliberations, although actual practice is not so egalitarian for women or for men with less wealth or skill. Nevertheless, egalitarianism is deeply embedded in the culture, as is individual freedom as a point of pride.[77] Thus Somalia holds the communitarian identity that characterizes much of Africa in tension with decidedly democratic mechanisms.

It is evident that Somalia has traditional resources that can hold together both communitarian and democratic forms of decision-making. What elements of Somali culture can strengthen democratic processes while affirming clan identity? Here I identify three: *mayida* (the corporate meal), poetry, and media.

In his novel *Links*, Nuruddin Farah describes the vital role that meal sharing plays in Somali culture. One of the characters, Bile, describes how in the midst of a chaotic situation bonds are formed with another Somali man who is visiting Mogadishu for the first time since the beginning of the war:

> "We've resorted to the traditional method of eating together daily from the same *mayida*," Bile said, "in the belief that we create a camaraderie and we'll all trust one another. Some might consider hogwash the idea that those who look one another in the eye as they eat together are bound closely to one another. But our experiment bears it out—anyone meaning to do harm to a fellow sharer of the *mayida* will not dare look him, or anyone else, in the eye. Around here we say that many people prefer staying away to coming and sharing the mayida when there is bad blood. And when we share the *mayida*, there can be no bad blood."[78]

77. Laitin and Samatar, *Somalia*, 42–43.
78. Farah, *Links*, 157–58.

Eating together is not simply a factor in strengthening peacemaking and fellowship between Somalis; it is a powerful sign of connection with outsiders as well. Fatima Jibrell, Somali Managing Director of Horn Relief Organization, offered this assessment of the Mennonite presence in Somalia: they educated many Somalis, advocated for Somali issues during times of crisis, risked their lives to be present, listened to Somalis, and demonstrated cultural humility by eating and sleeping in the same places as Somalis.[79] When Bonnie Bergey attended peace meetings, it was usually expected that she would be served with the men. It was often not possible or approved to eat with the women. When she was occasionally invited to eat with the women, it felt like an honor and a privilege, like being a special guest in the home. Fellowship shared over food is a catalyst for deeper mutuality among and with Somali people. In fact, one common greeting mentions both peace and food: *Nabad iyo ano* (peace and milk).[80]

Poetry is a distinctive point of pride for Somalis, whose rich oral tradition has spawned a venerable history of poets who serve simultaneously as community leaders, critics, and artists. This most impressive artistic achievement of the Somalis has now been adapted to modern technology. It can even be used to confront militant groups like al-Shabaab, as the poet Abdirashid Omar has done in creative ways.[81]

Lamar Witmer observes that the Somali art of poetry and great oration serves to bring conflict out in the open rather than allowing it to fester under the surface. Poetry is not simply art in a Somali context; the ability to speak eloquently and use alliteration demonstrates power and influence, which impacts many aspects of daily interaction. "I have always been very impressed with how Somalis deal with conflict on an interpersonal level," Witmer says. "We frequently heard people yelling as if they were incredibly angry with each other, and five minutes later they are walking down the street holding hands. They forgive readily when they are allowed to get it out in the open."[82] The Logans add that in Djibouti they observed that fighting people were quickly separated by onlookers. Once the fight was over, there was no residual resentment.[83]

79. Eby, *Fifty Years, Fifty Stories*, 116.
80. Bergey, interview.
81. Harper, *Getting Somalia Wrong?*, 26–28.
82. Witmer, interview.
83. Logan, interview.

Jonathan Rudy observes the power one can wield through words in an oral society. He was traveling to Hargeisa with a man from the refugee camp, and they were stopped at a checkpoint by a young soldier with a gun. The soldier began to question the man about whether he was an army deserter. The displaced man, whom Rudy assumed to be a quite powerless person, thoroughly rebuked and subjugated the young soldier using poetry. It was a seminal lesson on the force of words. Rudy realized that "there is more at work than what is visible. Somalis could teach us as a global community what it means to be animated but committed to talking to each other before we grab for our guns."[84]

After we studied the genre of American blues music in a class at the University of Djibouti, a student told me, "We have our own Somali blues." The similarities are striking; both employ a pentatonic scale and deal with themes of hardship and solidarity. Even in the absence of a central government, the central role of traditional spoken word has transferred easily into the twenty-first century, with the advent of cell phones and digital technology. Chantal Logan argues that Somali "oral political poetry," by which she means compositions dealing with issues in the life of the community (in contrast to love poetry), is mostly a vehicle for peacemaking rather than for war-making. Some poems express the desire for revenge, but the most prominent theme is calling for reconciliation and a unified society. Women's poetry is especially important in transmitting these messages.[85]

Poetry can have either a provocative or a calming effect. At a peace initiative in which the Logans were involved in the town of Beledweyne, the parties in conflict were airing grievances from the last fifty years. The atmosphere became tense, so an organizer asked a poet to intervene. The poet began composing verses on the spot dealing with the friendship between the two clans, and everyone calmed down. Following a peace treaty, a poet creates a poem about the agreement and it is dispersed, recited, and memorized all over the area.[86]

One venue in which peacemaking poets can gain a broader hearing is in the medium of radio, for which Somalis have a particular affinity. Radio is a significant way in which an oral society adapts to modern realities while maintaining its distinct character. A neutral radio station is a

---

84. Rudy, interview.
85. Logan, "Enduring Power," 355–56.
86. Logan, interview.

powerful peacemaking tool in Somali society. According to Said Samatar, "Somalis trade in news and hearsay like Americans trade on the stock market." He advocates poetry as one of the key features of peace-oriented radio because people listen to poets; "Poetry is how we ask the abiding questions—how are we, where did we come from, where are we going."[87] A neutral, unbiased station can also counter hate radio, which plays a powerful part in African politics, as Rwanda has demonstrated.[88] Similarly, Hussein Adam argues that one of the enabling conditions for lasting peace in Somalia is a free press. New newspapers in Mogadishu and Hargeisa indicate that such a development is occurring.[89]

Somali culture has a wealth of resources for peacemaking that can strengthen security as well as provide for the needs of everyone. Kinship performs both the positive social function of ensuring that all have their needs met and the positive political function of resolving conflict through the traditional channels of authority, the elders. The traditional social contract *xeer* is a vital tool in moving conflict from the vicious cycles of retaliation toward restitution and even reconciliation. According to the elicitive theory, these are the foundations on which a sustainable peace must be built. Now we turn to the question of how Mennonites engaged these traditional Somali peacemaking practices.

Peace from the Ground Up: Mennonites and Somali Peacemaking

A guiding principle of the way Mennonites view social change is that conflict and injustice are not remedied from the top down, but from the ground up. Lederach has argued that the only way to peace in Somalia is regional reconciliation that builds toward a national forum. The tools for restoring peace are not top-down but bottom-up and must focus on Somali society and its peace constituencies rather than on armed groups.[90] He identifies six tracks of MCC work in Somalia: relief and development (with equal attention to various groups), diaspora Somali peace initiatives (forming the peace group *Ergada*), UN/Life and Peace Institute resource group (keeping MCC in touch with Somali and UN leaders),

87. Samatar, "Poor Somalia," 80.
88. Stremlau, "Ending Africa's Wars," 364.
89. Adam, "Somalia," 276.
90. Lederach, "Toward a Sustainable Peace," 105–6.

in-country conciliation focused on bottom-up peacebuilding, education and awareness, and nonviolent peacekeeping and disarmament (in discussions with top officials at the UN and the US Institute of Peace). The underlying principles of this strategy include attention to long-term and short-term concerns, context and indigenous peace efforts, showing commitment to all people across lines of conflict, and remaining faithful to an ethic of nonviolence.[91]

In line with this strategy, MCC and EMM have sponsored various consultations focusing on the traditional clan elders, women, poets, and others who were trying to reach across clan lines and make peace.[92] They held Somali peace conferences in Nairobi and sought to address all aspects of the problem, including patterns of abuse in aid and development and the role of the narcotic *qat* in the disintegration of Somali society.[93] A 2003 MCC Peace Office Newsletter focused on the Mennonite interaction with traditional Somali peacebuilding.[94]

A way of seeing social change that starts from the ground up and draws from Somali peacemaking does not mean working exclusively with marginalized people. This approach also values higher education. For example, EMU and the University of Hargeisa in Somaliland agreed to an exchange of faculty from 2008 to 2011 in order to boost efforts for peace. A bottom-up approach to peacemaking emphasizes the importance of all kinds of activities and actors in building peace.

Here I explore reconciliation as a dynamic goal built on relationships, running much deeper than static, temporary solutions to violence. The following sections examine how Mennonites sought to facilitate the connection of Somali peacemaking practices to the goal of reconciliation.

Conflict and the Goal of Reconciliation

In *Building Peace*, Lederach argues that peacebuilding requires a comprehensive approach to conflict that pays attention to all levels of actors. He tells the story of two Somali friends at a UN-sponsored reconciliation conference, one of whom was working with NGOs, the other with a key political party. The former claimed, in typical poetic Somali fashion, that

91. Lederach, "Mennonite Central Committee Efforts," 141–48.
92. Eby, *Fifty Years, Fifty Stories*, 92.
93. Bergey, "'Bottom-Up' Alternative," 150–56.
94. "Struggling for Peace."

a head needs a strong body to support it. The warlord responded that the body needs a strong head. The grassroots leader then shifted the metaphor to a house that requires a foundation before it supports a roof. For Lederach, this exchange represents his fundamental argument that the nature of contemporary conflict requires an approach beyond statism; building the house of peace requires a foundation built by multiple actors and peacemaking activities.[95]

For Lederach, the key to every stage of building the house of peace is reconciliation. He defines reconciliation as creating relationships between antagonists. This includes dealing with past grievances and exploring future interdependence, the places where truth, mercy, justice and peace meet. Reconciliation aims to reframe the conflict so issues no longer take precedence over relationships.[96]

Part of what Lederach seeks to correct is the way conflict is understood. He challenges some assumptions about what is at the root of conflict. The number of intermediate armed conflicts has remained constant since the Cold War, indicating that ideology is not an adequate explanation. Neither do ethnicity or religion fully account for the several dozen intermediate conflicts around the world. And most wars are not between states but are intrastate affairs; since most are over control of state or dispute of border, it is more accurate to call them "identity conflicts" because they struggle for communal rights and needs. While international conflicts have gone down, minor, internal struggles between sharply defined identity groups have increased. This is why a regional perspective of a deeply divided society is often more useful than a national one. Deeply divided societies are characterized by the ready availability of smaller weapons, the diffusion of power among many political parties and leaders, and what Lederach calls "Somalization": the narrowing of identity and loyalty for the sake of a sense of security, even as central authority and infrastructure break down. In a situation like this, it is not difficult for inflammatory propagandists to build on the long-term fear and hatred of neighbors who are right next door. The statist approach assumes a hierarchy of power. But in contemporary conflicts where power is diffuse, leaders still seek legitimacy, which in the current international system requires an army.[97]

---

95. Lederach, *Building Peace*, xv–xvi.
96. Ibid., 34–35, 151.
97. Ibid., 8–16.

In addition to the misguided assumptions of a statist approach, Lederach also seeks to correct the view of conflict as static. Because conflict is always dynamic, peacebuilding is a process that requires working for more than a ceasefire. The dynamic view is better able to locate all kinds of peacebuilding activities—including education and health care—within the broader progression of conflict. An integrated framework sees the need for all kinds of analysis, including root causes, crisis management, and prevention of further conflict. Seeing conflict as a progression also allows one to view time differently. While there is a need for a humanitarian response to a crisis in the short term, these interventions rarely lead to sustainable solutions. The long-term objective of peacebuilding is moving from a war-system to a peace-system; "The goal is not stasis, but rather the generation of continuous, dynamic, self-regenerating processes that maintain form over time and are able to adapt to environmental changes."[98] These dynamic processes that make for peace are made up of a web of relationships between people doing different kinds of work. As Daniel Philpott writes, "Reconciliation encompasses peace settlements, human rights, democracy, and other key goals of negative and positive peace. It also includes . . . a broad restoration of right relationship involving a multiplicity of practices that each redress wounds of injustice in a particular way."[99]

Much of the work of peacebuilding, therefore, is creating points of contact between people working at different levels and activities. This is not done by a centralized peace authority, but it can still be done systematically. One important aspect is developing a peace inventory in order to discover who is doing what. Another is to create clear channels between the top range (influential political and religious leaders) and mid range (NGO workers, academics, less prominent religious leaders). Based on these connections, strategic resource groups can foster a cross-fertilization of ideas. It is also important to link internal and external peacemakers in order to catalyze creativity.[100]

---

98. Ibid., 71–84.

99. Philpott, *Just and Unjust Peace*, 48–49.

100. Lederach, *Building Peace*, 38–39, 99–102.

The Borama Peace Process

The most remarkable example of the clan elders exercising lasting influence was in the local peace conferences in Somaliland that culminated in the 1993 Borama Peace Conference. The process brought together more than five hundred elders and established a lasting peace in Somaliland.[101] With almost no involvement from UNOSOM, the elders framed a new constitution, elected a new president, and disarmed militias. Drysdale writes, "Unlike the UN-sponsored Addis Ababa conference in March, which cost US $1.3 million, the Borama conference, lasting four months, cost the UN virtually nothing, though some logistical help in the way of air transport was provided. By April 25, two major resolutions were adopted: on a countrywide security framework and on a national constitutional structure."[102]

Why was the Borama Peace Process so successful when conferences with more direct outside involvement were not? One answer is that the process strengthened and regularized rather than mitigated the role of the elders in peacemaking through the establishment of a kind of national *xeer*.[103] In contrast, the Addis Ababa, Arta, and Mbagathi conferences did not provide for the structural representation of the clan elders in decision-making. The success of the Borama Peace Process is due to its giving clan elders the authority to participate in decision-making during the negotiations. The process struck a creative balance between the traditional clan structures and a parliament elected by the people. As a result, Borama cultivated unprecedented ownership in the peace process on the part of Somalilanders. Borama demonstrates that clan structures can contribute to broad cohesion if they are approached from the bottom up.[104]

Another aspect of Borama's success was that outsiders, at the explicit request of the elders, played the role of observers, accompanists, and interpreters rather than actively participating in more obtrusive ways. As a result, the process took on particularly Somali traits rather than being constrained by Western limitations of time and budget. John Paul Lederach and Angela Lederach observe that four characteristics emerged

---

101. Ibid., 53.
102. Drysdale, *Whatever Happened to Somalia?*, 73, 143.
103. Lewis, *Modern History of the Somali*, 283.
104. Makhubela, "Conflict Resolution in Somalia," 91–97. See also Farah and Lewis, *Somalia, the Roots of Reconciliation*.

in such an unrestricted milieu. First, peace building assumed a circular form characterized by itinerant conversations, which the elders initiated repeatedly until consent could be reached. When the elders were not successful, a group of women initiated contact between conflicting groups and clans. In this sense, peace was built in a tangible, close-to-home way that people could observe in repeated cycles. Second, conversation was sustained around the rituals of eating, drinking tea, and chewing *qat*, "defying the notion of a 'meeting' and certainly defying the notion of 'effective use of time.' What seemed to matter was talk. Much of the interaction was public. Most meetings were open, under the tree in the village."[105] Third, the extended conversations evoked emotions, including anger, but also a sense of responsibility in response to the grievances of the past. Talk, even angry talk, means that one's interlocutors are being engaged and peace is still a possibility.

Finally, the local communities, rather than large international conferences, were the context for peace building. The elders understood that "their endeavor would take a long time and that outside intervention too often comes wrapped in agendas and time frames that offer help but which demand outcomes related to foreign understandings of purpose and results."[106] By starting regionally, they were able to build toward a national forum that included thousands of participants.

The Ergada Peace Group

The *guurti* (committee of elders) is one of the key components of a sustainable peacebuilding approach in Somalia. In the early 1990s a group of Somali intellectuals called *Ergada* (a Somali term meaning "peace delegation") brought together elders from each sub-clan and started to deal with issues at a local level. They then repeated the process at a higher level with other clans. These processes consisted of the creation of a forum of elders, lengthy oral deliberations (often lasting months), and negotiation over access to resources and recompense for deaths that would restore a balance among the clans.[107]

The *Ergada* group traces its roots to well before the collapse of the government. The experiences of providing aid in response to the

---

105. Lederach and Lederach, *When Blood and Bones Cry Out*, 103–4.
106. Ibid., 105.
107. Lederach, *Building Peace*, 52–53.

1984–85 famines in Ethiopia raised questions for MCC's Africa Department about the effectiveness of material relief apart from the longer-term transformation of conflict. In response to these concerns, the Horn of Africa Project (HAP) was established in 1987 at Conrad Grebel College's Institute of Peace and Conflict Studies. The purpose of HAP was to bring together representatives from Somalia, Ethiopia, Sudan, and Kenya, some of whom were living in East Africa and some of whom had relocated to North America. The project provided a forum for building trust, raising concerns from the different perspectives represented, developing a vision for the future, and engaging in specific conflict transformation activity as mandated by the forum participants.[108]

Somali participants in HAP emphasized the critical role of clan elders in resolving conflicts. Lederach, who was MCC's coordinator for international conciliation, began working with a core group of Somali exiles based in North America who eventually chose the name *Ergada* as a description of their goals of promoting dialogue and peacebuilding among Somalis at home and in the diaspora. Their first formal meeting was held at EMC on December 14–16, 1990, and in the following years they continued to hold regular meetings bringing together exiled Somalis. One meeting brought together five hundred Somalis in Toronto in May 1992, but most of the meetings were at a much smaller scale. Members of *Ergada* also travelled to Somalia to explore possibilities for building peace at a grassroots level.[109]

The distinctive grassroots approach of *Ergada*, which did not treat the warlords as the main political actors simply because they directed militias, attracted significant attention from parties seeking peace in Somalia at all levels. When UN special envoy Mohamed Sahnoun started work in Somalia in April 1992, the Swedish-based Life and Peace Institute raised funds for *Ergada* and established a resource group for them. Lederach writes, "The overall effort was aimed at providing a conceptual scheme and concrete plan of action that linked in-country efforts with external resources; enhanced the role of Somali reconciliation efforts, especially elders' conferences; and reinforced the efforts of the United Nations to broaden its peace initiative."[110]

---

108. Miller, "Peace Church Experience."
109. Ibid.
110. Lederach, *Building Peace*, 102–6.

In August 1992 Sahnoun invited Lederach to participate and provide counsel based on his conciliation experience, but Sahnoun's abrupt resignation in November 1992 disrupted some of the collaborative work that had been established. The slow but steady peacebuilding progress of *Ergada* was buried under the escalating calls for armed security and state-building in Somalia in late 1992. Harold Miller of MCC commented in late November 1992 on the impending arrival of 37,000 US and UN military personnel: "There is at this juncture not even the remotest parity between expenditures/efforts for relief food logistics, on the one hand, and conciliation/peacemaking efforts, on the other. Unfortunately, the latest UN initiative for Somalia is being mobilized without the benefit of serious consultation with the 'Ergada' or other organized groups of Somalis."[111]

Sahnoun's departure seriously damaged the possibilities of peacebuilding collaboration between *Ergada* and the UN. Throughout the intervention, the Uppsala Advisory Group at the Life and Peace Institute continuously advised the UN to follow a bottom-up approach in Somalia.[112] Nevertheless, Miller's grim assessment in 1992 proved to be the tragic trajectory of international involvement.

EMM/MCC Nairobi Office

When it became clear in December 1990 that personnel could not return as scheduled to Somalia, EMM and MCC established a joint Somalia concerns office in Nairobi to deal with ongoing Mennonite-Somali relationships and activities, including refugee and humanitarian assistance, community development, peace initiatives, and support for Somali believers. Harold Reed, EMM Director for Africa during this period, writes, "Included are brief periodic trips into various parts of Somalia which, in addition to assessing potential projects, have developed meaningful relationships with Somali organizations and families during this disastrous era."[113]

Bonnie Bergey, who had arrived in Somalia in March 1990 as an instructor at the Teachers' Training College, agreed to act as a representative out of the Nairobi office. In that capacity she made at least fifteen trips

---

111. Miller, "Peace Church Experience."
112. Woodhouse and Ramsbotham, *Peacekeeping and Conflict Resolution*, 168n58.
113. Reed, "Believers Fellowships," 403–4.

into Somalia over the next five years, trying to make or maintain good connections within the country. She met with the believer's fellowship and ensured that the employees of the mission were paid. Bergey's role turned toward relief and development, sometimes in partnership with World Concern and Swedish Church Relief in Mogadishu. She managed several aid projects for MCC in various parts of Somalia and Somaliland. She visited Hargeisa alone and with other MCC representatives in August 1991 to survey possibilities for food aid and peacemaking initiatives in the devastated city. Says Bergey, "I felt that EMM and MCC trusted me and my intuition, what I was choosing to do or not do. They gave me the authority to decide whether I felt good about traveling to Somalia. I recall that as a very good experience, very empowering and respectful." [114]

During a tranquil period in 1992 Bergey arranged for two EMM nurses, Verda Weaver and Marilyn Metzler, to work in Somalia with World Concern. As the three of them sat talking on the flat roof of the World Concern compound where they were housed in Mogadishu, the building was attacked with a bomb and gunfire. Although no one was injured, two days later the three women departed for Nairobi on a UN flight. [115]

On February 15, 1993, Bergey and MCC Canada overseas director Marvin Frey attended the opening session of the meeting of three hundred clan elders in Borama that led to the formation of a peace agreement for Somaliland. The meeting was partially sponsored by MCC, which provided 10 percent of the $100,000 expenses for the meetings. Participants from the five major clans in the north met at a secondary school, where they held informal meetings in the classrooms and corporate sessions beginning with poetry each morning. A major topic of discussion was how to make restitution for property stolen from one clan by another, especially because clans are responsible for even seemingly random acts of looting and vandalism committed by their members. Weapons are also considered clan rather than individual property, and according to Frey, "This is why Somalis tell us an earlier MCC proposal to swap food or some other commodity for guns probably wouldn't work without assuring clan security at the same time." [116]

---

114. Bergey, interview.
115. "World Concern Office in Somalia," 12.
116. Sensenig, "Somali Elders Meet."

In addition to the financial contribution, Bergey's role was to encourage some of the elders and others to have confidence in the possibility and effectiveness of a peace process. She also led some of them in budgeting food for a peace conference. After MCC backed the process, other entities began to take notice and offer their support, most notably the Life and Peace Institute. MCC thus served as a liaison between the Somali-initiated meetings and outside organizations, lending the process extra credibility in the eyes of NGOs. Bergey had little involvement in the meetings themselves (in part because some were closed to foreign presence and lasting several months), and some of the sessions she attended consisted mostly of speeches and other formalities.[117]

In her role with MCC and EMM Bergey attended many Somali-initiated peace meetings, as well as UN security meetings in Mogadishu and UN peace meetings in Addis Ababa. At times she was not invited into meetings with Somali men because she was a woman. But most of the time it did not seem to matter because she encouraged others to support the Somali efforts and she represented Mennonites, which gave her a certain platform that was beyond her status as a woman.[118]

Bergey took an intentional strategy of representing Mennonites in various parts of the country and with various clan groups, not just in Hargeisa or Mogadishu. She says, "I was giving a little bit of money to things, or listening to people, or sometimes trying to visit in different areas, in order to show that the Mennonite history had been for all Somalis anywhere. So I tried not to play into clannism." While she learned much about the various clans, she could play naïve if the situation called for it. Thus she found that interacting across a broad range of clans was not only more faithful to the Mennonite history in Somalia but also a personally safer approach than to be seen as aligning with one particular clan group.[119]

In an August 1993 memo Bergey noted that the political situation was unraveling with increased hostility against the US and UN presence in Mogadishu. A Somali acquaintance warned her that if the UN defeated Aidid, expatriates could expect retaliation from Somalis regardless of who they were. Despite these developments, Bergey expressed some hope at this time toward peace: "I met with Sture Normark of Life and Peace

---

117. Bergey, interview.
118. Ibid.
119. Ibid.

Institute. Between his information and some that John Paul has sent, I have a better picture of the rather positive approach of a segment of the U.N., for conciliation training and decentralizing Mogadishu, mainly through the opening of 21 district councils throughout Somalia. Unfortunately, the military interventions dominate the media and people's minds."[120] After a harrowing experience in Hargeisa in which she thought she would be killed along with Marvin Frey and two journalists, Bergey for the first time felt that her presence there sometimes was too great a risk.[121]

Bergey was influenced by Lederach, with whom she attended peace meetings in Addis Ababa, to promote peacebuilding that focused on cultivating relationships, in contrast to the peacemaking and peacekeeping terminology of the military. Instead of using peace terms that might be misunderstood, Bergey describes her five years of work in elicitive terms, encouraging traditional ways of resolving conflict. She learned to focus on the conversations that were happening in the "corridors," the informal networking that led to greater commitments to peace. This networking occurred both in Somalia and in Kenya; in Nairobi she connected displaced Somalis to services they needed through UNHCR, and often Somalis she had never met walked into her office to request information, support, or medicine. For Bergey, peacebuilding consisted of moments like these rather than focusing on a specific goal that was imposed from the outside.[122]

When Bergey ended her assignment in 1995, Bertha Beachy succeeded her as EMM and MCC representative in the Nairobi office. Chantal and Mark Logan took over the work in 2000, followed by Ann and Jerry King-Grosh.

Peace Initiatives in the Juba Valley

Chantal Logan observes that when Christians and Muslims gather together, "interesting and unexpected interfaith communication happens."[123] One catalyst for such communication was that the MCC Somalia office provided scholarships for Somalis to attend the African Peacebuilding

120. Bonnie Bergey to Somalia Concerns Office, memorandum, August 30, 1993.
121. Bergey, interview.
122. Ibid.
123. Logan, "Reflections," 63.

Institute in Zambia. During the Logans' term a conflict broke out within a minority sub-clan along the Shebelle River near the town of Beledweyne. The conflict erupted in violence, which was spreading and destabilizing the area. The peacemaking attempts by the majority clan elders were unsuccessful. A Somali man named Mustafa, who had been the first Muslim to attend classes at the Institute in Zambia, was from Beledweyne, near the area where the violence was taking place. He contacted the Logans and requested financial assistance in sponsoring a meeting of the local village elders. The funds happened to be available through the MCC/EMM office, and Mark was invited to attend the opening session. At that meeting the village elders checked their weapons at the door in a pile of knives and heavy sticks, and sat down to talk. They traced the history of the conflict and moments of resolution, starting fifty years before and proceeding to the most recent murder. A solution was proposed, and Mustafa sent the elders back to their villages to report, secure consensus, and return the next day for the final decision.[124]

At the meeting the next day Mark was asked to give a speech. Knowing that the primary identification and credential for Somalis is their ancestral lineage stretching back for generations, Mark introduced himself as part of the Mennonite Mission family. Unsure of how much interaction the people of this area had had with Mennonites, he explained that Mennonites are religious people who believe in one God, that God is great and the creator of the world. The gathered elders applauded enthusiastically. Mark continued by stating that we are all sons and daughters of Adam and Eve, and as sisters and brothers we should live in peace, and again received applause. Mark recounts,

> I was getting bolder, and went on. "I know that you follow the prophet Mohammad, but we follow the prophet Jesus." This time I didn't know what to expect. I was identifying myself as a Christian, without using the word. I was becoming the other, one from outside the group, confirming what my complexion already displayed. But again I was pleased, and somewhat surprised to hear applause. This was my cue, so I went on to explain. "We read in the Gospel that Jesus was a healer and a miracle worker, so when Mennonites came to Somalia they founded hospitals and clinics." At this I heard a voice quote the passage from the Qur'an which affirms that Jesus was a miracle worker. Then I said, "We also read that Jesus was a great teacher and so

---

124. Logan, "Sharing the Piece."

Mennonite Mission started schools in Somalia." At this point I heard someone mention the name of a town where a school had been. Next, I said, "We read that Jesus was a peace maker and even was called the Prince of Peace, and that is why we helped you have these meetings here in this place." Then I told them the story about the baby goat one of Chantal's students gave her in Djibouti and encouraged them to always work for peace.[125]

When Mark finished the elders announced that their villages were in agreement and that they had made peace. A joyful celebration followed, with laughing and hugging and food and everyone talking. Mark was surrounded by men who hugged him and stroked his beard. They told him that they would never forget how Mennonite Mission had helped to bring peace. About a year later, when Mark was introducing Jerry King-Grosh to some people in that area, some people whom he did not know and who had not attended the peace meetings approached them and said, "We know what you did for our people, welcome." Mark comments, "And if today, or ten years from now, or fifty, someone asks them how their conflicts were resolved, there will be the story of how peace was made with the help of the people who follow Jesus."[126]

A man from southern Somalia who worked with MCC in 2003–2004 recounts that the Logans assisted in transforming another conflict in the Juba Valley. There was a conflict between Somali Bantus and other Somalis in the area of Marere, near Kismayu. Through MCC's involvement in bringing together the elders of the villages, the situation was settled. In the years following, however, the presence of al-Shabaab once again stirred up the old conflict, and this time it was not possible for any Western organization to come to the area.[127]

Ahmed Ali Haile, a Mennonite Peacemaker in Action

Ahmed Ali Haile's life crossed borders of many kinds—cultural, religious, and geographical. As a peacemaker committed to Christ, he actively explored the possibilities and limitations of clan identity, Somali culture and traditions, and the religious resources for peace. His willingness to

125. Ibid.
126. Ibid.
127. Hersi, interview.

risk his own life for the sake of peace demonstrates the costliness, but also the fruit, of a bottom-up, elicitive approach.

Born and raised in a Muslim context in Bulo Burte, Somalia, Haile became a Christian at age seventeen. For Haile, identifying with Jesus and the church meant no longer identifying with the mosque. Yet he resolved never to speak ill of Islam, because Islam had prepared him to meet Jesus and planted in him the desire for God that was fulfilled in Jesus and for community that was fulfilled in the church, which Haile compared to a spiritual house like an *udub*, a traditional Somali hut.[128]

Shunned by members of his own clan and threatened by the Somali authorities, Haile struggled with his identity as a Somali Anabaptist follower of Jesus. He continued to seek inclusion among his fellow Somalis, sustained by his conviction that Jesus' disciples are called to reflect the incarnational presence of Christ. As the political situation unraveled, Haile's calling to be an ambassador of the gospel of peace brought him back to Somalia again and again. J. Dudley Woodberry notes that the first recorded Muslim convert to Christianity was a migrant in East Africa; "Yet, unlike the first Muslim convert to Christ, who is generally understood to have gone to East Africa to avoid conflict in seventh-century Mecca, the contemporary convert Ahmed returned to the region repeatedly to mediate conflict."[129]

Ahmed Haile and his wife Martha Wilson Haile lived in Mogadishu for three years in the mid-1980s. During this time Haile provided some leadership to the small group of Somali believers. The anti-Christian sentiment in the city had not heightened as it later would, but there was a general atmosphere of suspicion as the Barre regime crumbled. One night a small group of believers was meeting at the home of Elizabeth and Ken Nissley when the police knocked on the door. They took Haile outside, and he did not return. The others did not know what had happened to him. So Ken Nissley sought out Haile's brother and they drove around Mogadishu all evening, searching the police stations until they found where Haile was being held. They brought him some food and a blanket, and the next day Haile's brother managed to convince an official not to press any charges and to release him.[130]

---

128. Woodberry, preface to *Teatime in Mogadishu*, 34–37.

129. Haile and Shenk, *Teatime in Mogadishu*, 9.

130. Nissley, interview. The Nissleys suspect that their night guard was complicit in Haile's arrest.

After moving to Elkhart, Indiana, in October 1991 Haile was called by Somali colleagues, under the auspices of the newly formed inter-clan peace group *Ergada* (which was sponsored by MCC), to return to Somalia for two weeks of peacemaking work, especially between the divided factions of the United Somali Congress (USC). *Ergada* requested his presence at this volatile time for a number of reasons. Haile shared a vision with *Ergada* of a just, peaceful Somali state built on good clan relations, which he saw as the only possibility for a functioning government.[131] He was recognized both for his boldness in engaging the clan system and for his abilities in mediation, and he had master's degrees in peace studies and public administration. Additionally, Haile was from the Karanle sub-clan of the Hawiye clan. Both the interim president Ali Mahdi and General Farah Aidid were also from the Hawiye clan. The Karanles are considered the "elder brothers"[132] of the Hawiye clan according to Somali tradition, and they play a key role in settling disputes. These qualities, both of pedigree and personality, put Haile in a unique peacemaking position. He served as the only Christian on a team of Muslims. Of his Muslim companions, Haile states, "We were joined by a love for our people, believing that something stronger than guns could bring peace."[133]

As Haile was attending a negotiation near the fighting zones in Mogadishu in January 1992, the house where the meeting took place was attacked by Aidid's forces. Haile's leg was severely wounded in the attack and was later amputated. Yet he continued to be involved in peacemaking among his Somali people, in Somalia, Kenya, and North America. Haile taught for years at Daystar University in Nairobi, where he founded a peace studies program. He also helped to lead the growing Somali Christian community in Eastleigh, driven by a vision for a thriving Somali fellowship. By the time he returned to Eastleigh, where he had previously worked with David and Grace Shenk, the situation had changed to the extent that he could not work openly at the Eastleigh Fellowship Center. But he continued to fellowship with Somalis in his home and in other ways in Eastleigh.[134] Haile also gathered Muslim and Christian scholars together to read and discuss their scriptures.[135]

131. Shenk, interview.
132. Eby, *Fifty Years, Fifty Stories*, 94.
133. Kraybill, *Apocalypse and Allegiance*, 96.
134. Shenk, interview.
135. Logan, interview.

Although his background was known to many, in his memoir Haile chose not to identify his clan, seeking to emulate his father's example of treating all people equally regardless of heritage.[136] He recounted his expectations of positive treatment from his own clan members due to their special bond. He was discouraged to discover that rather than embracing him they rebuked and rejected him because of his commitment to Christ. The experience served as a catalyst for Haile to transform his view of clans based on Philippians 2:1–11, even as the country was disintegrating into inter-clan warfare. "What would happen if clans honored rival clans more than they honored themselves? What if people were ready to die for the enemy rather than seek to dominate the enemy?" Haile asked. Like the Apostle Paul, Haile recognized that he had an enviable heritage but that his genealogy could not offer salvation or peace. It was not long after his conversion that his new commitments were tested by the appearance of a visitor from a rival clan, which was considered by some to be inferior to his own. The visitor was amazed that Haile offered him his bed while he slept on the floor.[137] Haile's life offers a vision and example of a sense of kinship that transcends clan ties even as it acknowledges them.

Haile engaged all of the peacemaking tools he could find: pre-Islamic systems of justice, colonial courts and laws, the *qadi* and *sharia* courts, and social sciences. More than only peacemaking theories, they were the fundamental tools for acting in the midst of tremendous challenges and resistance, such as the imam who called for his execution for apostasy and later became his protector. Haile discovered, however, that "ultimately it was the gospel that could end the cycle of retaliation as it was absorbed by Christ and his cross and the Holy Spirit who through the church reconciled people to God and each other."[138]

The North American Mennonites learned from Ahmed and Martha Haile what it might mean to employ an elicitive approach in Somalia, particularly the importance of hospitality and conversation. Elizabeth Nissley says, "Watching Ahmed work with traditional Somali peacemaking was significant for us. Even when he had some hostile family members come, he invited them to eat together, and served tea."[139]

---

136. Haile and Shenk, *Teatime in Mogadishu*, 20.
137. Ibid., 49–50.
138. Woodberry, preface to *Teatime in Mogadishu*, 10.
139. Nissley, interview.

Haile was diagnosed with cancer in 2006, and died in 2011. After he learned that his cancer was terminal, he told EMM leaders, "When Orie O. Miller [early Mennonite mission leader] was dying he said, 'Don't forget the Somalis.' I want to say the same thing. Do not forget the Somalis."[140]

The fruit of Ahmed Haile's life continues in both Africa and North America. His memoir was released just days after his death. It is now available in several languages, including Somali.

In July 2011 a group of Somalis, including poets and politicians, gathered in Toronto with North American mission workers and others to celebrate Haile's life and the release of *Teatime in Mogadishu*, and to consider the ongoing work of peacemaking in Somalia.[141] Haile's remarkable life is a catalyst for the sharing of stories across some surprising boundaries. Somalia is a nation of poets, and the weaving of words is prized above any other art form. Upon Haile's passing, an unidentified Somali friend penned these words, rendered here in English:

> The departed Ahmed Haile
> The sagacious one
> Whom the Lord took away . . .
>
> He was a peacemaker
> Whom we honored well
> He was widely respected . . .
>
> He said these abhorrent actions
> The endless civil wars
> Will one day cease . . .
>
> He said to hold fast to the rope of God
> Without any distractions . . .
>
> He strolled away with dignity
> And returned to paradise
> The cherished expert.[142]

I have argued that Mennonites can understand their task and role in a post-government Somali context in terms of *salt* and *light*. In a climate in which military solutions were popular and compelling, especially

---

140. Showalter, "Eternal Home for a Somali Nomad."
141. Leaman, "Somali Community in Toronto."
142. "Xog Warran."

when they were driven by a narrative of Western heroism and a doctrine of intervention that dominated both the UN and the US, Mennonites appealed to other possibilities for lasting change in Somalia. Their quiet work in education and healthcare in the decades leading up to the civil war prepared them for a different approach from the dominant appeals to force. The peace convictions fostered across generations allowed the Mennonite clan to bear witness in salty, distinctive ways. The urgency of the civil war led Mennonites to solidify their commitments to an elicitive approach that learned from Somali cultural forms of peacebuilding.

Moreover, the recognition that any sort of presence as guests in a host country is only possible because of relationships translated, in the context of escalating conflict, into the insight that only healed clan relations can yield a sustainable peace in Somalia. Once again, the previous work of the Somalia Mennonite Mission, especially the bringing together of clans in the schools, served as a foundation for an ongoing peace witness as inter-clan violence increased. These relationships made possible both the support for *Ergada* and the involvement in the Borama Peace Process. As an alternative to violence and force, Mennonites attempted to prove that God can use the best practices of a given culture to heal divisions, establish peace, and abolish war.

Any serious appeal to cultural peacemaking resources, however, cannot ignore the driving force of faith, especially when it serves as a pillar of identity. We turn now to consider the role of Somali Islam in building peace.

6

Saints and Soldiers

Somali Islam and Peacemaking

IN THIS CHAPTER I interrogate how Mennonites operating in an elicitive mode can find resources for peace within Somali Islam. Several observations by Mennonite workers in Somalia bring into focus both the challenges and possibilities of this task:

1. *Somalis generally have a non-anxious form of Islam, with Islamic piety fluidly built into the culture.* In Somaliland, for example, a high level of devotion exists and the flag bears the *shahada*. Yet Islamist groups have trouble getting a foothold, and a foreign Christian presence for the purpose of educational collaboration is tolerated.[1]

2. *Somalis have historically been resistant to any form of outside dictation of their faith and piety, whether Christian, secular, or Islamic.* There is inbuilt resistance to highly political Islam. Bonnie Bergey predicts that a more authentically indigenous Somali Islam will regain influence in the coming years, a less restrictive form of Islam that will again give greater cultural voice to poets, women, and advocates of education.[2]

3. *Interaction with popular piety is much more likely than Muslim-Christian dialogue at a scholarly level.* The sorts of high-level conversations between Mennonites and qur'anic scholars in Iran are not

---

1. Rudy, interview.
2. Bergey, interview.

possible in a Somali context.[3] Attention must be given rather to the popular forms that Islam takes for Somali Muslims.

These observations provide some clues for how Mennonites might engage Islam as a peacemaking resource in Somalia. I contend that three elements—a) historical analysis of the tensions within Somali Islam, b) constructive readings of the Qur'an that promote peace, and c) peacemaking examples from within Somali Sufism—are essential ingredients in the articulation of a peace-oriented Somali Islam.

The roughly thirteen million Somalis around the globe are almost 100 percent Muslim, with a small Christian minority stemming from missionary activity and the proximity to Ethiopia. Islam is deeply embedded in Somali culture and identity, to the extent that many Somalis view Islam as one of the defining characteristics of what it means to be Somali. For this reason, a peacemaking approach that seeks to draw from the resources within Somali culture must identify the peacemaking possibilities and impetus within Islam and the Qur'an.

Like other areas of the majority-Muslim world, over the centuries Somalia has developed its own unique blend of traditional elements and orthodox Islam. One of the most important aspects of Somali Islam is the prominent position that Sufi orders have played in popular belief and practice. In some instances a particular branch of Sufism takes an explicitly political form as in the case of the Salihiyah reformer Sheikh Mohammed Abdullah Hassan, who in the early twentieth century led followers known as Dervishes in waging a *jihad* against Ethiopian, British, and Italian colonialists. Political Islam, however, was mostly dormant in Somalia from the defeat of the Dervishes in 1920 until the 1990s.[4] The years since the collapse of Siad Barre's government have seen a rise in Islamism in various forms. Here I use the term Islamism to refer to the vision of Islam as a framework for a new worldwide political and social order. Such avowedly political Islam can be militant or moderate. The more militant kind of Islamism often finds itself at odds with the less political Sufi traditions in Somalia.

The introduction of Islam into the Horn of Africa occurred between the late seventh century and the ninth century, facilitated by Muslim merchants and to a lesser degree by missionaries. Due to the proximity to the Arabian Peninsula, Islamization happened fairly rapidly along the

3. Rudy, interview.
4. Bradbury, *Becoming Somaliland*, 20.

coast, where Muslim city-states like Zeila, Merka, and Mogadishu developed along ancient trade routes. It was only after centuries of Arab missionary efforts, in about the thirteenth century, that the near-universal acceptance of Islam was evident among the nomadic and agricultural peoples of the interior.

The relationship between Muslims and Christians in the region was tense from the beginning. In Islam's nascent years the protection offered to persecuted Muslims by the Abyssinian king prompted a hadith prohibiting *jihad* against Abyssinia, laying the ground for a positive relationship between Muslims and Christians in the Horn. The early expansion of Islam in the region was essentially peaceful because the lack of a navy precluded the kind of wars of conquest happening in Byzantium and Persia at the time.[5] But a two-century struggle between the expansionist Christian state in Ethiopia and the Muslim city-states for control of the Horn of Africa contributed to the cultural and emotional ties Somalis felt to the Arab world. These ties were only strengthened in the late nineteenth century when Italy, Britain, France, and Ethiopia established colonial rule over the Somalis. The experience of colonization at the hands of Christians prompted a revival of Islam in the region; ancient Sufi orders such as the Qadiriyah intensified their activities, and newer reformist Sufi orders were established in Somalia for the first time.[6]

The years since the collapse of the government have prompted yet another resurgence of interest in Islam. Religion has emerged as a source of comfort for many Somalis in an unstable and distressful environment. Vinodh Kutty describes the common ground of Islamic values as a "valued point of reference that transcends parochial, political, and [clan]-based interests."[7] Many Somalis perceive Islam and *sharia* as pillars of the new society and its government. According to Hussein Adam, one of the enabling conditions on which sound governance for Somalia could be built is Islamic revival. He acknowledges that there are pockets of fundamentalism in areas, but that revivalist spirit of most Somalis is based on the Somali Sunni tradition of avoiding radical politicized Islam. "Somalia's Islamic revival promises to strengthen civic values and institutions of civil society and should be reinforced. Unlike the centrifugal politics of clan division, Islamic beliefs and behavior manifest a latent

---

5. Jhazbhay, "Islam and Stability," 177–78.
6. Kapteijns, "Somalia."
7. Kutty, "Tol, Xeer, and Somalinimo," 210.

centripetal political tendency of integration."[8] What kind of Islam will gain traction, however, depends upon the understanding of Somalis as to the nature of their faith. Mosques and religious leadership play an important role in the country and the diaspora in determining whether Somali Islam takes on militant or more peaceful forms.

The diaspora experience can have the effect of increasing the significance of Muslim identity for Somalis. Because they can no longer take their religion for granted as they did before immigration, their faith becomes an important anchor in their lives in the midst of dislocation. Kutty writes of the Somali community in the US: "Many refugees study the *Quran* and ensure that *Quranic* education is an important part of their child's education, and that women dress in accordance with Islam in ways that they would not have done when they were in Somalia . . . . [They] did not want their children to have a 'rootless' identity and a confused attachment, or no particular attachment, to Somalia and Islam."[9] As a result, for young Somalis in the US their Muslim identity becomes the "cornerstone of their self-identification. It proves to be a single, permanent and unifying identity. The phrase 'I am Muslim first and foremost' is one that young Somalis relate to."[10]

Another reason that the nature of Islam in Somalia is important is that radical Islam often serves as the rationale for Western-backed military intervention. The alliance between the US and Ethiopia that formed as part of the George W. Bush administration's "war on terror" is calculated to eradicate Islamic fundamentalism in the Horn of Africa.[11] Religions are here to stay and the interface between religions, especially the most liberal adherents, is expanding. At the same time, radicalization within religions will likely continue as global inequalities grow and human needs remain unmet. In light of this challenge, we must avoid the temptation to retreat into safe enclaves of like-minded people. Peacemaking in Somalia or any context requires engaging the heart of what drives religious people to conflict or peace: their faith. Peacemaking does not demand leaving one's particular faith at the door in the quest for universal principles; on the contrary, it emerges from the deeply held beliefs that fundamentally shape the way people of faith view the world.

8. Adam, "Somalia," 276.
9. Kutty, "Tol, Xeer, and Somalinimo," 210.
10. Ibid., 220.
11. Rutherford, *Humanitarianism Under Fire*, 190.

Rather than appealing only to academic elites, peacemaking solutions must speak to the average person's sense of what is true.[12] In the case of Somalia, this means engaging even those who feel the attraction of involvement with militant Islamist groups.

My intention is not to argue that Islam is always or by nature a peaceful religion. It is necessary to acknowledge that the Qur'an is read in violent ways, and the ideals of Islam articulated in militant terms, by some Muslims around the world. Further, some who interpret Islam in this way wield great political and social power and put it to pernicious ends. I have no wish to excuse the violence performed by some Muslims. I contend rather that Islam has tremendous resources for peace, both within its foundational Scriptures and throughout its history. Peacemaking in Somalia must benefit from these resources, even as peacemakers acknowledge the tension within the practices and ideologies of Islam in Somalia. After exploring this tension, I will survey examples of peacemakers within Somali Sufism.

Islams in Tension: Sufism and Islamism in Somalia

The relationship between Islam and Somalia is complex. The European colonial powers were not alone in exploiting the region; one significant yet overlooked aspect of Somali history is the slave trade. According to a twelfth-century Moroccan scholar, in the northern town of Zeila the main exports were slaves and silver. By the early nineteenth century the Islamic powers Egypt and Zanzibar extended their rule into the Horn and expanded the slave trade in all of northeastern and eastern Africa. In 1892 the Sultan of Zanzibar ceded control over the Benadir coast to Italian commercial interests, along with decrees against slave trade. But by 1903 Italy's Benadir Company was openly collaborating with local slave dealers and almost a third of Mogadishu's 6,700 inhabitants were slaves, mostly owned by wealthy Arabs and Somali merchants. When the Italian government took over in 1906 there were between twenty-five and thirty thousand slaves in the colony. The impact of historical divisions in society along racial lines is long lasting; the free labor provided by slaves in the pre-colonial era became menial and dangerous labor for low pay

---

12. Gopin, *Between Eden and Armageddon*, 15, 223–26.

during colonial rule, and resulted in persistent poverty through independence and up to the present.[13]

Somali Islam tends to be resistant to two kinds of external forces: Western secularism and Arab-influenced Islamism. The former, epitomized in the Somali context by Siad Barre's revolution toward scientific socialism in 1969, proved unpopular and devastating for the country. The latter fails to make inroads because Somalis have practiced a fairly tolerant form of Sunni Islam for centuries, and generally do not support militant Islamism. This mediating position is not therefore simply a rejection of foreign options but the product of a long history of Sufi belief and practice that is well suited to Somali society.

In recent times several factors have contributed to the reaffirmation of a middle path. Islamist hopes for Somalia were crushed by the move toward scientific socialism and the execution of religious critics. The effect of these executions, however, was that religion became a form of resistance to Barre.[14] The political instability of the last two decades has further contributed to the return of many Somalis to greater faith and piety. But many Somalis also resent the foreign roots of Islamism, especially in its strictest forms, such as the Wahhabism from Arabia. The suggestion that their Islamic beliefs, entrenched over centuries and influenced by pre-Islamic culture, are inadequate or heretical is offensive. Sufism is a long contested tendency within mainstream Islam, and Arabian Islamism's refusal to accommodate Sufi practice reveals how foreign it is in Somalia. For example, militant Islamist groups tend to eclipse the divergent view of *jihad* among the Sufi orders, which is the struggle of the individual's soul for union with God rather than in political terms.[15] The perception of condescension is only heightened by the fact that Africa has a severely limited role in Islamist political imagination, marked by stereotypes of African cultures and traditional religions. The conflict between African Islamists and Arab Islamists is demonstrated in the latter's difficulty in co-opting Somali Islamism.[16]

Another factor is resistance to the clear political agenda to establish a conservative Islamic Somali state. Vinodh Kutty writes, "Islam's potential to overcome Somalia's divisions and to nurture a lasting peace is thus

13. Segal, *Islam's Black Slaves*, 96, 187–90.
14. Harper, *Getting Somalia Wrong?*, 76.
15. Lewis, *Saints and Somalis*, 43–45.
16. De Waal, *Islamism and its Enemies*, 18.

at odds with the divisiveness and violence represented by competing fundamentalist ideologies. Most disturbing, perhaps, is the overt ambition of the most vigorous movements to reintroduce the kind of centralized, authoritarian leadership Somalis have fought so hard to overthrow."[17]

Perhaps most significantly of all, Islamism has difficulty in navigating a context in which clan is a highly mobilized and political identity. Even where Islamism was able to gain some traction it was divided by clan affiliation, and thus al-Qaeda and other militant Islamist organizations found themselves up against not only the resistance of the more moderate Sufi brotherhoods but also the confounding complexities of the Somali clan system.[18] Lidwien Kapteijns notes that even when Islamist groups are recognized in Somali politics, they are relegated to a role secondary to clans; "Of the fourteen formal, large-scale reconciliation efforts that have taken place since 1991, the thirteenth, in 1999–2000, was significant in that it allowed for the participation of Somali civic organizations and for the first time explicitly recognized an Islamist movement and constituency. However, this same conference adopted representation on the basis of clan, thus denying civil society groups (such as women, Islamists, and others) any right of representation except through the clans into which they had been born."[19]

In Somaliland the system of clan elders is a pragmatic solution to the tension between Islam and secular nationalism. Religion plays a stabilizing role in society in that it keeps in check extremes of any kind, either to exclude Islam from the realm of politics or to make Islam the only basis for politics. This is because the role of *wadaad* (religious man) is not inherently tied to any brand of Islam. In that sense a *wadaad* can choose for or against Islamist politics without undermining his legitimacy within Somaliland society. In recent years some religious leaders have been calling for a return to traditional Somali Sufi Islam and a rejection of Wahhabism. The stabilizing effect of Somaliland's brand of Islam can be seen in the support it receives among all sectors of society. The qur'anic schools enjoy popular support as long as they temper any extremist inclinations. And popular support for a mixture of *sharia* and customary law remains strong; for most Somalilanders it is enough to

---

17. Kutty, "Tol, Xeer, and Somalinimo," 211–12.
18. Mantzikos, "African Version of the Taliban?," 121.
19. Kapteijns, "Somalia."

consider *sharia* the center of the legal system even as preference is given to customary law at a practical level.[20]

Somali Sufism

Sufism has a long history in the Horn of Africa and is well suited to Somali society. According to I. M. Lewis, some sort of affiliation to Sufi orders is "practically synonymous with the profession of faith" in Somalia; "The Somali approach to the Prophet and worship of God is almost exclusively channeled through Sayyid 'Abdul Qaadir or through Sayyid Ahmad. The Orders know no linage boundaries, and Somali of different and often hostile clans and lineages worship God through the same 'brotherhood.' Attachment is to a particular Order to which their ancestor adhered."[21]

Lewis notes, however, that "True Sufism is considered by some authorities to have fallen into decadence in [the twentieth] century.... Amongst the Somali, after a period of great activity and general expansion up till the 1930s, the Dervish movement seems to be on the wane."[22] Nevertheless, Somalia has been deeply shaped by Sufi thought and practice, which can serve as a unifying force in society. Sufism provides a framework for peaceful arrangements between moderate Islam and a government characterized by religious tolerance.

Somalis are Sunni, adhering to the Shafi'i school of Islamic jurisprudence. Somali Islam is characterized by veneration of Islamic saints, belief in the mystical powers of charismatic itinerant holy men, and allegiance to Sufi brotherhoods.[23] The role of Sufi orders in Somali Islam is significant and has deep historical roots in the region. The introduction of Islam, and along with it the three Sufi orders—the moderate Qadiriyah and more reformist-oriented Idrisiyah and Salihiyah—started on the northern coast and reached the Ethiopian Ogaden before disseminating south. The relationship between the three Sufi brotherhoods was rarely congenial, at times devolving into violence.[24]

---

20. Jhazbhay, "Islam and Stability," 198–99.
21. Lewis, *Saints and Somalis*, 60.
22. Ibid., 9.
23. Laitin and Samatar, *Somalia*, 45.
24. Lewis, *Saints and Somalis*, 60. See also Johansen and Talib, "Sufism and Politics."

The anti-colonial movements following World War II were articulated in terms of secular Somali nationalism, informed by a liberal Islam that saw Islamic faith as compatible with modern secular education and statecraft. It was therefore Muslim leaders influenced by the more moderate Qadariyah version of Islam who established the independent Somali republic in 1960, with the help of the women's branches of their parties.[25]

Sufism is structurally well suited to a clan-based society. Adherents of Sufism belong to congregations or communities known in Somalia as *al-jama'ah*, following various Orders called *al-tariqa* ("the way") with different doctrines and practices. The spiritual goal of *tariqa* is *ma'rifah*, which literally means *knowledge* in Arabic but within a Sufi context carries the meaning of absorption in God. Those who have traveled the furthest are nearest to God, by the *baraka* (translated as grace or blessing) that God gives them. *Baraka* passes to the followers who walk in the true path of the founder of the Order. There is religious prestige connected with the Prophet Muhammad's Qurayshitic lineage in that his *baraka* flows most in the blood of those descended from him, a notion that fits well with Somali emphasis on lineage.[26] Although membership in a brotherhood is theoretically a voluntary matter unrelated to kinship, in reality kinship lines are often affiliated with a specific Order and a man usually joins his father's Order.[27]

David Shenk describes Sufism as a quest for the power that comes from mystical union with God, in contrast with orthodox spirituality. Rather than the "I-thou" relationship that characterizes Christian theology, Sufis aspire to be caught up in union with the divine (*fana'*). While affirming the concept of *tanzil* (that no partnership can exist between God and humans), Sufis insist that the qur'anic notion of friendship with God can serve as a model for spirituality.[28] The union that comes from being a close associate (*wali*) with God is the source of power in the life of a Sufi Muslim.

One aspect of Somali Sufism that lends itself to peacemaking, therefore, is its alternative account of power, in contrast with a warrior society. Sheikhs, known locally as *wadaad*s, act as mediators between persons and also between person and God. The *wadaad* also treats sickness, divinates,

25. Kapteijns, "Somalia."
26. Ibid., 9–10.
27. Jhazbhay, "Islam and Stability," 179.
28. Shenk, *Journeys*, 214.

and officiates at religious ceremonies as the possessor of liturgical lore. *Wadaad* is not usually a political office but serves a peacemaking and arbitration function, such as recommending compensation according to *sharia* and *xeer*, and administering Muslim principles of inheritance. The distinction drawn between *wadaad*s and warriors demonstrates a dichotomy of pastoral warring life and the peaceful ideals of Islam. Any man who has sufficient religious knowledge is given the title *Aw* before his name; as a man of God and no longer a warrior, he is now expected to fulfill religious roles like directing the Friday and special Sufi services. Although *wadaad*s are not primarily political leaders, they participate by blessing leaders who make decisions. But they can also resist violence by withholding their blessing from hostile parties, binding them by an oath to do no more violence. When conflict gets too acute, however, the sheikhs reach the limits of their authority and secular courts may be required to use force. According to Lewis, Somalis regard *wadaad*s and warriors as having access to different types of power; the latter relies on the number of fighting men, and the former on the power of God and the spiritual authority he bestows. Yet the two categories always mix to some extent and depend on one another for the functioning of society; the distinction between the spheres is not rigid.[29]

The relationship between Somali Sufism and Orthodox Islam is dynamic. One aspect of this tension is the extent to which spiritual and political authority is merged. In cases of conflict people sometimes turn to the leaders of the *jama'ah*, rather than to the heads of the clan, to act as mediators in a dispute. In this way in which the Sufi community can actually infringe upon clan structure. Like most manifestations of mysticism, Sufism focuses on the relationship of the individual to God. Many interpretations of *sharia*, on the other hand, assume an Islamic state. But in nomadic Somalia, application of *sharia* is often limited to intra-clan affairs and certain personal matters, and is limited by local custom (*xeer*). *Sharia* views guilt as the individual's responsibility, while Somali traditional law considers guilt the responsibility of the kin group. By way of summary, Lewis describes Somali Islam as comprising several layers and standards. One layer is Islamic conduct as it is prescribed in the Qur'an. A second is the popular morality or Somali custom. The third layer is

---

29. Lewis, *Saints and Somalis*, 48, 62–70.

the actual popular practice. All three are interrelated, with the last two referring to the first for their legitimacy.[30]

Another point of tension between Somali Sufism and Orthodox Islam is the extent to which Sufi saints can take on the role of intercessor to God in popular thought and practice. David Shenk recounts that in Somalia, the sense that God does not hear the prayers of sinners leads people to seek the saints as intercessors, even as they acknowledge that this is not "good Islam" according to orthodox theology. Shenk interprets these Sufi practices as expressions of the desire for contact with the Creator.[31] In some cases, the search for God's forgiveness takes the form of animal sacrifice in Sufi-influenced areas of Somalia.[32]

Within the mystical traditions known as Sufism there are also points of similarity and contrast beyond the competition for adherents and influence. The Orders share in common a belief that the founder of the Order is near God through his virtue and true devotion, which his followers must adopt in order to receive the blessings of the founder. But differences in practice often put the Orders at odds with one another. The Idrisiyah and Salihiyah Orders are more puritanical, prohibiting smoking and the chewing of *qat*. The Qadiriyah do not prohibit these practices and have more flamboyant services, including processions of singing and chanting en route to the mosque. Because of these differences, each Order has its own mosque in any given town, and the interaction between them is minimal. Despite the peaceful ideals of the founders, at times the disagreements give rise to hostility and even violent conflict. The bitter rivalry during the uprisings in the early twentieth century led the competing groups—including the famous Salihiyah reformer Mohammed Abdullah Hassan—to compose incendiary poems against each other. In some cases loyalty to *tariqa* transcended even clan.[33] Sufi history in Somalia demonstrates how even those who condemn violence can forsake their ideals when conflict arises.

---

30. Ibid., 11, 24–25, 51–56.
31. Shenk, *Journeys*, 215–16.
32. Haile and Shenk, *Teatime in Mogadishu*, 34.
33. Lewis, *Saints and Somalis*, 61–66.

Islamism in Somalia

The distinction between Sufism and Islamism is not a rigid one. Indeed, some of the most radical Islamic revivalist movements like the Dervish movement in the early twentieth century have been Sufi reactions to colonialism and rejection of their more moderate fellow Orders. It is therefore more comprehensible to speak of the extent to which a movement embraces a vision of Islam as a framework for a new worldwide political and social order. Such avowedly political Islam can be militant or moderate. The more militant kind of Islamism often finds itself at odds with the less political Sufi traditions in Somalia.

To what extent is Somalia's long history with Sufism compatible with the sort of Islamism encroaching from other parts of the Muslim world? Islamic sects with Saudi Arabian, Sudanese or Iranian connections and resources, particularly Wahhabism, began to compete for followers among the Somalis who had suffered from the consequences of the civil war in the 1990s.[34] Wahhabism is therefore not indigenous to the Somali Islamic value system. Nevertheless, formations aligned with Wahhabism, such as the al-Itihaad al-Islamiya organization, have had the infrastructural capacity to influence the politics of Somalis, especially after the collapse of the state in 1991 created a political vacuum.[35]

One Islamist movement by the name of Waxda had some success in Somaliland. Launched in August 1969 in Hargeisa, it was established as an Islamic institution whose primary influences were Islamists such as Sayyid Qutb of Egypt, Sayyid Abul A'la Maududi of Pakistan, and other new Islamist thinkers. When the nation took a decidedly secularist path under Barre, Waxda went underground and began publishing treatises against the socialist state. They spread south during the 1970s, and after the devastation of Hargeisa and Burco in 1988 became supporters of Somaliland's premier liberation organization, the Somali National Movement (SNM). Apart from Waxda, other Islamist groups in Somalia originated and operate mostly in southern Somalia in and around Mogadishu.[36]

The Siad Barre regime played a significant role in creating the foment that led to the emergence of Islamist groups. In proclaiming scientific socialism as the official ideology of the state, Barre set out on an

---

34. Lewis, *Understanding Somalia and Somaliland*, 20.
35. Makhubela, "Conflict Resolution in Somalia," 40.
36. Jhazbhay, "Islam and Stability," 180.

active course of development. Islamism was dealt a blow in 1974, when the state declared that the Latin script would be used for Somali orthography rather than the Arabic script or the Somali-created Osmaniya script, a choice that opponents declared *la din* (without religion). But the straw that broke the camel's back was a new family law in 1975 that granted women more rights. Closely resembling the secular Tunisian version, the law provoked radical opposition from religious circles. When members of the religious establishment (*ulama*) openly condemned the law by peaceful protests, Barre executed ten sheikhs by firing squad in January 1975. The regime engaged in a campaign against all the "religiously backward" people who sided against progress. According to Lidwien Kapteijns, "Coinciding with a period of extensive labor migration to the Arab oil states, this event marks the beginning of a new turn to a deepened personal Islamic piety and the rise of fundamentalist Islam in Somali society."[37] Rather than repressing Islam, the regime's hostility sparked a revival in which many Somalis committed themselves to religious dress and to regular prayers and fasting.

Barre's actions touched a nerve in Somali society. His disrespect for the institutions of the Islamic faith added to the general public's resentment of the regime, driving a wedge between state and society that only deepened over time.[38] Between 1989 and 1990, Barre ordered his troops to murder hundreds of religious leaders and their followers, prompting many Somalis to demand his resignation and fuelling clan-based opposition groups that challenged the regime from bases in Ethiopia. Although a number of Islamist groups were organized in the 1980s, there is little information about them because they were driven underground during the Barre era.[39]

The fear that the military regime was moving the country toward atheism drove many Somalis to reject secularism. At the same time, Somalia was no longer isolated from the Arab world, joining the Arab League in 1974. More students trained in Sudan, Egypt, and Saudi Arabia, where new Islamist trends were developing. The Ogaden War against Ethiopia in 1977 and the Iranian Revolution of 1979, along with increased trade with Dubai and regular flights to the Arabian Peninsula, further contributed to a cultural affiliation with the Arab world. Despite

37. Kapteijns, "Somalia."
38. Makhubela, "Conflict Resolution in Somalia," 40.
39. Jhazbhay, "Islam and Stability," 180.

these new connections, political Islam failed to gain much support from youth and urban populations in the 1980s. In part this was because clan alliance ran deeper than religious loyalties. Leading figures lacked the moral authority of clan elders, and Arab Islamist propaganda was seen as somewhat alien to Somali society. In the words of Roland Marchal, "As the framework for political activities became increasingly clan-based, militant Islamic militants had little to offer."[40]

One way in which Islamists and their organizations have gained public support in recent years is by pursuing a clear-cut social agenda that reaches out to people who are weary of war. Kutty writes, "Underpinned by extensive holdings in the private sector, including hotels, *xawalaad* (money transfer/wiring services), and import-export concerns, the most sophisticated organizations offer medical care, schooling, and training, as well as support to struggling entrepreneurs."[41] Islamic NGOs often respond effectively to education, health care and disaster relief needs without the benefit of state control, making them popular with the people.[42]

Islamic Courts Union

The abuse of power in the Barre regime was so great that it cultivated a deep distrust of centralized authority. A central army is perceived as threatening in light of the uses to which Barre put the Somali military in the waning years of his control. Somalis turned to Islamic revival in lieu of a centralized government, which led to the emergence of alternative institutions without any external support. The court movement in and around Mogadishu in the mid 2000s, which became known as the Islamic Courts Union (ICU), is one such alternative institution.[43]

The circumstances under which the ICU emerged are due in part to the imposition of a Transitional Federal Government (TFG) on the Somali people by the international community in 2004, which continued to be based on clan. Some members of the new government turned against it soon after its formation, leaving it relatively powerless to restore order to the capital city. Although the U.S. helped to install the TFG, rather than working with the weak government it secretly hired Mogadishu warlords

40. Marchal, "Islamic Political Dynamics," 117–21.
41. Kutty, "Tol, Xeer, and Somalinimo," 211.
42. De Waal, *Islamism and its Enemies*, 12–14.
43. Adam, "Somalia," 274–75.

to capture and kill al-Qaeda operatives in Somalia. The ICU was officially formed in June 2006 in order to combat these US-supported warlords. The courts succeeded in bringing peace to the streets of Mogadishu and earned some international favor as a result. The internal contradictions of the ICU, however, soon caught up with it; it was characterized both by hard-line Islamist ideology and by notorious warlords related to clan affiliations. When the ICU attempted to displace the TFG by force in late 2006, international sympathy shifted to the TFG, and a coalition including Ethiopia, Burundi, and Uganda provided military assistance in the fight against the ICU, once again throwing Mogadishu into violent conflict.[44]

Why did the ICU initially experience such success in unifying Somalis and establishing stability? One reason is that the political vacuum left by the collapse of the Barre regime in 1991 paved the way for clan-based militant factions to carve up the capital. Exhausted by a long period of lawlessness, Somalis saw the ICU as a force of liberation from the tyranny of the competing militias. The ICU portrayed itself as bringing order to chaotic Somalia, and the Islamic leaders earned legitimacy in the eyes of the people by effectively administering court functions, mostly based on *sharia*, in lawless areas. Like the Taliban in Afghanistan a decade earlier, the ICU capitalized on the absence of nationally accepted leadership, presenting itself as the only government the people needed.[45]

In the aftermath of Barre's departure from power, identification with Islam and its practices was a way in which Somalis sought security and identity. Yet religious leaders were not integrated into the process of seeking peace agreements early on in the conflict. In a January 1993 meeting hosted by Boutros-Ghali, for example, the high-level actors did not include religious leaders, who were given space to play only a weak role.[46] The increased religiosity of the Somali population therefore did not have a political outlet. Religious practices in the form of clothing, prayer, and fasting accompanied a general willingness to concede greater authority to the Islamic courts, which prohibited the chewing of *qat* and implemented elements of *sharia*. Marchal writes, "For a few years, security in North Mogadishu reached a quasi-normal level that the population had not enjoyed since the late 1980s. For several years, it became rare

44. Kapteijns, "Somalia."
45. Mantzikos, "African Version of the Taliban?," 114–18, 127.
46. Toft et al, *God's Century*, 194.

to see people moving with weapons in Karaan."⁴⁷ The ICU was also able to clamp down on the prevalence of piracy of the coast of Somalia, a feat that has not been replicated since.⁴⁸

The fact that the ICU contained radical elements made it easy for external powers, particularly Ethiopia, to draw a link to al-Qaeda. The Ethiopian government emphasized this link in order to appeal to the US and the UK for military, financial, and moral support. But the claims lacked any solid evidence, especially because the ICU was such a fragment coalition comprising a wide range of ideologies. The notion that some radical elements within the ICU might be sympathetic to al-Qaeda's ideology does not change the fact that a large percentage of the moderates in the organization, including Sheikh Ahmed, were staunchly opposed to any structural links to Wahhabism and other foreign radical Islamist groups.⁴⁹ Nevertheless, US American and British claim of ties to terrorism, combined with Ethiopia's fears that Somalia might be reuniting under a powerful Islamic movement, garnered enough support that on Christmas Eve 2006 tanks rolled into Somalia. The ICU proved to be no match for US and Ethiopian forces, who killed rather than captured.⁵⁰

The invasion by Ethiopia and the US achieved the opposite of its intended outcome. Journalist Eliza Griswold describes both the invasion and the Bush administration's policies in Somalia, including supporting notorious warlords and launching Tomahawk missile strikes against civilians, as a complete backfire. The fighting stemming from the invasion killed at least 8,500 people by the end of 2009, leaving 1.5 million homeless and 3.8 million at risk of famine. The battle for the hearts and minds of Somalis was lost, allowing al-Qaeda to plant a "friendly flag" among a population increasingly willing to side with anyone against the barbarity of the West. The long hatred for the Ethiopians (and subsequently Christians) was rekindled; Griswold reports widespread sentiment regarding the thousands of dead, including many civilians, that "Muslims wouldn't do anything like this."⁵¹

Al-Shabaab, a radicalized offshoot of the ICU, responded positively to the cooperation of al-Qaeda, which opened up new possibilities for

---

47. Marchal, "Islamic Political Dynamics," 123–35.
48. Makhubela, "Conflict Resolution in Somalia," 99.
49. Ibid.
50. Dowden, *Africa*, 125.
51. Griswold, *Tenth Parallel*, 128–30.

sophisticated media and equipment. As in Sudan, what had been a local conflict became globalized through a common ideology and military technology. Still, the conflict was mostly ignored in the rest of the world, because Somalis were dying rather than Americans, as in Iraq and Afghanistan.[52] The US and its allies had ushered in the enemy they had claimed to be destroying. Somalia was back to square one on insecurity and anarchy, with new groups like al-Shabaab and Hizbul Islam forming in the wake of the ICU's decimation.[53]

Just as tragically, the invasion and overthrow of the ICU was a lost opportunity for peacemaking. If the international community had recognized that the ICU was a genuine grassroots government with broad support from the Somali people, the focus could have turned to peacebuilding strategies rather than the endless tasks of state-building. It was an ideal moment to construct a genuinely Somali, bottom-up government, a moment that was utterly squandered by the Bush administration's war on terror, which painted all kinds of Islamic organizations with broad and often deeply mistaken brushstrokes. The deployment of the AU troops also demonstrated that the lesson of UNOSOM—that Somalis unite against foreign military intervention, to the benefit of groups like al-Shabaab—was still not learned.[54]

Al-Shabaab and Militant Islamism

The overthrow of the ICU left a vacuum in which more radicalized groups could emerge. Although the attempts to link the ICU and al-Barakat to extremist organizations like al-Qaeda has been overstated or even fabricated, there are Somali organizations with explicit ties to foreign jihadist groups. In the 1990s warlords, not groups driven by religious ideologies, were the primary players in Somalia. The events following September 11, 2001, including the Bush administration's war on terror and the 2006 destruction of the ICU, brought together people with jihadist ambitions and led to the formation of al-Shabaab.[55]

Although in recent years al-Shabaab has dominated the Somali jihadist landscape, it had influential predecessors. One prominent

52. Ibid., 135.
53. Harper, *Getting Somalia Wrong?*, 85.
54. Makhubela, "Conflict Resolution in Somalia," 99–100.
55. Harper, *Getting Somalia Wrong?*, 77.

organization that formed soon after the collapse of the Barre regime is al-Itihaad al-Islamiya. Al-Itihaad came into being as a merger of organizations following Wahhabi Islam from Saudi Arabia. Originally a group devoted to *dawah*—the responsibility to call Muslims and non-Muslims to faith—al-Itihaad transformed into a military force in Kismayo and the Ogaden region in 1994. Some members of al-Itihaad had fought as mujahidin in the Afghan war against the Soviet Union, a connection that shaped al-Itihaad's polity and strategy, and also served as the basis for association with al-Qaeda. Al-Ansar al-Sunna, a faction of al-Itihaad, established the first court in Mogadishu in 1993, and some within al-Itihaad became affiliated with the ICU, most notably Hassan Dahir Aweys.[56] Already weakened by the Ethiopian military response to their attacks, al-Itihaad dissolved around the time that the ICU was formed.[57] In Somaliland, al-Itihaad's decline can be attributed to a number of factors: the dismantling of their military capabilities; the adoption of nonviolent methods of proselytizing by some members; and improved relations with neighbors, especially Djibouti. Because of this, al-Itihaad's influence mostly disappeared from Islamic charities and religious education in Somaliland.[58]

Al-Shabaab, the successor to al-Itihaad, is the Somalia-based cell of al-Qaeda. The group comprises many disparate ideological goals and variations in tactics. At its peak in early 2011, al-Shabaab had thousands of militants and controlled large areas of southern Somalia, including much of the capital. Somewhat weakened by a lack of leadership and loss of public support, al-Shabaab withdrew from Mogadishu in August 2011. Tension with al-Qaeda caused a split in early 2012. In September 2012 AMISOM troops captured the city of Kismayo, the group's headquarters, further weakening its influence. Nevertheless, al-Shabaab continues to attract recruits, many of whom are children who are indoctrinated and initiated early into the group's brutal tactics. Many foreign fighters join al-Shabaab, often criminals on the run in their own countries. Somalia and Yemen provide each other with fighters, and extremists from Kenya ensure a steady import and export of jihadist militants.[59] Even US citizens and Somalis from Minneapolis and other areas have been known

---

56. Mantzikos, "African Version of the Taliban?," 118.
57. Harper, *Getting Somalia Wrong?*, 79.
58. Jhazbhay, "Islam and Stability," 195.
59. Harper, *Getting Somalia Wrong?*, 86–99.

to join al-Shabaab. Venodh Kutty documents the way in which Somali youths' relationship to Islam can differ from that of their parents: "They ask questions about their faith and actively search for an Islam that is pure. They search the internet and read books to determine for themselves how to be a good Muslim in a Western society.... This quest for deep faith may in turn lead some to bond with radical elements whose agenda is not always peaceful."[60]

Although there are signs that al-Shabaab's influence is in decline, the group continues to operate campaigns of violence against both Somalis and foreigners. Mary Harper notes, "It is possible that the increased monitoring and targeting of Somalis around the world will, like the Ethiopian invasion of 2006, further radicalize the Somali community, leading to more attacks at home and abroad."[61]

Not all commentators see the decline of al-Shabaab as a primary goal in peacemaking. In a 2011 document produced by Life and Peace Institute, Ryne Clos presents three reasons why al-Shabaab is part of the solution to Somalia's problems, even as he denounces the widespread violence done by the organization. Al-Shabaab can be a force for peace in that it is a successful social movement that is compelling to Somalia's youthful population. It is also a political voice that cuts across clan lines. Third, al-Shabaab is an indigenous movement that draws on the history and aspirations of the Somali people, in contrast to the self-interested involvements of the international community. Clos writes, "As peacebuilders, we must extract what is good and deploy it in our efforts to transform society from enduring war to sustainable peace, even if this means engaging with those accused of crimes against humanity or other 'undesirable' actors."[62] Clos documents a decided transition of al-Shabaab from an ideological court militia consisting of hardcore mercenaries, to a "widespread political organism, hydra-headed and willing to negotiate a power-sharing agreement to maintain territory without wastefully deploying its resources." Al-Shabaab is not so much a single movement as a "youth-based, anti-clannish avalanche of multiple voices and manifold visions."[63]

In the same vein, John Paul Lederach argues that it is a mistake to employ a strategy of isolation rather than engagement with groups like

---

60. Kutty, "Tol, Xeer, and Somalinimo," 220.
61. Harper, *Getting Somalia Wrong?*, 103.
62. Clos, "Al-Shabaab," 20.
63. Ibid., 24.

al-Shabaab. He criticizes the tactic of creating wide ranging terrorist lists that seek to control acts of terrorism but have no long-term strategy for transforming the factors that cultivate terrorism. What is needed instead is a multi-faceted approach grounded in a compelling theory of social change.[64] Neither isolating al-Shabaab nor pursuing the organization militarily will have any lasting impact for peace.

Somali Sufi Saints

In addition to historical analysis of Somali Islam and constructive readings of the Qur'an that promote peace, a third essential ingredient in the articulation of a peace-oriented Somali Islam is attention to examples of peacemaking from and within Islam.

Known in Somalia as "friend of God" from the Arabic *weli*, Sufi saints are considered channels of God's favor and peace. Their lives and legacies are often characterized by miraculous events (*karamat*) that emphasize God's provision and protection for those who are near him. The *baraka* of the saints was bestowed on their followers through physical following and contact or obedience to their *tariqa*.

A host of miracles are attributed to Sheikh 'Abdirahman Zayla'i (d. 1882). Because food security was a major issue in parts of Somalia in the nineteenth century, as it is now, many of these miracles concern food. In one instance the sheikh fed nine of his followers with a single sheep shoulder. Other accounts demonstrate the spiritual powers of the sheikh to cure illnesses such as smallpox and tuberculosis through prayer, restore sight to the blind by rubbing their eyes, be in two places simultaneously, and astound foreign scholars with his insight. He was reportedly able to hear and respond to the cries and prayers of those in need even at great distances.[65]

In one account Sheikh Zayla'i had a golden camel that carried his library from place to place. The camel was impervious to attacks from wild animals, but went astray and was found one day by some wicked herdsmen. Some wanted to slaughter the camel, but others resisted because it belonged to the sheikh. One wicked man insisted on killing it, but in the process his own spear killed him as well as the camel. When his companions tried to bury him, the grave refused to accept the body. After

---

64. Lederach, "Addressing Terrorism," 17.
65. Martin, "Shaykh Zayla'i," 19–21.

seven failed attempts, they finally sought out the sheikh and confessed what they had done. Sheikh Zayla'i said to them, "I have forgiven the man who killed my camel and the grave will now receive him."[66]

In some cases, the Sheikh Zayla'i's supernatural deeds are linked to his poetic powers. When a student of the sheikh's was killed by an Ethiopian, and his head cut off with a sword, the sheikh did not seek revenge but went immediately to the body of his student. Placing the severed head on the neck, he chanted seven times, "Prophet of God, I have no Protector / Save you, who guards me / From severe torment." The man was brought back to life, and the sheikh became known from that point as *Hadiyat al-Arwah*, the "Camel-herder of Souls."[67]

The Somali saints played an important role in the evolution of the traditions of *xeer*, mediating disputes, assessing compensation (*diya*) for bloodshed, and assisting at rituals of reconciliation. A founding saint of the Rahanweyne clan of southern Somalia, Sheikh "Sagaal Hajile" ("Nine Pilgrimages"), was renowned as an organizer, agriculturalist, and peacemaker. He established many of the customs of *xeer*, showing people how to resolve disputes and preserve the peace without formal government.[68]

The most celebrated local saint in Somaliland is Sharif Yuusuf Barkhadle. Visiting his tomb near Hargeisa three times is equal to one pilgrimage to Mecca, and his birthday celebration is an important holiday in the region. God's blessing was upon Sheikh Yuusuf, so that God would reject those who were hostile to him and would answer his prayers for peace among the people. Upon visiting his tomb, one receives the sheikh's final blessing by which his image is placed in one's heart as a reminder to trust in God's protection, to love each other regardless of wealth or clan, and to live without fear. Sheikh Yuusuf's emblematic trust in God rather than in weapons is illustrated in a widespread myth in which he is confronted and asked to prove his authority by Qanana, the Oromo leader. The sheikh responded that his adversary had more men and weapons, and should therefore go first. Qanana passed through a mountain twice as proof of his powers, but on the third attempt Sheikh Yuusuf imprisoned him by reciting the *surat al-Yasin* (Sura 36, known as the "Heart of the Qur'an).[69]

66. Lewis, *Saints and Somalis*, 40.
67. Martin, "Shaykh Zayla'i," 23–24.
68. Cassanelli, *Shaping of Somali Society*, 127–30.
69. Lewis, *Saints and Somalis*, 89–95.

According to anthropologist B. W. Andrzejewski, the popularity of local Sufi saints is connected to the fact that they are considered to be protectors against foreign invasion. At the shrine of Sheikh Garweyne of Gendershe there are rocks that are said to be Portuguese soldiers, petrified by the Sheikh who rose from his grave as they landed on the coast. Similar accounts have Sheikh Uweys (the founder of the local Qadiriyah Order in Somalia) appearing along with the Prophet Muhammad and two other Sufi saints to route the invading Ethiopians.[70] The motif resembles the reliance on divine intervention in the Exodus and conquest narratives, imprecatory Psalms, and prophetic literature of the Hebrew Bible.

Other Somali Sufi saints represent peacemaking between clans, ethnicities, and nationalities. Sheikh Hussein of Bale is a multifaceted symbol of local Islamic identity, bringing together Oromo, Somali, and Arab peoples in his remembrance. Located in the Oromo region of Ethiopia, the Sheikh's tomb draws Ethiopians and Somalis together in a similar way to that of Sheikh Yuusuf; visiting his shrine three times is equivalent to one pilgrimage to Mecca.[71] The veneration of multi-ethnic saints like Sheikh Hussein of Bale is a potential catalyst for peaceful relations in the midst of national hostility between Ethiopia and Somalia.

Sufi mysticism could also serve as a link to mystics of other faiths. The English Christian John Ethelstan Cheese, who wandered unarmed in East Africa in the early twentieth century as an independent, self-appointed missionary, was called by one Somali chief "without doubt the holiest man in all Somalia."[72]

Other saints were venerated specifically as peacemakers. According to Andrzejewski, "The power of effective cursing and blessing which is attributed to the saints is often said to be put to a socially beneficial use, particularly in preventing or stopping internecine warfare." This

70. Andrzejewski, "Veneration of Sufi Saints," 17.

71. Lewis, *Saints and Somalis*, 99–104.

72. Salvadori, "St. Ivel." Salvadori ponders what Somalis thought of "this English Christian, staunch Trinitarian, a self-appointed missionary wandering in their midst? The very fact that he was able to walk not merely unharmed but actually welcomed is evidence enough of their appreciation of him. But what did they talk about? Angels on heads of pins? Houris in Paradise? Probably not! Islam as practised by the Somalis has a long train of Sufism, and it is credible that, as Cousins quotes a chief who once said, 'He is without doubt the holiest man in all Somalia.' I expect the Somalis simply recognized the peripatetic English gentleman as a fellow mystic and as such there was no need to discuss religion at all. They lived it" ("St. Ivel").

peacemaking role is especially praised in Sheikh 'Ali-Gure, of whom it was said:

> Whenever he was afraid that two clans would fight one another or when people told him that two Somali clans were actually fighting, he used to send either his ablution vessel or his rosary to them; he would hand it to his students and say: "Stand in front of each clan with it and say: 'Here is the rosary of the Sheikh Cali-Guure! If you go and attack those other Muslim people, may God confound you! If you refrain, may God keep you safe!'" They used to take it to the other clan. Once his ablution vessel or his rosary was seen there was no clan that would make preparations for war. They used to stop at that point.[73]

One remarkable aspect of this account is that the Sheikh not only earned a reputation as a peacemaker, but he also actively taught his students how to do peacemaking among the clans in conflict.

The Sufi saints that have been influential in Somali Islam are a peacemaking resource because they represent an alternative account of power, in contrast with military strength. Union with God, trust in God's protection and provision, and reluctance to embrace external forms of political Islam provide a buffer against militant Islam in a Sufi society. Moreover, Sufism offers an alternate account of *jihad* as the struggle of the individual's soul for union with God rather than in political terms. Islam in Somalia, if the Sufi traditions are strengthened, can therefore have a stabilizing function in society in keeping in check extremes of any kind, whether the exclusion of Islam from the realm of politics or making Islam the only basis for politics. Moreover, Sufi Islam can help to sustain attention for the value of all people, especially the marginalized, the hungry, and the poor.

Conclusion

I have argued that three elements—historical analysis of the tensions within Somali Islam, constructive readings of the Qur'an that promote peace, and peacemaking examples from within Somali Islam, particularly Sufism—are essential ingredients in the articulation of a peace-oriented Somali Islam.

---

73. Andrzejewski, "Veneration of Sufi Saints," 23.

In this equation the second element is a critical ingredient that must be further developed. The marginalization of Islamic scholars under Siad Barre continued into the era of the warlords, and even throughout the establishment of Western-backed federal governments. As a result voices in the middle, between Salafi-influenced Islamism and secular government, have been mostly silenced.

Nevertheless, there are striking examples of Islamic peacemaking in the face of tyranny and violence. In July 1989 Catholic Bishop Salvatore Colombo, an outspoken critic of the Barre regime, was gunned down in the cathedral, an act believed to be ordered by the president. Days later, government forces killed 450 protestors at a Mogadishu demonstration, leading to a manifesto for Barre's resignation. Barre sentenced to death nearly half of the 114 signers of the manifesto but was forced to back down by demonstrators surrounding the court, in a remarkable display of nonviolent direct action.[74]

After the conflict escalated between Mahdi and Aideed in 1991, Somalia's most famous Islamic scholars—Sheikh Mohammed Moallim, Sheikh Ibrahim Suley, and Sheikh Sharif Sharafow—met with the two warlords to advise them against war. "When the two sides started exchanging heavy gunfire the scholars continued traversing the frontlines in the midst of crossfire in a symbolic effort to urge ceasefire."[75]

How can Mennonites engage Somali Islam's deep peacemaking resources? I suggest that one way is by more intentionally integrating Islam and the Qur'an into the Mennonite peacebuilding collaboration, such as the partnership with the University of Hargeisa described in the next chapter. If EMM's decision to permit the teaching of Islam in its schools yielded positive outcomes for decades, how much more powerful could it be if a Mennonite-influenced peacebuilding program would help to elicit Somali interpretations of the Qur'an and Islam that promote peace?

The assumption with which I have been working is that Islam, along with the other Abrahamic faiths of Christianity and Judaism, can hermeneutically rework the violence in their tradition while maintaining the religious commitment, seeing "the sacred as operating at a deeper level than the overt violence or hatred that may appear on the surface of a particular text."[76] War does not happen in a vacuum but has a causal chain

---

74. Samatar, "Historical Setting," 52.
75. Bradbury and Healy, "Islam and Somali Social Order," 96.
76. Gopin, *Between Eden and Armageddon*, 68.

leading up to it, and intersects with other sorts of human interaction. This is why the practices of peacemaking before war begins, like those articulated in just peacemaking theory, are so crucial. War does not take place in a vacuum, but takes many relationships to fail and values to be violated before it happens. A significant challenge is to discover the interpersonal values in a culture that were violated at some point by an enemy, which are vital indicators of how wars started in the first place and how they are justified.[77] Much work remains to be done in Somalia on the question of what sorts of moral violations have taken place that could have facilitated such intense and persistent violence, which formerly the cultural and Islamic values could contain.

Above all, what I hope my analysis demonstrates is that religious values, like the cultural values of the previous chapter, cannot be imposed from above but must emerge from the most profound part of people's religious identity. In Somalia, the deep Sufi roots, the powerful peacemaking impetus found in the Qur'an, and the people who give them legs in exemplary practice have great potential to shape Somali religious identity now and in the future.

77. Ibid., 74, 84.

7

Bridge-Builders

*Mennonite Peacebuilding Education
and Women Peacemakers*

Women take a broad view of a peaceful society, where children can be fed and educated, and where people can live in right relationships with each other.

— DEKHA IBRAHIM, "WOMEN'S ROLES IN PEACE-MAKING"

JANICE JENNER DESCRIBES HER first visit to the University of Hargeisa in Somaliland in this way: "I knew nobody there. I walked into the university and thought I was going to have to really explain myself. But as soon as I said Eastern Mennonite University, it was just this welcome, it was amazing, an open door. A couple of the older professors starting talking, and they had been educated in Mennonite schools in the south. One of them had actually started his career teaching in one of the Mennonite schools. It was just amazing!"[1]

What Jenner discovered in Somaliland, and what other Mennonites have realized in countless interactions with Somalis, is that the two communities are woven together in ways that are not quickly forgotten. The Mennonite schools of the past are reduced to rubble; the first generation of Mennonite teachers are elderly or home in glory; but Mennonite education lives on.

The most recent Mennonite connections to Somalia, particularly the work of the Center for Justice and Peacebuilding at EMU, have been

---

1. Jenner, interview.

focused on peacebuilding education, with special attention to women as peacebuilders. This is not a new orientation for Mennonites in Somalia. Judith Gardiner states that Anabaptists have a long historical experience at the margins, and maintain an orientation to the margins that stresses God's "preferential option for the poor."[2] Justice requires special concern for the vulnerable and poor, in many cases women and children. During the Somalia conflict MCC and EMM persisted in focusing on the most vulnerable, conducting an AIDS workshop in Mogadishu in 2002. Emphasis on working with women was strategic as well as theological. In 1997–1998 MCC gave $50,000 for work in Somalia, most of which went to women's peace conferences. MCC recognized that women are uniquely positioned to work for peace because they are not tied to clan politics and often support entire families. Women play a central role in education, small business, and healthcare in a war-torn area.[3]

Bertha Beachy, who represented MCC and EMM from 1995 to 2000, became aware that women act as the primary facilitators of peace between clans. During her previous work in Mogadishu from 1958 to 1976, she brought together girls and women from different clans for activities like classes, tea, and outings like attending events at the National Theater. In this way she built up trust not only between herself and the women, but among the women. In her later work based out of Nairobi, Beachy continued to view her role as a catalyst for relationship-building between women of different clans. She developed a special relationship over many years with a Somali peacemaker named Fatima Jibrell, who offered Beachy valuable insight into the experiences of women in Somali culture. They attended peace conferences and UN-sponsored meetings together, and Jibrell traveled from Nairobi to speak along with Beachy at a meeting the MCC UN office organized for all organizations working in Somalia. Beachy comments, "It was far more powerful because an American and a Somali shared the opportunity."[4]

2. Gardiner, "Getting Stuck In," 376.

3. Eby, *Fifty Years, Fifty Stories*, 102. See also Bergey, "'Bottom-Up' Alternative," 155.

4. Beachy, interview. Another close friend of Mennonite Mission is Fatima Omar Hashi, who was a member of the Somali parliament during the Barre era. When the government fell she began working with World Vision in Washington, DC (Nissley, interview.)

EMU and Somali Peacebuilding

EMU and the Center for Justice and Peacebuilding (CJP) have a long history of involvement with Somali people. In the last several decades EMU has cultivated a strong connection to Somalia, both institutionally and informally. Somalis have attended and taught in programs at CJP, particularly the Summer Peacebuilding Institute. Many of the Mennonite workers in Somalia from all eras are graduates of EMU. According to Janice Jenner, former director of CJP's Practice and Training Institute, more than ninety EMU graduates have worked in Somalia, Somaliland, or Northeast Kenya. USAID is so heavily EMU-influenced in the region that people refer to the EMU mafia, because every organization hires people who were connected with the university in some way.[5]

While the early Mennonite work in education was in the south, in Johar, Mahaddei, and Mogadishu, EMU's recent partnerships have been in Somaliland. A major reason for this shift is the relative stability of the north compared to the south. As a result of this stability, the rate of enrollment in upper primary school (grades 5–8) in Somaliland is almost double that of greater Somalia. None of the primary schools in Somaliland are operated by international NGOs, whereas in greater Somalia nearly a quarter of the schools are run by aid agencies. In Somaliland more schools are operated by local authorities and parents. While Islamic charities from Egypt, Sudan, Libya, and the Arabian Peninsula also contribute significantly to education, Somalilanders take pride in minimizing their reliance on outside help. These efforts have roots in the colonial era, when Somaliland guarded its education carefully and resisted the efforts of British officers to set up schools in the early twentieth century.[6]

In light of this history, it is all the more remarkable that some actors within the government of Somaliland have actively sought to partner with Mennonites in education. The Ministry of Education has issued a request to EMM and other Mennonite agencies for secondary school teachers in English, music, physical education, and conflict resolution. Universities in the country have embraced collaboration with EMU and other universities in the areas of peacebuilding, social work, and health care.

---

5. Jenner, interview.
6. Jhazbhay, "Islam and Stability," 191–93.

Summer Peacebuilding Institute

EMU's Summer Peacebuilding Institute has trained many Somalis in the last fifteen years, including people who later attained prominent political positions. Khadija Ossoble Ali, who became a member of the Somali cabinet, earned a master's degree at EMU in conflict transformation in 2001. She encouraged Hassan Sheikh Mohamud, who was later elected President of Somalia, to attend EMU in 2001 as well. Mohamud was a university professor and dean before turning to civil activism and politics. Ten years after studying peacebuilding in traumatized societies at EMU, he founded the Peace and Development Party, the platform from which he launched his successful bid for the presidency. The BBC describes Mohamud as a "peace activist and educational campaigner" [7] who, unlike many Somali intellectuals, remained in Somalia during the most difficult years of the conflict. Mohamud emphasizes the importance of including civil society groups in any strategy for lasting peace. He has a record of working across clan lines to establish partnerships between NGOs. As a Muslim who rejects militant Islamism, Mohamud's life is regularly threatened; two days after his election an assassination attempt by al-Shabaab killed several of the African Union soldiers guarding him.

While EMU does not claim to know in what way he was impacted by his time in SPI, there is hope among the Somali women in EMU's program that President Mohamud will continue to seek a more peaceful, secure Somalia through increased participation, development, and consensus from the people rather than the strong-armed tactics that have characterized Somalia in the past. A position like a presidency exerts enormous pressure that is more powerful than any individual. The greater hope for Somalia is thus that peace will be built from the ground up rather than by the strength of the top leader, which is why EMU chooses to focus on peace education for women in particular.[8]

Partnership with the University of Hargeisa

In 2008 EMU began a partnership with the University of Hargeisa to develop a peacebuilding program. The project was funded by a four-year grant from USAID through Higher Education for Development (HED),

---

7. Lofton, "New Somali President."
8. Rhodes, interview.

an organization that matches universities in the US and the developing world. The intention was to exchange faculty between the universities. Three faculty members from Hargeisa came to the Summer Peacebuilding Institute in the first year of the grant, but in the following years every visa was denied by the US government. The University of Hargeisa decided to make their program a master's certificate rather than undergraduate, but their professors were not equipped to teach at that level. So the UN Peace University Africa Division based in Addis Ababa sent five of the faculty to do a master's course in Costa Rica. In their absence CJP professors, most frequently Barry Hart, traveled to Hargeisa to teach courses.[9]

Along with Muhyadin Said, Hart conducted a research project comparing conflict transformation and traditional Somali peacebuilding. They concluded that Somali customary law (*xeer*) is flexible enough to integrate the strategies of conflict transformation, which would allow for deeper analysis of conflict and a transformation of structural causes rather than simply resolving conflict after the fact. The traditional strengths of *xeer*, especially the emphasis on integrity, interdependence, and listening, can combine with the conflict transformation framework to address the issues Somaliland faces.[10]

The university partnership resulted in the formation of the Institute for Peace and Conflict Studies. The program has educated nearly two hundred people, and is running its seventh cohort of students. Since the HED grant expired in 2011, the institute is funded on tuition. The institute has trained government officials in various Ministries, including the first vice president of Somaliland and the Speaker of the House, as well as UN and NGO workers. The faculty and student body is from different clans and from all over Somaliland, reflecting the diversity of Hargeisa, and the institute is working to include more people from Somalia and northeast Kenya as well. In October 2011, the institute published the inaugural issue of *Somaliland Journal of Peace and Development*, the first professional journal out of Somaliland, which included articles on traditional Somali governance, peacebuilding by Somaliland women, and the difference in approach and outcomes in Somalia and Somaliland.

Jonathan Rudy, who worked in northern Somalia with MCC in the late 1980s, has developed a partnership between the University of Hargeisa and Elizabethtown College, where Rudy teaches. As a graduate

---

9. Jenner, interview.
10. Hart and Saed, "Integrating Principles," 17.

of EMU, Rudy had an automatic entrée into a working relationship with the University of Hargeisa, and was invited to visit in March 2013. There he met with the leadership of the university, who enthusiastically welcome new international partners.[11] He has returned to Hargeisa three times to teach short courses on peacebuilding in civil society, conflict analysis, and designing peace education.

Like the CJP program, Rudy operates out of a conflict transformation framework that focuses on relationships. He has developed a model that consists of current analysis and past analysis, and then asks participants to describe their perfect world. Peacebuilding is everything in between that gets one from the present to the imagined future, with the assumption that the values, process, and structures are consistent with the outcome. Because peacebuilding pays attention to both the means and the ends, Rudy relies on both a pragmatic and a principled nonviolence.[12] He resonates with the broader trend within the field that sees peacebuilding as a wider-reaching community of practice than just organizations focusing on conflict resolution. The new doctrine *Peacebuilding 2.0* states, "Durable peace requires efforts at the intersection of many fields, including conflict resolution, development, democracy and governance, human rights, and many more."[13] This means that every intervention in divided societies, including work in medicine and education, can either reduce or augment violence.

Peacebuilding is about connecting the various pieces that contribute to a more durable society. In that sense, peacebuilding education incorporates all sorts of activities, including art, music, ecology, writing, and much more. In peacebuilding classes, whether at Elizabethtown or in Somaliland, Rudy's approach is to present the various frameworks and models, then ask the students what it means for them in their personal and communal context. When students consider how their talents and social locations might contribute to peacebuilding, they think in more expansive and creative terms than the narrow goals of violence reduction.[14]

---

11. Rudy, interview.
12. Ibid.
13. *Peacebuilding 2.0*, 7.
14. Rudy, interview.

Women as Peacemakers in Somali Culture

As in many conflict situations, women in Somalia have a unique role as peacemakers. In the face of persistent barriers of discrimination and oppression, women are acting in remarkable ways to resolve conflicts and care for those with the deepest needs. Women act as mediators in a Somali context in two ways: through marriage according to the Somali tradition of exogamy, known as *hidid*; and as middlepersons between the political authorities and the community.

Women in Somalia face difficult circumstances. Maternal and infant mortality rates rank among the highest in the world. A lack of adequate healthcare and the widespread practice of Female Genital Mutilation (FGM) make Somalia one of the most dangerous places in the world to become pregnant. Women also suffer disproportionately as victims of the fighting and as refugees.[15] During food crises women bear the brunt of caring for families. Even in times of relative prosperity the economic burden falls on women. One contributing factor to this is the amount of household income that is spent, mostly by men, on the narcotic *qat*. When I asked my students at the University of Djibouti about their views of *qat*, they were divided almost completely along gender lines. The reason is simple; the women are opposed to the drug because they carry the burden of caring for families who need the money that the men spend.

Women were granted voting rights according to Somalia's original constitution in 1960. Fae Miller was in Jamama at the time of independence. She was invited to say a few words at a celebratory event, and her Somali hosts were delighted when she stood up and said, "When America became independent the women had to wait one hundred and fifty years for voting rights. You have it right away!"[16]

Somalia's new administration has taken some steps toward greater inclusion of women in the political process. In November 2012 Somalia Prime Minister Abdi Farah Shirdon appointed two women to his cabinet. Fowsiyo Yussuf Haji Aadan was named Deputy Prime Minister as well as Foreign Minister, the first woman to have been selected for this position. Maryam Kassim was appointed Minister of Social Development. Nevertheless, the socio-political process in Somalia remains mostly the realm of men. Lidwien Kapteijns is critical of the ways in which customary law (*xeer*) actually violates some of the protection of women's inheritance in

15. Harper, *Getting Somalia Wrong?*, 24–25.
16. Miller, interview.

Islam, imposing rules that are nonexistent in the Qur'an and sidestepping some of its legal provisions for women. In traditional Somali society women cannot establish households or hold formal positions of political and religious authority. Their moral capacities are considered inferior to that of men; according to one proverb, "Knowledge cannot come to reside in a bosom that has contained milk." Urbanization brought several positive changes for women. Banks meant that wealth could be accumulated, creating less dependence on one's kin group to increase capital. Labor could be obtained through paying wages, establishing more equality in opportunity and pay. For Kapteijns, Islamic law is more desirable for women than *xeer* because it allows a middle-class man to privilege his nuclear family (both males and females) rather than bequeathing the inheritance to distant male relatives.[17] Despite some increased opportunities, women in Somalia remain second class citizens both in popular perception and in the realities of political power.

Within such a strongly patriarchal society, however, some women find alternative sources of power and remarkable space to operate. Kinship (*tol*) in Somalia comprises two principle elements: the shared identity of a common male lineage, and marriage ties (*hidid*). *Hidid* determines obligations to the kin of a wife that actually privileges the mother's relatives in any benefit from the offspring.[18] While pre-colonial, non-state Somali society was unquestionably patriarchal, dividing women's loyalties between her family of origin and of marriage, she did have institutionalized value in the practice of exogamy. The prescription that men obtain wives from outside their own clan or sub-clan enhanced the likelihood of peaceful conflict resolution and the sharing of scarce economic resources. In this way "each married woman became a significant bearer of social capital in that she represented to both communities the rights and duties of reciprocal sharing."[19] A special son-to-mother bond in Somali culture provides some counterbalance to the weight of patriarchy. As a result, Somali leaders often construct key alliances with their mothers' clans, facilitating a constant reconstruction of clan identity.[20] When their children marry, older women have access to an even greater number of clans. They can operate as messengers between clans

---

17. Kapteijns, "Women and Crisis," 216–19.
18. Samatar, "Curse of Allah," 109.
19. Kapteijns, "Women and Crisis," 217.
20. Laitin and Samatar, *Somalia*, 31.

because they have greater freedom of movement.[21] Women also have a special responsibility to keep peace at a household level, granting them a measure of authority in addressing disharmony within the family, before a conflict expands to a wider circle. Women are thus in a natural position to act as bridge builders both within the family and between clan groups that may be hostile to one another.[22]

A second way in which women serve as peacemaking mediators is between high-level political actors, who are almost exclusively men, and the grassroots level. Lederach emphasizes the importance of middle-range players in any conflict who are "uniquely situated to have the greatest potential for constructing an infrastructure for peace" because they can access both the top and the grassroots levels. Middle-range actors are critical because they can be recognized as valid, trustworthy actors by the international community, they have unique capacities to relate to middle-range players of other clans, and they are more inclined to own their loyalties as peacemakers rather than to seek the elusive goal of "objectivity." Women have proven adept at filling this role in Somalia, rebuilding inter-clan communication and preparing the way for clan conferences that led to local peace agreements.[23] In recognition of this fact, when the Life and Peace Institute established district council training centers throughout Somalia, they included at least one woman on each district council.[24] Women are more likely than men to drive conflicts toward reconciliation and away from violence.

While women were not very visible in many of the official meetings of the Borama Peace Process, they played an important role in facilitating many aspects of the proceedings. Bonnie Bergey was taken to a nearby school where food was being prepared for the meeting. There she observed pregnant women working hard for the sake of transforming the conflict; the women of Somaliland "prepared and sacrificed themselves so that the men could come together and talk about peace."[25]

According to Siham Rayale, the experience of women in Somaliland is unique in that they participated in innovative ways in the political establishment of the state, even as they stayed mostly within the boundaries

---

21. Ibrahim, "Women's Roles in Peace-making," 167.
22. Adam, "Somalia," 275.
23. Lederach, *Building Peace*, 94–95, 151.
24. Prendergast, "Applying Concepts," 178.
25. Bergey, interview.

of their traditional roles. During the Borama conferences women composed poems known as *baraanbur* to express their frustration with the ongoing inter-clan conflicts and bring the impact of displacement and violence on women to the forefront. In this way, women helped to sustain the impetus for peacemaking throughout the process.[26]

Women also enhance the effectiveness of relief efforts. Despite the disintegration of many facets of Somali society, during the famine some Somali women with a gift for reconciliation were instrumental in operating the food distribution centers established by NGOs.[27] Even in the face of oppression and the dictates of a deeply patriarchal society, women in Somalia act as peacemakers through marriage and as mediators between top-level and grassroots communities.

Edna Adan Ismail's remarkable life has included a post as Somaliland's Foreign Minister (the only woman in the Somaliland government from 2003 to 2006), Somaliland's Minister of Family Welfare and Social Development, and founding and directing the Edna Adan Maternity Hospital in Hargeisa. She was married to Somali Prime Minister and President of Somaliland Mohamed Haji Ibrahim Egal. Her work as an activist in the struggle for the abolition of female genital mutilation (FGM) and as a pioneer in maternal health has earned her the nickname "Muslim Mother Theresa."[28] She is also President of the Organization for Victims of Torture.

Adan began building a hospital in Mogadishu in the mid-1980s, but was forced to leave the country by the civil war. In the ensuing years she worked for the World Health Organization (WHO), training midwives and addressing issues affecting the health of women and children. When she was able to return to Somaliland in 1997 she built the Edna Adan Maternity Hospital, which opened in 2002 and continues to operate. With almost no educated nurses in the region, Adan focused on training dozens of local nurse-midwives in order to combat one of the highest maternal and infant mortality rates in the world.[29] The hospital treats fistula and has delivered over 12,000 babies in the last decade. Drawing on both the expertise of Somali women and the benefits of Western medicine, Adan's work facilitates cooperation across clans to meet the needs of

---

26. Rayale, "Participation through Peacebuilding," 29–32.
27. Metz, *Somalia*, xxxiv–xxxvi.
28. Grant, "Muslim Mother Theresa."
29. Kristof and WuDunn, *Half the Sky*, 123–30.

the most vulnerable people in Somali society. She also represents to the world the ability of Somalis (even more effectively since being featured in the 2012 PBS documentary *Half the Sky*), with help from friends in other parts of the world, to address the many challenges facing their society.

Women's Peacebuilding Leadership Program

The latest iteration of EMU's involvement with Somali people is focused on training and equipping women with peacebuilding tools. The Women's Peacebuilding Leadership Program emerged out of a brainstorm among a group of women connected in various ways to CJP, as students, teachers, and associates, with the goal of supporting women who did not have access to higher education. CJP alumna and 2011 Nobel Peace Prize laureate Leymah Gbowee funded four Liberian women to attend the program, and CJP staff also raised funds for Somali and South Pacific cohorts.[30]

The program was designed to bring the cohorts to EMU's campus, where they would earn a graduate certificate. When eight of the women from the Somali cohort were refused visas by the US government, it became impossible for them to complete the courses as expected. In response to the problem, two faculty members and the director of CJP traveled to Hargeisa in fall 2012 to teach the courses in conflict analysis and strategic peacebuilding to the group of women from Somaliland, Mogadishu, and northeast Kenya.

CJP's Peacebuilding Education Approach

Jenner sees peacebuilding education as giving people frameworks and language for what they already know intuitively. Peacebuilding education is building on the work people have already been doing, providing new ways of thinking about and articulating conflict and peace. In a Somali context, therefore, the emphasis is on combining traditional Somali and Islamic understandings with global, modern, secular concepts, "putting them together in a package that works."[31] According to CJP professor Jayne Docherty, the program's purpose is to foster a network of women

---

30. Rhodes, interview.
31. Jenner, interview.

peace leaders within a specific country or region, who can "relate to one another as 'lost sisters from the same clan.'"[32]

Unlike CJP's normally diverse Summer Peacebuilding Institute, the class in Hargeisa was a relatively mono-cultural group. As a result, the students could focus mostly on their own context for case studies, and integrate the alternative models presented by the professors into the Somali context they knew thoroughly. The CJP faculty had to be flexible in tailoring the curriculum of the program to meet the needs of the Somali women, who are largely practitioners rather than academics. Both the women and the funders wanted hard outcomes in the form of concrete social change, which is a lot to expect from an eighteen-month program. Additionally, although they all have undergraduate degrees, the same kind of support is not available for them as there would be on EMU's campus (such as the library and writing services). The result is that the limitations of distance learning are combined with the further challenges of language, distance, cultural and religious differences, and limitations on women's access to Western education. Nevertheless, the basic structure of the program serves the needs of the women. It consists of core courses in conflict analysis, peacebuilding practice at a general and strategic level, theory, and research.[33]

Jenner acknowledges that differences exist between CJP's sociological approach and that of EMU's theology faculty. That is not to say that CJP does not have a theological foundation, which is grounded in respect and value for all people as God's creations. But rather than perceiving knowledge primarily in terms of revelation, a sociological approach sees knowledge and theory as built on experience. One of the realities that must shape our theology and the way we articulate what it means to follow Jesus is that we are globally interconnected more than ever before in history, giving us new responsibility to understand and build peace with one another. Jenner describes how her work in conflict situations like Sierra Leone and Somalia have changed her understanding of pacifism from a principle or rule-based concept; "My pacifism has come down to whatever moves from more violence to less violence in this broken and violent world is what we have to support."[34]

---

32. Edwards, "EMU Peace Profs."
33. Rhodes, interview.
34. Jenner, interview.

The situation in Hargeisa is dynamic and complex, bearing little resemblance to the city it was two decades ago. Bonnie Bergey had some of her most dangerous personal experiences in Hargeisa in the early 1990s. On one trip she arrived in the city one day after three women were stoned to death. In that instance, Somalis kept her out of the public eye and she had to move cautiously around town and back and forth to the airport.[35] Jonathan Rudy recalls an atmosphere of paranoia around the city in the late 1980s, fostered by Soviet-trained secret police sent by Barre to quell any resistance to the government in the south. Twenty-five years later, the contrast is immense; it is an open environment with a thriving economy and money pouring in from the diaspora, and Somalis are resettling in the country along with their families. Many Somalilanders welcome the presence of foreigners and the international visibility they can bring.[36] At the same time, Saudi influence is increasing in Somaliland and is especially apparent in the areas of education and dress. Women make personal changes for various reasons, including the influence of family and spouses, fads, and other social pressures. Some are also motivated by personal convictions and piety, emphasizing that their faith is their own choice. The women in WPLP reflect this range, but most identify strongly with their Islamic faith. Jenner observed in the fall course in Hargeisa that all six women cited their faith as a source of power and a point of identity.[37]

The heavily sociological approach to conflict analysis leads the CJP faculty to view the Islamic faith of the Somali women primarily in terms of identity and power. The analytical model helps people to create models of who is involved, stakeholder mapping, identity group mapping, and other identity tools. The students analyze who holds power—whether economic, religious, political, or gender—and how identity contributes to power dynamics and conflict. They also look for what connects and divides people across identity lines, identifying in what setting religion is a resource for peace or for conflict, and who are the key actors in Muslim

---

35. Bergey, interview.

36. Rudy, interview.

37. Jenner, interview. On an individual basis the role of faith can change over time. A longtime Somali associate of the center became more religious over the two decades in which she related to CJP, so that eventually she would not shake hands with a man. After performing the Hajj several times she began to pray and fast regularly. She and a number of other women fasted two days a week because they felt that traveling for peace work without their husbands risked violation of their faith.

religious groups. For example, two women in the program have a good educational background and a deep interest in political science, but still lack political access as women. Following the conflict analysis course, the women then consider their peacebuilding options in light of the power dynamics of their situation, along with the range of outside models they might engage. They develop a strategic peacebuilding plan with a specific timetable, in which they translate their new insights about their connections and limitations as women within the Somali clan and religious systems into a course of action. This is particularly significant in a classroom setting that brings women of different clans together. For example, one of the women was recently married to a man from a different clan. She exclaimed, "Ok, now I have a strategic relationship!"[38]

Part of what drives CJP's approach is the urgency of establishing viable alternatives to violence. The phenomena of militant groups like al-Shabaab and piracy along the Somali coast are both rooted at least in part in unmet basic human needs. These needs must be satisfied, and people will resort to violence if they cannot meet them any other way. What begins as the need for livelihood that drives people to act in increasingly desperate ways can become entrenched in patterns of identity and self-determination, as in the cases of piracy and militancy.[39] The gift that Somali women offer is the living proof that basic human needs are better met through peacebuilding and development than with guns.

Signs of Hope

Finding hope in a decades-old conflict can be difficult, but the Somali women in WPLP are brimming with ambition and optimism. One reason is that the increasing interconnectedness of the world, and the contacts they make within the program, give them new awareness of the work of women around the globe. CJP alumna Leymah Gbowee's Nobel Peace Prize brought new recognition of the ways in which women are creating their own corridors of power, even in traditionally patriarchal societies. Just as importantly, Somali women are sharing their own stories of resisting violence and building peace, such as 2012 Nobel Peace Prize nominee Hawa Abdi. Abdi's work in a refugee camp raised the ire of al-Shabaab, who came and confiscated her keys in order to isolate her. When they

38. Rhodes, interview.
39. Ibid.

came back to return them later, Abdi responded, "'I don't want to take them unless you write a letter of apology.' And they did. She knew that if she'd just take them, they'd just be back whenever it suits their fancy. That's a bold move, but it's by a woman who understands that she is able to make a difference, and that she believes in her own people."[40]

The hope displayed by the women in the WPLP was a pleasant surprise to Gloria Rhodes. The legacy of the US military involvement and the intransigence of the warlords, despite the work of Lederach and others two decades ago, make the conflict appear intractable. From the perspective of conflict analysis and peacebuilding, there seems to be little to build on in terms of a functioning government and social services. Moreover, many of the women in the program have been displaced for much of their lives, and have witnessed violence, poverty, and war. It is difficult to imagine how some of them managed to earn undergraduate degrees, let alone pursue a graduate program in the midst of all their other family and work involvements. But the classroom experience with the women gives Rhodes a glimpse of the way in which Somali society, even in Mogadishu, has continued to function even apart from the standard measures of stability. On some level the clan system is working to provide social security where the government cannot. One student from Mogadishu is training others in what she is learning, working with youth, and developing plans for her home area. One of her projects is to run peace clubs in the local schools.[41]

The women are well-informed about the history of their own context and its conflicts. They absorb and analyze every piece of information, which they see as another way they can know about their context, or another tool that can be applied. Their education is also enriched by the interaction with the other CJP cohorts from Liberia and the South Pacific. During one course in Monrovia the women visited a gathering of children from both a Muslim and a Christian school. Rhodes recounts, "All the Muslim school children really lit up when all the Somali women walked in with the hijab. And the women in our program lit up too because they were sensing, 'It's ok; these Muslim children are here in this church, and it's ok.' I'm very hopeful for what is going to happen."[42]

---

40. Beachy, interview.
41. Rhodes, interview.
42. Ibid.

CJP is an education and training organization and therefore does not focus on peacebuilding programming. When the first cohort completes the WPLP, therefore, Jenner hopes that CJP can continue to support the women and their organizations that are running programs. One possible avenue for further involvement is Peace III, a cross-border program between Kenya, Somalia, and other borders in East Africa. USAID East Africa is heavily Mennonite-influenced, especially since four of the key staff and consultants are graduates of CJP. USAID is requesting CJP's involvement in training key leaders in the program, specifically on trauma and justice issues.[43] Trauma awareness and healing as a component of peace education is a growing edge in Mennonite involvement. In 2015 Elizabeth and Ken Nissley, who have worked in a victim-offender reconciliation program in the US, led short courses in the Somaliland cities of Hargeisa and Berbera for civil society leaders who are doing trauma healing work.

Breathing Peace: Dekha Ibrahim

Dekha Ibrahim, an extraordinary Kenyan peace leader of Somali origin, was an important ambassador between Mennonites and traditional Somali peace initiatives. Ibrahim had a longstanding relationship with CJP, first as a student and later as a colleague and teacher. She was recognized by many for her gifts both as a peacebuilding theorist and a practitioner.[44]

Ibrahim comes from Wajir, in the north eastern province of Kenya. From 1992 to 1998 a violent conflict between clans threw the area in turmoil. While the conflict was aggravated by the instability in neighboring Somalia, the central issues were local and national, including drought, displacement, water and grazing rights, and lack of political representation. By 1993 clan relationships had degenerated to the extent that people could not visit towns or areas of the city under the control of rival clans, and the market became a place of tension and fighting. Ibrahim and two other women began to visit the prominent and educated women of various clans, and called a general meeting for "all women in Wajir who love peace."[45]

At that meeting the group Wajir Women for Peace was formed. Starting in the marketplace, they worked to strengthen peaceful relationships

---

43. Jenner, interview.
44. DeBoer, *No Failure in Peace Work*.
45. Ibrahim, "Women's Roles in Peace-making," 168–69.

between women of different clans and social strata. Realizing that peace is the responsibility of all parties, in 1995 they took initiative to include men who had the same goals as well as the government of the District. The coalition had a transformative effect on the community, leading to a cessation of the fighting and normalizing of businesses and trade.[46] The women also realized that peace and development depend on one another, because without economic stability peace is impossible.[47] The insight that everyone in a communal culture—men, women, and children in all positions—have duties to make peace led the Wajir initiative to embrace the motto, "Peace is a communal responsibility."[48]

The success of the women's initiative resulted in the formation of the Wajir Peace and Development Committee, whose goal was to address the ongoing concerns of the three major clans in nonviolent ways. The committee acted as first responders to conflicts that arose. For example, in July 1998 two clans had a dispute over access to a water pan for camels. A rapid response team of three elders, two women, and a government representative traveled to the area to meet with village leaders. They included all concerned parties in the discussions and reached an agreement before any violence erupted.[49]

Another crisis arose in the region in January 2008, with widespread violence following Kenya's election. The women's movement served as a precedent for successful communal action at a number of levels. Five prominent Kenyan civil society peace workers established an initiative called Concerned Citizens for Peace (CCP), which worked to encourage dialogue during the crisis. Because of her extensive experience and leadership skills, Dekha Ibrahim was chosen as chair of the initiative. At the outbreak of the violence, CCP played a crucial role in demonstrating "at that early stage that dialogue was the only way out of the crisis. The initial focus was to plead publicly and privately with the political leadership to dialogue, while calling upon Kenyans to stop the violence and wanton destruction of property."[50]

Mennonites were involved on the edges throughout these peace initiatives. Ibrahim was closely connected to EMU and CJP staff from the

46. Ibid., 169–73.

47. Asha Hagi Elmi et al., "Peace is Milk." See also Jenner, "Development and Peace."

48. Jenner, interview.

49. Babu Ayindo et al., *When You are the Peacebuilder*, 49–51.

50. Wachira et al., *Citizens in Action*, x.

early 1990s onward. MCC funded some of the meetings surrounding the establishment of the Wajir groups. In the 2008 crisis one of the founders of CCP was George Wachira of Nairobi Peace Initiative, an organization that MCC worker Harold Miller had helped to establish decades earlier.[51]

Bridget Ann Walker describes Ibrahim's peacebuilding approach in this way: inclusive and open to all affected parties; reflective on past successes and mistakes; willing to take risks; allowing sufficient time for processes; and respecting and drawing from the values of the participants.[52] According to Ibrahim, Somali women work within the clan system almost intuitively. They draw on Islamic and Somali cultural peace resources, because they recognize that local initiatives are the main instrument of peace work. Women act as horizontal bridge-builders between clans and as vertical connectors between top-level leaders and grassroots movements. But women also join a wider framework of peacebuilding, with many other actors at different levels. In this sense the peace work of women is just one part of an integrated and multi-faceted approach to peacebuilding. Ibrahim writes that women "take a broad view of a peaceful society, where children can be fed and educated, and where people can live in right relationships with each other."[53]

Ibrahim's influence and her connection to Mennonites continue after her death in 2011. Her friends and colleagues on the CJP faculty hold up the Wajir story and her involvement as a peacebuilding example in their courses. Ibrahim's Somali and Kenyan protégées are now involved in CJP's programs.[54] Remembering Ibrahim, a colleague writes, "She does not just do peacebuilding because she gets paid or gets a name or whatever other reason, but because she genuinely wants, lives and breathes peace."[55]

51. Harold Miller, e-mail message to author, February 14, 2013.
52. Walker, "Some Approaches to Peacebuilding," 12–13.
53. Ibrahim, "Women's Roles in Peace-making," 173.
54. Rhodes, interview.
55. Shuria, "Final Word," 137.

―――― 8 ――――

Peace Clan Past and Present

A Kenyan friend of Mennonites working in Nairobi decided to go to Somaliland as a Christian teacher. He made contact and secured a job, but when the officials discovered that he was a Christian they asked what kind of a Christian he was. They told him, "If you are Mennonite, you can come."[1]

This story is one among many illustrating a mutual aspiration between Somalis and Mennonites to re-imagine and renew a fruitful partnership. Mennonite agencies and personnel have expressed the desire to build upon the history of involvement with Somali people. The civil war and instability of the past two decades threaten to undermine the previous decades of work unless Mennonites are able to find a vision and strategy for continuing the relationship. The ongoing work with Somalis will be different from that of the past, especially in the context of different political realities. But it will also resemble the work of the past in important ways. Here I explore what those ways may be, based on how Mennonite theology and practices have developed. I also return to the question with which we started: What can it possibly mean when someone identifies as a Somali Muslim Mennonite? The identity of membership in a peace clan is sufficiently inclusive and fluid, yet also substantive, to provide an imaginative framework for an enduring partnership.

1. Logan, interview.

A Good Name

Each generation of Mennonites who works in Somalia observes that they are standing on the shoulders of those who came before. The rapport that has been established between Mennonites and Somalis over the last six decades, as turbulent as these years have been, is built on love, respect, and mutual gratitude. Rhoda Lind, who set foot in Somalia sixty years ago with her husband Wilbert as the first Mennonite missionaries in the country, expresses this sentiment on the part of the Mennonite clan. Despite the challenges of living in a foreign place, learning a new culture, and even surviving a nighttime knife attack, Lind declares, "Living among Somalis was a privilege—never a burden, never a burden!"[2]

Chantal Logan notes the inestimable value of a good name in an African culture. Several incidents demonstrate that the Mennonite name continues in Somalia. When Logan and Mike Brislen visited Somaliland, the Minister of Education implored them to send teachers. A man sitting beside them leaned over and whispered, "We don't want just any teachers; we want *Mennonite* teachers." On another visit to the Lower Juba region by the Logans, people came from the town of Ras Kamboni to ask the Mennonites to start a school there. They even offered to give them an island on which to build the school.[3] In the recent educational partnerships, likewise, Jan Jenner and Jonathan Rudy found that the Mennonite name was an open door. Rudy observes, "Somalis are networked, and for one's reputation to be attached to a larger one is really a good thing."[4]

Bonnie Bergey is certain that the Mennonite connections in Somalia protected her and opened doors wherever she went. In contrast to the Western military personnel she saw in Somalia, some of whom never left the airport, she was taken by Somalis all over the city and was able to visit many places in the country. At the time, there were many who knew Mennonites were supporting peace efforts. Somalis then started informing her of other peace meetings that were going to be held by women's groups or clan leaders. Some involved dances and other cultural events. In this way, the Mennonite history gave her special access to Somali culture and peacebuilding initiatives. She states, "I did not even have to know people directly connected to that history, but if I said I was with Mennonite mission, I could find someone in that little town, wherever it

2. Lind, interview.
3. Logan, interview.
4. Rudy, interview.

was, who would take me in or help me make my next connection if I had any trouble. There was this kind of network because of the history. It was beautiful, and I wish we could see that happen in other places and believe in that kind of building of society, among people with different cultural practices and understandings."[5]

Although Bergey's experience was vastly different from the Mennonite educational and medical work in previous decades, and the elicitive and conflict transformation language was new, she felt all along that her presence in Somalia was a continuation of the earlier story. EMM's willingness to allow Islam to be taught in the schools, for example, had a lasting bridge-building effect that no one could have predicted. Moments such as these indicate that history is more relational than linear. Bergey notes, "Somali oral culture broadened my perspective on history, time, and how people can know they are connected to each other."[6]

Even those who know the shared history of these two peoples can be surprised by encounters along the way. When I arrived in Hargeisa to teach peace and conflict studies in early 2015, I was immediately taken under the proud protection of a former teacher and a former student at one of the Mennonite schools. I had never met these two venerable Somali men, yet I was *their people*.

Holistic character ethics reminds us that we are deeply shaped by our loyalties to certain people, practices, or ideas.[7] Somalis and Mennonites forged a deep sense of loyalty to one another over six decades. The mutual recognition that our communities have benefited deeply from one another builds a sense of trust that holds promise for the future.

The Task of Renewal

A good name does not last forever without the constant renewal of relationships. The disruption of Somali society by the conflict has made it necessary to start over in building many aspects of infrastructure, government, and civil society. By all accounts that process is well under way, as Mogadishu and other areas of the country experience an unprecedented boom in repatriation and construction. In the same way, even long-standing relationships must be built again. Chantal Logan is concerned that many

---

5. Bergey, interview.
6. Ibid.
7. Stassen and Gushee, *Kingdom Ethics*, 59.

North American Mennonites are unaware of the Somalia connection, which is tragic because there are so few examples of Muslim and Christian cooperation that is sustained across half a century. Such relationships are needed more than ever because when the two groups come together, "interesting and unexpected interfaith communication happens."[8] Unless Mennonites continue to partner with Somalis in significant ways in the next decade, the tremendous heritage will be lost. Many of the people in leadership when the Logans were in Somalia ten years ago had studied in Mennonite schools, but the new generation of leadership has not.[9]

Logan's concerns are echoed by many of the former Mennonite workers in Somalia. Bertha Beachy says, "What would I like Mennonites to be doing? Connecting—in any way or every way possible."[10] Fae Miller advises that the Somali people are in the best position to determine what the partnership should look like; "At the beginning, low-key until you learn to know the people, the culture, and the language. Then see needs where you are, which may be education. And probably like at the Jamama hospital, teaching nurses and training lab technicians."[11] Ken Nissley agrees that the model for Mennonite involvement should be supporting a university, training efforts, or hospitals in conjunction with a local organization.[12]

Some of what Mennonites do could resemble the work of the past. A Christian from southern Somalia urges Mennonites not to lose hope: "Some projects like a health project here, a peace project here, agricultural project here, all of this Mennonites are doing. Also assisting refugees in returning to Somalia. Most of the Somali people know about Mennonites. I am encouraging Mennonites to continue what they are doing, not to give up at all. It is sixty years now since they went there. So let them continue what they are doing. I don't think there is another organization that is working in Somalia for such a long period. Even when they were kicked out from there, they were looking behind at Somalia. And I'm sure one day they will be on that goal."[13]

---

8. Logan, "Reflections," 63.
9. Logan, interview.
10. Beachy, interview.
11. Miller, interview.
12. Nissley, interview.
13. Hersi, interview.

There is recognition, however, that the nature of the relationships in the past cannot be exactly replicated in the present context. Carl Wesselhoeft observes, "Through our schools, they said the students are a tribe. They have something in common. And they recall being in Mahaddei, or being also in Mogadishu, and they are Mennonite Mission Somalis. And that is a connection that would be sad to lose if there is no continuation. But it will never be like the boarding school again, where they were with us twenty-four hours a day."[14] Omar Eby adds, "I'm not sure that the question is ours to decide. When they say, come back and be teachers—we're never going to build schools again. We see the Johar Secondary School just bombed."[15] The hollow shells of the destroyed Mennonite schools and clinics symbolize the inimitability of the past. Little physical evidence remains of the Mennonite presence in Somalia. The future resides in the friendships that can be cultivated, which has always been the case even when that friendship was facilitated by physical structures.

Security in Relationships

Mennonites seek security in relationships and community. I have argued that the community loyalty of Mennonites informed their sense of calling to mission, but also allowed the deepest values and commitments of their tradition—especially following Jesus in love, forgiveness, and costly discipleship—to be transmitted into a new cultural setting. When the broader Mennonite church shifted its attention to activism over quietism and the changing political context made questions of justice and peace more acute, Mennonites maintained their commitment to nonviolence.

Bonnie Bergey traveled to Somalia in the early 1990s with the knowledge that if she were taken hostage there would not be a ransom paid or an armed rescue operation. She says, "It was already part of my understanding of how EMM worked, and my own faith perspective, that I was willing to risk that."[16] The sometimes extreme vulnerability demanded by Somalia puts nonviolent convictions to the test and broaches the basic issues of personal security. Should Mennonites willingly place themselves in areas where anti-foreigner militant groups are active, or where travel advisories have been issued? Mennonite personnel have

---

14. Wesselhoeft, interview.
15. Eby, interview.
16. Bergey, interview.

worked in dangerous situations, particularly in Mogadishu, where they faced armed teenagers, gunfire, and bombs. Three points of consideration emerge from my interviews.

First, while trends can be observed, security is not an objective category that is fully measurable to any one person or organization. Governments and embassies make judgments based on limited information, and can ignore factors that are more relational and subjective. The best form of security a foreigner can have in Somalia, argues one Somali Christian who escaped with his life only because of help from Muslim friends, is to have close relationships with Somali neighbors.[17] In this sense, a good name is the best protection one could desire in a place like Mogadishu or Hargeisa. In a communal culture, security is communal as well. Even in the face of grave danger, Bonnie Bergey found great hope in a faith and heritage that reaches out to others in a vulnerable way, going the second mile, not using violence in defense, and viewing security in entirely different terms than the power of weapons. Says Bergey, "I just believe in a whole different way. Guns are a deterrent to peace because they take conflict in an entirely different direction. But dialogue and discussion and peaceful approaches, trying to assess local people and local families and local situations, is a lot more hopeful. This became real to me as I needed to be vulnerable to the families who gave me food or provided a place for me to stay. Peacemaking and mission connect for me, in many little ways."[18]

Second, the legacy of US involvement has surely contributed to Somalia's failure to stabilize. In that sense, globally minded US Americans bear an element of responsibility for the actions of their country in Somalia. In considering the risks of her travels to Hargeisa, Gloria Rhodes observes, "If we can send people there or anywhere to do war, then all of us should be willing to also go and work at constructive approaches to problems. I cared how dangerous it was, but we send people into harm's way all the time to do our military's bidding."[19]

Third, and most importantly, safety cannot be a primary consideration in following Jesus. In urging Mennonites to continue work in Somalia, Chantal Logan identifies security concerns as the biggest obstacle for North American Mennonites. She asks why Mennonites are

17. Hersi, interview.
18. Bergey, interview.
19. Rhodes, interview.

now afraid to risk their lives for their faith. In 2003 the Logans helped to place a woman from a non-Mennonite background in a teaching position through MCC. She took a sabbatical from teaching nursing and moved to Puntland with her twelve-year-old daughter. When the US began bombing Iraq in March, all the foreigners began to leave Puntland. Mark Logan arranged a space on the last flight out for the woman and her daughter. But after consulting with Somali colleagues, she decided to stay and continue to teach her classes. Up to that point she had been known by everyone in town as "the white woman who cooks with charcoal like we do." Because she worked with MCC she was known from that point on as "the Mennonite woman who stayed." Chantal comments, "It's just amazing how God used this woman. The 'real Mennonites' were not willing to go, but she went. She was willing to take a risk." She adds, "When you go to a place where you can get killed, you have to be sure that it's really the Lord calling you. Don't go for any other reason; you can't call yourself, you can't go because of pressure from the outside."[20]

Bergey recalls being introduced by one Somali woman to another: "This is Bonnie, she has been with us in the war." The idea that she had been present as a co-sufferer gave her legitimacy and a level of honor. But the risks are real; Bergey concurs with Logan, "You can't be in a Somali context and be unsure about whether you have purpose. I literally felt like people sometimes assessed my legitimacy. It wasn't that I had to be strong all the time, but I had to have enough confidence that I didn't appear weak or like I had some hidden agenda. It takes a lot of energy. A lot of energy and vulnerability."[21] Jonathan Rudy agrees, stating that his time in Somalia pushed him to seek spiritual direction and deeper contemplation. "It was at the point of a gun that I realized I didn't have the internal spiritual resources to actually face this kind of world that I had embraced. My sense is that Somalia was that place for so many missionaries. It was a tough place, so in-your-face with who you are, like a mirror. You didn't leave anything behind, you brought it all with you."[22] Some of the Mennonite missionaries found joy and strength in fresh encounters with the Holy Spirit. They testify to a powerful outpouring of the Holy Spirit that radically transformed their ministries during the sometimes tumultuous

---

20. Logan, interview.
21. Bergey, interview.
22. Rudy, interview.

times.[23] Rudy observes that people who worked long-term in Somalia had a solid sense of purpose there, like Bertha Beachy. Perhaps Somalia attracted Mennonites who were not afraid of facing who they were at the core. Or perhaps Somalia made them into that kind of person.

Yet even internal spiritual resources, as vital as they are, are not sufficient. Bergey was inspired in her difficult work by the knowledge that a whole network of people was behind her and praying for her, even many people she did not know. She wonders if that possibility has changed with the shift away from mission organizations and toward individual or congregational support of individual missionaries. At various times when Bergey faced life-threatening situations, she sensed peace with herself and with God, and felt that even the moments of fear were worth that moment. She describes it as a feeling of "synergy," but adds that "it's hard to have that if you don't have a wider or broader perspective, if you don't have history working with you, if you don't have a network of people behind you, if you don't believe that peace and negotiation can actually work."[24]

In a context of vulnerability, a peace theology depends on the hope that Jesus' commands to turn the other cheek can actually effectively disarm the person with evil intent (Matt 5:38). The clarity of the gospel of peace can be most evident in these moments. For example, a fundamentalist Somali man entered the EMM/MCC Nairobi office and demanded that Chantal Logan give him the names of Somalis who were Christians. He interrogated her intentions and the reason for her presence, accusing her of wanting to convert Somalis. Logan responded, "I came because I look for the will of God in my life, and I think God wanted me to come. I don't know exactly why." She continued, "I don't know if you come here as a friend or as an enemy. But Jesus taught us to bless and love your enemies, so I'm treating you as a friend." The man responded, "You would make a good Muslim." Logan replied, "I'm flattered you would say that, but in Jesus I have everything I need." The man seemed perplexed and intrigued by the idea of blessing one's enemy. He left with a changed demeanor. When Logan told her Muslim friends about the man's visit, they chastised her for talking with him without calling for help, as he was a dangerous person.[25] They did not realize that she had access to a different, deeper kind of security.

23. Shenk, interview.
24. Bergey, interview.
25. Logan, interview.

The same sense of history and community that provides strength and purpose also makes it possible for work to continue even if the same people do not return. As Stanley Hauerwas has argued, ethics and theology only exist for and in a community. Only by sharing in a larger story can a person respond faithfully to God's calling.[26] Participating in a storied community provides meaning even when one's internal resources run dry. For Bergey, there came a time when her certainty wavered, and she began to ponder whether some things were worth dying for and some were not. When a number of her Somali friends and associates were murdered in just one year, including a married couple with whom she stayed on trips to Mogadishu, she knew that it might be time to leave. Kenyan pastor Philip Okeyo gave her the gift of telling her, "Bonnie, you've been here long enough—it's ok for you to go home."[27] His words were a liberating reminder that she did not have to see resolution or success for her work to have been worthwhile.

Without Knowledge there is No Light

At the request of Somalis, Mennonites focus on education. Prominent Somali studies scholar Said Samatar surmises that education has been the most important Mennonite contribution in Somalia. Education has a world-opening effect, and the Mennonite schools brought together different clans in a way that created lasting bonds and spread to the larger society.[28]

Somalia's disrupted history has limited the possibility of sustained, widespread educational efforts. This is not representative, however, of the central role of education in the Somali value system. The heady optimism at the time of independence centered on the advancement of the country through applied knowledge and literacy. The radio was a powerful way to transmit messages to the public, and the signature tune of Radio Mogadishu was Abdillahi Qarshi's musical rendition of a well-known proverb:

> Without knowledge there is no light
>
> No home, no life
>
> Care for the schools, care for them

---

26. Hauerwas, *Community of Character*, 1–2.
27. Bergey, interview.
28. Said Samatar, interview by author, South Orange, NJ, January 15, 2013.

O do care for them

And brothers, go to school.[29]

I propose that the reason Mennonites are always drawn back into education work, no matter the political situation, is that their involvement focuses on the needs identified by the Somali people. In many areas of the world, including other parts of Africa, Mennonite missionaries started by asking the question: How can we help? This unique stance ensured that the work would be centered on relationships, not on the agenda of a foreign mission agency.[30] A posture of humility was absolutely critical in establishing rapport with Somalis, who eagerly requested English classes, schools, and other partnerships for the sake of education. Constructing and operating schools was a primary feature of the Mennonite work from the time of their arrival until all the schools were nationalized in 1972.

Even after the collapse of the Somali government and the withdrawal of US and UN troops, MCC continued to support SAACID, a primary and secondary school in Mogadishu that provided education for hundreds of children. Most of the country's academics fled the country, leaving the future of education in jeopardy. Schools funded by fundamentalist groups from the Arabian Peninsula sought to fill the gap. Mohammed Abdi Mohammed, a Somali-born university professor in France whose peace activism has earned him the nickname "Gandhi," stated in 2002, "If we don't establish standardized public schools, within ten years Somalia will be completely fundamentalist."[31] Professor Mohammed helped develop an MCC-supported peace training manual drawing on traditional Somali, Islamic, and international peacemaking principles, for use in the Mogadishu schools. Several of the teachers in SAACID studied in the EMM schools and have created their own conflict resolution curriculum.

More recently, the EMU partnership with the University of Hargeisa from 2008 to 2011 and the further work with the Women's Peacebuilding Leadership Project indicate the extent to which both Somalis and Mennonites value collaboration around education. In August 2013 EMU held a consultation in Nairobi to discuss the shape of its involvement in the Somali region in the future. Mennonite teachers have traveled to Hargeisa as individuals and small groups to teach peacebuilding, trauma awareness and healing, and English.

29. Logan, "Enduring Power," 364.
30. Rudy, interview.
31. Miller, "Learning Peace," 17–19.

One avenue for relationship is Mennonite schools in the US, where a significant number of Somalis have studied over the decades, including Said Samatar, Ahmed Haile, Khadija Ali, and Hassan Sheikh Muhamud. Glen Roth recommends that Mennonites continue to facilitate Somali students attending EMU and Goshen College.[32] Such an approach would be most effective if a scholarship program made it possible for multiple Somali students to attend a Mennonite college at the same time, representing different clans. In this way the program could reflect in a new era the inter-clan relationship building that occurred in the Mennonite-run schools in Somalia in the past.[33]

A Welcoming Peace Clan

Mennonites operate as a welcoming peace clan within wider society. I contend that the strongest link between the Mennonite work of the past and present is that Mennonites see their calling as cultivating vital communities whose impact spreads in the broader society. This moral imagination is often articulated in two food metaphors, both drawn from Jesus: salt and yeast. Salt, as I have argued, refers to communal practices that are distinct from the dominant wisdom of the world. Yeast implies the disproportionate and unpredictable effect that one small ingredient can have on the metaphorical bread, in this case a society. Both metaphors communicate a sharp contrast to the overt power that operates from the top down. Salt and yeast imply a minority status that necessarily works from the bottom up and the middle out.

The identity of a salty, yeasty community links more than just the past and the present. It also reveals commonalities even within the tensions in Mennonite work. Both church planting and peacemaking endeavors rely on a small community of people who take on a new identity—whether as followers of Jesus or as peacemakers, or both. Furthermore, the salty, yeasty minority identity bridges the geographical gap between North America, Somalia, and anywhere else in the world. Understanding their identity as a community that resists the dominant patterns of the broader society in North America made it easier for Mennonites to assume the same posture in a Somali context. Grounded in convictions about power and social change in the Reign of God, Mennonites saw their task as

---

32. Roth, interview.
33. Rudy, interview.

extending an invitation to a few Somalis to take on a peacebuilding identity, becoming leaven in their society just as Mennonites have attempted to be in other parts of the world.

It should not be surprising, therefore, that inherited boundary markers are challenged and reconstructed in novel ways over the course of a sixty-year relationship. The identity of "Mennonite Muslims" that emerged at the school in Johar, for example, indicates a startling defiance of the assumed identity options. Less astonishing but equally profound is the number of Somalis who take on the identity "peacemaker" after studying in a Mennonite program.

Any discussion of identity in Somalia cannot ignore the reality of the clan system. In light of some striking similarities between the oral culture of Somalis and the traditional culture of North American ethnic Mennonites, I find it helpful to think of Mennonites as a clan. Both find it important to trace their lineage back many generations, and family connections play an important role in traditional communities. The importance of heritage and familial memory is assumed and prioritized.

Ashley Lyn Greene argues that peacebuilding is not about replacing clan or Muslim identity with a national allegiance. Greene writes, "No single identity can offer a sustainable solution to conflict and state formation in Somalia. Sustainable peacebuilding efforts must rely on approaches that foster inclusion and participation among multiple Somali identities. . . . Peacebuilders must identify the strengths of traditional Somali social structures while promoting government institutions that compensate for their weaknesses."[34] In the same way, the invitation to join the Mennonite "clan" is not contingent on leaving behind the cherished refuge of biological clan.

It is worth noting that a kind of adoption between clans is sometimes practiced in Somali culture. Most often it occurs when a weak or scattered clan seeks protection from a stronger clan, resulting in a contractual agreement known as *gaashaanbuur*, meaning "pile of shields."[35] Even in the context of a power differential, however, there is a sense of mutual dependence between the patron and client clans. For example, agriculturalists might give to a clan of pastoral people exclusive rights to river access points close to their village, in exchange for protection

---

34. Greene, "Re-thinking Somali National Identity," 41–42.
35. Kutty, "Tol, Xeer, and Somalinimo," 61.

against the intrusion on their fields by other foreign shepherds.[36] In some cases, the adopted people formally renounce their birth clan and promise to accompany the adopting clan forever. They also assume the rights and duties of their new *diya*-paying group. These arrangements serve to benefit groups with traditionally excluded lineages, like the Bantu peoples.[37]

The notion of joining a Mennonite "clan" can play on this traditional practice of adoption, but with one significant difference. Rather than the powerful majority clan subsuming a weak and scattered clan, here the minority clan extends an invitation to take on a new identity without necessarily shedding one's familial allegiances. In this sense, Mennonites frame clan identity as inclusive of people from all different clans. Rather than joining a bounded set that excludes one's previous identifications, the Mennonite clan centers on the identity of peacemaking.

Even before Mennonites were thinking in terms of active peacemaking, they were facilitating peaceful coexistence between clans in the context of the Mennonite schools. Fighting between clans was not tolerated, and as a result clan differences were never pronounced or even very visible. In the classrooms and the dormitories the students established friendships across clans that allowed them to refer to themselves as the "Somali Mennonites." The school experience had a transformative effect on the way that they perceived people from other clans. They learned the value of peace, and that formation stayed with them for the rest of their lives.

Some of the boys who studied at Johar in the 1960s and 1970s, including the poet Mohamed Togane, gather in Toronto to reminisce about their time in the Mennonite school. According to Elizabeth Nissley, the self-designated Somali Mennonites tell the Mennonite missionaries, "We came from many different tribes, and we had to live together in the dormitory. Some of the tribal things did cause trouble, and we're aware of that. But you treated us all the same. And so we became one tribe, the Mennonite Mission tribe. If we could do it then, why can't we do it now? Why don't you come back and let that happen again?"[38]

Jonathan Rudy notes that conflict transformation and peacebuilding are concepts around which people can and do form a new identity. In his work with MCC in the Philippines, Rudy observed that after a nonviolent

---

36. Declich, "Fostering Ethnic Reinvention," 20. Cited in Kutty, "Tol, Xeer, and Somalinimo," 61.

37. Lewis, *Peoples of the Horn of Africa*. Cited in Kutty, "Tol, Xeer, and Somalinimo," 61.

38. Nissley, interview.

struggle ousted Marcos, a highly polarized political and social situation between the government and the communist groups nearly tore the country apart. But certain Filipinos developed a peace constituency that attracted enough people in civil society that it became a viable third way, and actually became an identity marker where they had previously identified with the government or the communists. Rudy asks, "Is there a framework or an issue or an orientation that can draw Somalis into a new way of being, that has Mennonite DNA but that resonates with Somalis?"[39]

My contention that Mennonites present themselves as an inclusive peace-oriented clan assumes not that Somalis will become any less a part of their own clans, but rather that a transformation of vision can occur that ties them together with peacemakers of other clans and cultures. This transformation continues through the Mennonite involvement in peacebuilding education in Somaliland, which draws together peace-oriented people not only of different clans but also of different nationalities. The women who participate in the Women's Peacebuilding Leadership Program, for example, form inter-cultural and inter-clan bonds that would not otherwise occur. They join the Mennonite peace clan as Muslims, Christians, or whoever they may be.

The emphasis of the Mennonite clan is not on numerical dominance but on the quality of relationships. John Paul Lederach issues the reminder that what is needed in Somalia is not critical mass, but critical yeast consisting of the right people in the right places.[40] This was Lederach's strategy as a mediator for MCC in early 1993 in the Horn. He did not participate in the official UN-sponsored meetings in Addis Ababa but engaged in "corridor facilitating," assisting those who were excluded from the discussions—including clan elders, poets, and women—to connect with each other. Lederach then continued this leavening work in Somaliland, operating under the conviction that traditional Somali voices of authority were being excluded in ways that would thwart the effectiveness of the UN process.[41] The failure to include clan elders did indeed doom the Djibouti and Addis Ababa conferences. In contrast, the successful Borama Process provided for the structural representation of the clan elders in decision-making. The MCC strategy of working steadily in

39. Rudy, interview.
40. Lederach, *Moral Imagination*, 90–91.
41. "Lederach to Assist Mediation in Somalia."

the corridors proved to be more effective in the long run than the hasty, expensive UN conferences.

It is impossible to determine the exact effect that Lederach and other Mennonite workers had on such a complex process. Chantal Logan states that Mennonites had a much more prominent role than the official history indicates. The chaos in the south was due in part to the fact that the greater number of clans splintered the region into so many pieces. Although MCC attempted to mediate in the south, it was impossible to establish any cohesion in all the multiple localized conflicts. The fact that the north had only two major clans is one reason that the north succeeded in reaching a peace agreement while the south failed. But just as significantly, in order to gain international recognition and a platform in any peace process in the south, a clan had to have a warlord and a militia. Logan recalls one clan that did not have a warlord stating that perhaps they needed to get one in order to gain a listening ear. The internationally community ignored the traditional clan authority structures and reinforced the warlords by assuming that the people in power were the ones with guns. Logan asserts, "That mistake was not made in Somaliland. Why?—because the Mennonites were involved. In 1991, after the big mess, Somalilanders started fighting among themselves. And that's when Lederach and Life and Peace got all of those people to be trained, and they didn't get involved beyond organizing and funding the meetings among the elders. And the elders just worked it out."[42]

The fact that the Mennonite involvement is rarely mentioned in the official historical accounts is perhaps an indicator of the extent to which Mennonites operate within a yeasty, bottom-up framework rather than in more conspicuous ways.[43] Jonathan Rudy suggests, "Maybe this is a hallmark of Mennonite education, that it's invisible. It has to be such, otherwise it's about us. In the history of southern Africa as well, and what Mennonites did in terms of solidarity and promoting ideas of reconciliation, it never shows up the official annals. But it's the background work, the training and connecting people, that enables people to succeed. We have to tell these stories among ourselves, without overstating them."[44]

A critical component of the Mennonite peace clan approach is seeking out peacemakers in any place and role they are found. Bergey

---

42. Logan, interview.

43. Harper (2012), Drysdale (1994), Peterson (2000), Lewis (2002), and Bradbury (2008) make no mention of the Mennonite involvement in Somalia and Somaliland.

44. Rudy, interview.

recounts that at the Hargeisa meeting there was an influential Somali man who had a long association with Mennonites, who became one of the early appointees of the Somaliland government that was borne out of the peace meetings there. Bergey recalls, "He had quite a bit of respect from the other Somalis, and he was influential in that meeting. I always knew that regardless of what little I knew, there were others who seemed to know I was coming or were making connections because of respect for the Mennonite history and long-time presence. It was bigger than me, the way word got around."[45] Mennonite peace clan members like this man provided Bergey with natural connections wherever she went.

Another member of the Mennonite peace clan in Somalia is Mohamed Abdi Mohamed, the French-educated politician and peace activist mentioned above who was known by the nickname "Gandhi." Together with MCC and a team of Somali scholars, Gandhi published a book of qur'anic passages and traditional Somali proverbs and songs that was used to teach human rights in the schools and in workshops.[46]

I highlight these examples to illustrate that when the Somali Mennonites of Johar and Toronto, Ahmed Haile, Mohamud Togane, Fatima Jibrell, Mohamed Abdi "Gandhi" Mohamed, Dekha Ibrahim, and countless others take on the identity of peacemaker, they join a peace clan whose impact extends far beyond its small numbers. They become salt and yeast for their society, as Mennonites strive to be in any part of the world where they find themselves as pilgrims.

Peacemaking is a precarious identity and a precarious calling. The Mennonite story in Somalia is a reminder that peacemaking is as much about remembering rightly as it is about discerning the future. Mark Logan writes, "Only seeds planted in love and watered by the grace of God will bring forth a harvest. This knowledge keeps Mennonites working in a country that has demoralized many. It is faith that keeps us going when the world around us seems to have gone suddenly mad."[47] Over the vicissitudes of six decades as guests in the Somali home, Mennonites have understood rightly that the seeds of peace are sown in relationships, founded on hope that God is calling out a peace clan who can teach one another how to walk in the light of the Lord.

45. Bergey, interview.
46. Logan, interview.
47. Eby, *Fifty Years, Fifty Stories*, 115.

Appendix

List of Interviews

Ali, Ahmed, and Mohamed Farah (pseudonyms). Columbus, OH. January 2, 2013.
Beachy, Bertha. Goshen, IN. January 3, 2013.
Bergey, Bonnie. Alexandria, VA. April 29, 2013.
Eby, Omar. Harrisonburg, VA. April 6, 2013.
Gehman, Mary. Lancaster, PA. October 1, 2012.
Hersi, Daoud (pseudonym). Lancaster, PA. February 8, 2013.
Jenner, Janice. Harrisonburg, VA. April 8, 2013.
Leaman, Ivan and Mary Ellen. Lancaster, PA. November 14, 2012.
Lind, Rhoda. Lancaster, PA. December 3, 2012.
Logan, Chantal and Mark. Bridgewater, VA. April 7, 2013.
Miller, Fae. Orrville, OH. January 1, 2013.
Nissley, Elizabeth and Ken. Lancaster, PA. March 19, 2013.
Rhodes, Gloria. Harrisonburg, VA. April 7, 2013.
Roth, Glen. Lancaster, PA. February 4, 2013.
Rudy, Jonathan. Manheim, PA. April 15, 2013.
Samatar, Said. South Orange, NJ. January 15, 2013.
Shenk, David. Denver, PA. February 12, 2013.
Wesselhoeft, Carl. Logan, OH. January 2, 2013.
Witmer, Barbara and Lamar. Lancaster, PA. March 9, 2013.

Bibliography

Abu-Nimer, Mohammed. *Nonviolence and Peace Building in Islam: Theory and Practice.* Gainesville, FL: University Press of Florida, 2003.

Adam, Hussein. "Somalia: International Versus Local Attempts at Peacebuilding." In *Durable Peace: Challenges for Peacebuilding in Africa*, edited by Taisier Mohamed Ahmed Ali and Robert O. Matthews, 253–81. Toronto: University of Toronto Press, 2004.

Afrax, Maxamed D. "The Mirror of Culture: Somali Dissolution Seen Through Oral Expression." In *The Somali Challenge: From Catastrophe to Renewal?*, edited by Ahmed I. Samatar, 233–51. Boulder, CO: Lynne Rienner, 1994.

"Aid Groups Support US Effort in Somalia." *Christian Century*, November 3, 1993.

"Aiding Somalia." *Christian Century*, September 9, 1992.

Alexander, Paul. *Peace to War: Shifting Allegiances in the Assemblies of God.* Telford, PA: Cascadia, 2009.

Ali, Taisier Mohamed Ahmed, and Robert O. Matthews, eds. *Durable Peace: Challenges for Peacebuilding in Africa.* Toronto: University of Toronto Press, 2004.

Anderson, Mary B. *Do No Harm: How Aid Can Support Peace—or War.* Boulder, CO: Lynne Rienner, 1999.

Andrzejewski, B. W. "The Veneration of Sufi Saints and its Impact on the Oral Literature of the Somali People and on Their Literature in Arabic." *African Language Studies* 15 (1974) 15–53.

Anglade, Michael. "Somalia: A Country Without a State." In *Geopolitics of Hunger, 2000-2001: Hunger and Power*, edited by Action Against Hunger, 35–42. Boulder, CO: Lynne Rienner, 2001.

Ansel, Douglas. "Civilian Support and the Foundations of al-Shabaab Expansion." In *Somalia: Creating Space for Fresh Approaches to Peacebuilding*, edited by Life & Peace Institute/Kroc Institute, 28–32. Uppsala, Sweden: Life & Peace Institute, 2011.

Appleby, R. Scott. *The Ambivalence of the Sacred: Religion, Violence, and Reconciliation.* Lanham, MD: Rowman & Littlefield, 2000.

Appleby, R. Scott, and Angela J. Lederach. "Conversion, Witness, Solidarity, Dialogue: Modes of the Evangelizing Church in Tension." *Review of Faith and International Affairs* 7 (2009) 11–19.

Ayindo, Babu, et al. *When You are the Peacebuilder: Stories and Reflections on Peacebuilding from Africa*. Harrisonburg, VA: Eastern Mennonite University, 2001.

Bahadur, Jay. *The Pirates of Somalia: Inside their Hidden World*. New York: Pantheon, 2011.

Beachy, Bertha. "My Pilgrimage in Mission." *International Bulletin of Missionary Research* 35 (2011) 208–12.

———. "The Somali Journey: Presence and Patience." In *Anabaptists Meeting Muslims: A Calling for Presence in the Way of Christ*, edited by James R. Krabill et al., 235–40. Scottdale, PA: Herald, 2005.

Bergey, Bonnie. "The 'Bottom-Up' Alternative in Somali Peacebuilding." In *From the Ground Up: Mennonite Contributions to International Peacebuilding*, edited by Cynthia Sampson and John Paul Lederach, 149–64. New York: Oxford University Press, 2000.

Bonhoeffer, Dietrich. *Discipleship*. Minneapolis: Fortress, 2001.

Bowden, Mark. *Black Hawk Down: A Story of Modern War*. New York: Atlantic Monthly, 1999.

Bradbury, Mark. *Becoming Somaliland*. London: Progressio, 2008.

Bradbury, Mark, and Sally Healy, eds. "Islam and Somali Social Order." In *Whose Peace is it Anyway? Connecting Somali and International Peacemaking*, 94–97. Accord 21. London: Conciliation Resources, 2010.

Brander, Bruce. "Somalia: A Deadly, Dusty Hell." *Christianity Today*, October 26, 1992.

Brislen, Mike. "Djibouti." In *Anabaptists Meeting Muslims: A Calling for Presence in the Way of Christ*, edited by James R. Krabill et al., 213–14. Scottdale, PA: Herald, 2005.

———. "Pacifism Among Muslims in Africa." In *Anabaptists Meeting Muslims: A Calling for Presence in the Way of Christ*, edited by James R. Krabill et al., 264–72. Scottdale, PA: Herald, 2005.

Burkholder, J. R., and Ted Koontz. "When Armed Force is Used to Make Relief Work Possible." *Gospel Herald*, January 12, 1993.

Cassanelli, Lee V. *The Shaping of Somali Society: Reconstructing the History of a Pastoral People, 1600–1900*. Philadelphia: University of Pennsylvania Press, 1982.

Checole, Alemu, and Samuel Asefa. "Mennonite Churches in Eastern Africa." In *Anabaptist Songs in African Hearts*, edited by John Allen Lapp and C. Arnold Snyder, 221–33. Global Mennonite History. Intercourse, PA: Good, 2006.

Chenoweth, Erica, and Maria J. Stephan. *Why Civil Resistance Works: The Strategic Logic of Nonviolent Conflict*. New York: Columbia University Press, 2011.

Clos, Ryne. "Al-Shabaab, Part of the Solution to the Problems Faced by Somalia?" In *Somalia: Creating Space for Fresh Approaches to Peacebuilding*, edited by Life & Peace Institute/Kroc Institute, 20–27. Uppsala, Sweden: Life & Peace Institute, 2011.

Cook, Martin L. "Just Peacemaking: Challenges of Humanitarian Intervention." *Journal of the Society of Christian Ethics* 23 (2003) 241–53.

Cragg, Kenneth. *The Call of the Minaret*. 3rd ed. Oxford: Oneworld, 2000.

———. *The Christian and Other Religion: The Measure of Christ*. London: Mowbrays, 1977.

De Waal, Alex. *Islamism and its Enemies in the Horn of Africa*. Bloomington, IN: Indiana University Press, 2004.

DeBoer, Patricia. *No Failure in Peace Work: The Life and Teaching of Dekha Ibrahim Abdi*. Siem Reap, Cambodia: Centre for Peace and Conflict Studies, 2012.

Declich, Francesca. "Fostering Ethnic Reinvention: Gender Impact of Forced Migration on Bantu Somali Refugees in Kenya." *Cahiers d'Études Africaines* 157 (2000). Online: http://etudesafricaines.revues.org/2.

Detweiler, Richard C. *Mennonite Statements on Peace, 1915–1966: A Historical and Theological Review of Anabaptist-Mennonite Concepts of Peace Witness and Church-State Relations*. Scottdale, PA: Herald, 1968.

Dowden, Richard. *Africa: Altered States, Ordinary Miracles*. New York: Public Affairs, 2009.

———. "Covering Somalia—Recipe for Disaster." In *Somalia, Rwanda, and Beyond: The Role of the International Media in Wars and Humanitarian Crises*, edited by Edward Girardet et al., 91–97. Geneva: Crosslines Global Report, 1995.

Driedger, Leo, and Donald B. Kraybill. *Mennonite Peacemaking: From Quietism to Activism*. Scottdale, PA: Herald, 1994.

Drysdale, John. *Whatever Happened to Somalia?* London: HAAN Associates, 1994.

Dula, Peter. "A Theology of Interfaith Bridge Building." In *Borders and Bridges: Mennonite Witness in a Religiously Diverse World*, edited by Peter Dula and Alain Epp Weaver, 160–70. Telford, PA: Cascadia, 2007.

Eby, Omar. *Fifty Years, Fifty Stories: The Mennonite Mission in Somalia, 1953–2003*. Scottdale, PA: Herald, 2003.

———. "Testimony." *Missionary Messenger*, 1957.

———. "Triumph in Suffering." In *Called to be Sent: Essays in Honor of the Fiftieth Anniversary of the Founding of the Eastern Mennonite Board of Missions and Charities, 1914–1964*, edited by Paul N. Krabill, 123–30. Scottdale, PA: Herald, 1964.

———. *A Whisper in a Dry Land; A Biography of Merlin Grove, Martyr for Muslims in Somalia*. Scottdale, PA: Herald, 1968.

Edwards, Chris. "EMU Peace Profs Go to Women in Somaliland." *EMU News*, November 20, 2012. Online: http://emu.edu/now/news/2012/11/emu-peace-profs-go-to-women-in-somaliland/.

Elmi, Afyare Abdi. *Understanding the Somalia Conflagration: Identity, Political Islam and Peacebuilding*. London: Pluto, 2010.

Elmi, Asha Hagi, et al. "Peace is Milk, Peace is Development, Peace is Life: Women's Roles in Peacemaking in Somali Society." In *Rethinking Pastoralism: Gender, Culture and the Myth of the Patriarchal Pastoralist*, edited by Dorothy Hodgson, 121–41. London: James Curry, 2001.

Erb, Paul. Introduction to *Called to be Sent: Essays in Honor of the Fiftieth Anniversary of the Founding of the Eastern Mennonite Board of Missions and Charities, 1914–1964*, edited by Paul N. Kraybill, 5–8. Scottdale, PA: Herald, 1964.

Farah, Ahmed Yusuf, and I. M. Lewis. *Somalia, the Roots of Reconciliation: Peace Making Endeavours of Contemporary Lineage Leaders: A Survey of Grassroots Peace Conferences in Somaliland*. London: ActionAid, 1993.

Farah, Nuruddin. *Links*. New York: Riverhead, 2004.

Friesen, Duane K. "In Search of Security: A Theology and Ethic of Peace and Public Order." In *At Peace and Unafraid: Public Order, Security, and the Wisdom of the Cross*, edited by Duane K. Friesen and Gerald Schlabach, 37–82. Scottdale, PA: Herald, 2005.

Friesen, Duane K. and Gerald Schlabach, eds. *At Peace and Unafraid: Public Order, Security, and the Wisdom of the Cross.* Scottdale, PA: Herald, 2005.

Friesen, Ivan. *Isaiah.* Believers Church Bible Commentary. Scottdale, PA: Herald, 2009.

Gardiner, Judith A. "Getting Stuck In: Anabaptist Involvement in Local Politics." In *At Peace and Unafraid: Public Order, Security, and the Wisdom of the Cross,* edited by Duane K. Friesen and Gerald Schlabach, 365–85. Scottdale, PA: Herald, 2005.

Gettleman, Jeffrey. "The Most Dangerous Place in the World." *Foreign Policy* (2009) 61–69.

Gingerich, Jeff. "Breaking the Uneasy Silence: Policing and the Peace Movement in Dialogue." In *At Peace and Unafraid: Public Order, Security, and the Wisdom of the Cross,* edited by Duane K. Friesen and Gerald Schlabach, 389–403. Scottdale, PA: Herald, 2005.

"Glimpses of Somalia." *Missionary Messenger,* 1953.

Gopin, Marc. *Between Eden and Armageddon: The Future of World Religions, Violence, and Peacemaking.* New York: Oxford University Press, 2000.

———. *Holy War, Holy Peace: How Religion Can Bring Peace to the Middle East.* New York: Oxford University Press, 2002.

Grant, Kate. "The Muslim Mother Theresa." *Huffington Post,* October 1, 2012. Online: http://www.huffingtonpost.com/kate-grant/edna-adan_b_1925711.html.

Greene, Ashley Lyn. "Re-thinking Somali National Identity: Nationalism, State Formation and Peacebuilding in Somalia." In *Somalia: Creating Space for Fresh Approaches to Peacebuilding,* edited by Life & Peace Institute/Kroc Institute, 33–42. Uppsala, Sweden: Life & Peace Institute, 2011.

Grill, Peter James. *Introducing the Camel: Basic Camel Keeping for Beginners.* Desertification Control Programme Activity Centre, United Nations Environment Programme, 1987.

Griswold, Eliza. *The Tenth Parallel: Dispatches from the Fault Line between Christianity and Islam.* New York: Farrar, Straus and Giroux, 2010.

Guthrie, Stan. "Somalia: Warlords Await UN Withdrawal." *Christianity Today,* January 9, 1995.

Haile, Ahmed Ali, and David W. Shenk. *Teatime in Mogadishu: My Journey as a Peace Ambassador in the World of Islam.* Harrisonburg, VA: Herald, 2011.

Harper, Mary. *Getting Somalia Wrong?: Faith, War and Hope in a Shattered State.* New York: Zed, 2012.

Hart, Barry, and Muhyadin Saed. "Integrating Principles and Practices of Customary Law, Conflict Transformation, and Restorative Justice in Somaliland." *Africa Peace and Conflict Journal* 3 (2010) 1–17.

Hauerwas, Stanley. *A Community of Character: Toward a Constructive Christian Social Ethic.* Notre Dame, IN: University of Notre Dame Press, 1981.

———. *Matthew.* Grand Rapids: Brazos, 2006.

Hege, Nathan B. *Beyond Our Prayers: Anabaptist Church Growth in Ethiopia, 1948–1998.* Scottdale, PA: Herald, 1998.

———. "Communicating the Message." In *Called to be Sent: Essays in Honor of the Fiftieth Anniversary of the Founding of the Eastern Mennonite Board of Missions and Charities, 1914–1964,* edited by Paul N. Kraybill, 85–94. Scottdale, PA: Herald, 1964.

Holzgrefe, J. L., and Robert O. Keohane, eds. *Humanitarian Intervention: Ethical, Legal, and Political Dilemmas.* New York: Cambridge University Press, 2003.

Hostetler, Marian. *They Loved Their Enemies: True Stories of African Christians.* Scottdale, PA: Herald, 1988.
Huebner, Chris K. *A Precarious Peace: Yoderian Explorations on Theology, Knowledge, and Identity.* Waterloo, ON: Herald, 2006.
Ibrahim, Dekha. "Women's Roles in Peace-making in the Somali Community in North Eastern Kenya." In *Somalia—The Untold Story: The War Through the Eyes of Somali Women*, edited by Judith Gardner and Judy El Bushra, 166–74. London: CIIR, 2004.
Ignatieff, Michael. "State Failure and Nation-Building." In *Humanitarian Intervention: Ethical, Legal, and Political Dilemmas*, edited by J. L. Holzgrefe and Robert O. Keohane, 299–321. New York: Cambridge University Press, 2003.
Ilesanmi, Simeon O. "So that Peace May Reign: A Study of Just Peacemaking Experiments in Africa." *Journal of the Society of Christian Ethics* 23 (2003) 213–26.
Iye, Ali Musse. *Le Verdict de L'Arbre (Go'aannkii Geedka): Le Xeer Issa Etude d'une Democratic Pastorale.* Djibouti: n.p., 1990.
Jardine, Douglas James. *The Mad Mullah of Somaliland.* London: H. Jenkins, 1923.
Jenner, Janice. "Development and Peace: You Can't Have One Without the Other." In *Development to a Different Drummer: Anabaptist/Mennonite Experiences and Perspectives*, edited by Richard A. Yoder et al., 97–111. Intercourse, PA: Good, 2003.
Jennings, Willie James. *The Christian Imagination: Theology and the Origins of Race.* New Haven, CT: Yale University Press, 2010.
Jhazbhay, Iqbal. "Islam and Stability in Somaliland and the Geo-politics of the War on Terror." *Journal of Muslim Minority Affairs* 28 (2008) 173–205.
Johansen, J. E. A., and Mohammad Talib. "Sufism and Politics." In *The Oxford Encyclopedia of the Islamic World*, edited by John L. Esposito. New York: Oxford University Press, 2009. Online: http://www.oxfordislamicstudies.com/article/opr/t236/e0760.
Kamau, Wairimu. "A Study of Eastleigh Fellowship Center's Muslim-Youth Ministry Methods from a Christian Cross-Cultural Perspective." MA thesis, Nairobi Evangelical Graduate School of Theology, 2005.
Kanagy, Conrad L. *Road Signs for the Journey: A Profile of Mennonite Church USA.* Scottdale, PA: Herald, 2007.
Kanagy, Conrad L., et al. *Winds of the Spirit: A Profile of Anabaptist Churches in the Global South.* Harrisonburg, VA: Herald, 2012.
Kapteijns, Lidwien. "Somalia." In *The Oxford Encyclopedia of the Islamic World*, edited by John L. Esposito. New York: Oxford University Press, 2009. Online: http://www.oxfordislamicstudies.com/article/opr/t236/e0751.
———. "Women and the Crisis of Communal Identity: The Cultural Construction of Gender in Somali History." In *The Somali Challenge: From Catastrophe to Renewal?*, edited by Ahmed I. Samatar, 211–32. Boulder, CO: Lynne Rienner, 1994.
Kateregga, Badru D., and David W. Shenk. *A Muslim and a Christian in Dialogue.* Scottdale, PA: Herald, 1997.
Keener, Craig S. *A Commentary on the Gospel of Matthew.* Grand Rapids: Eerdmans, 1999.
King, Martin Luther, Jr. *Strength to Love.* Philadelphia: Fortress, 1963.
Krabill, James R., et al., eds. *Anabaptists Meeting Muslims: A Calling for Presence in the Way of Christ.* Scottdale, PA: Herald, 2005.

Kraybill, J. Nelson. *Apocalypse and Allegiance: Worship, Politics, and Devotion in the Book of Revelation*. Grand Rapids: Brazos, 2010.

Kraybill, Paul N. "Preface." In *God Led Us to Somalia*, edited by Dorothy Smoker and Merle W. Eshleman, 2. Salunga, PA: Eastern Mennonite Board of Missions and Charities, 1956.

———. "Prologue." In *Called to be Sent: Essays in Honor of the Fiftieth Anniversary of the Founding of the Eastern Mennonite Board of Missions and Charities, 1914–1964*, edited by Paul N. Kraybill, 11–12. Scottdale, PA: Herald, 1964.

Kristof, Nicholas D., and Sheryl WuDunn. *Half the Sky: Turning Oppression into Opportunity for Women Worldwide*. New York: Alfred A. Knopf, 2009.

Kutty, Vinodh. "Tol, Xeer, and Somalinimo: Recognizing Somali and Mushunguli Refugees as Agents in the Integration Process." PhD diss., University of Minnesota, 2010.

Laitin, David D., and Said S. Samatar. *Somalia: Nation in Search of a State*. Boulder, CO: Westview, 1987.

Lapp, John A. "Foreword." In *Fifty Years, Fifty Stories: The Mennonite Mission in Somalia, 1953–2003*, edited by Omar Eby, 7–9. Scottdale, PA: Herald, 2003.

———. "The Mennonite Engagement with Muslims: A Historical Overview." In *Anabaptists Meeting Muslims: A Calling for Presence in the Way of Christ*, edited by James R. Krabill et al., 89–121. Scottdale, PA: Herald, 2005.

Leaman, Ivan. "A Mustard Seed." *Missionary Messenger*, November 1965.

Leaman, Mary Ellen. "Somali Community in Toronto Hosts Book Launch." *The Mennonite*, August 25, 2011.

Lederach, John Paul. "Addressing Terrorism: A Theory of Change Approach." In *Somalia: Creating Space for Fresh Approaches to Peacebuilding*, edited by Life & Peace Institute/Kroc Institute, 7–19. Uppsala, Sweden: Life & Peace Institute, 2011.

———. *Building Peace: Sustainable Reconciliation in Divided Societies*. Washington, DC: United States Institute of Peace, 1997.

———. "The Doables: Just Policing on the Ground." In *Just Policing, Not War: An Alternative Response to World Violence*, edited by Gerald W. Schlabach, 175–91. Collegeville, MN: Liturgical, 2007.

———. "Mennonite Central Committee Efforts in Somalia and Somaliland." In *From the Ground Up: Mennonite Contributions to International Peacebuilding*, 141–48. New York: Oxford University Press, 2000.

———. *The Moral Imagination: The Art and Soul of Building Peace*. New York: Oxford University Press, 2005.

———. *Preparing for Peace: Conflict Transformation Across Cultures*. Syracuse, NY: Syracuse University Press, 1995.

———. "Toward a Sustainable Peace in Somalia." In *Fifty Years, Fifty Stories: The Mennonite Mission in Somalia, 1953–2003*, edited by Omar Eby, 105–6. Scottdale, PA: Herald, 2003.

Lederach, John Paul, and Angela Jill Lederach. *When Blood and Bones Cry Out: Journeys through the Soundscape of Healing and Reconciliation*. St Lucia, Queensland: University of Queensland Press, 2010.

"Lederach to Assist Mediation in Somalia." *Gospel Herald*, January 26, 1993.

Leeuwen, Arend Theodoor van. *Christianity in World History: The Meeting of the Faiths of East and West*. New York: Scribner, 1966.

Lehman, Chester K. "Jesus Christ—The Lord of the Church." In *Called to be Sent: Essays in Honor of the Fiftieth Anniversary of the Founding of the Eastern Mennonite Board of Missions and Charities, 1914–1964*, edited by Paul N. Kraybill, 13–22. Scottdale, PA: Herald, 1964.
Lewis, I. M. *A Modern History of Somalia: Nation and State in the Horn of Africa*. London: Longman, 1980.
———. *A Modern History of the Somali: Nation and State in the Horn of Africa*. 4th ed. Oxford: James Currey, 2002.
———. *Peoples of the Horn of Africa: Somali, Afar and Saho*. London: International African Institute, 1969.
———. *Saints and Somalis: Popular Islam in a Clan-Based Society*. Lawrenceville, NJ: Red Sea, 1998.
———. *Understanding Somalia and Somaliland: Culture, History, Society*. New York: Columbia University Press, 2008.
Lofton, Bonnie Price. "New Somali President Studied Peace at EMU." *EMU News*, October 4, 2012. Online: http://emu.edu/now/news/2012/10/new-somalia-president-studied-peace-at-emu/.
Logan, Chantal. "The Enduring Power of Somali 'Oral Political Poetry': Songs and Poems of Peace in the Midst of Chaos." In *Songs and Politics in Eastern Africa*, edited by Kimani Njogu and Hervé Maupeu, 355–76. Dar es Salaam, Tanzania: Mkuki na Nyota, 2007.
———. "Reflections on Mennonite Interfaith Work in Somalia." In *Borders and Bridges: Mennonite Witness in a Religiously Diverse World*, edited by Peter Dula and Alain Epp Weaver, 57–65. Telford, PA: Cascadia, 2007.
Logan, Mark. "Sharing the Piece." Unpublished sermon. Ridgeway Mennonite Church, Harrisonburg, VA, 2013.
Lybarger, Loren Diller. "Defining Presence: The Formation of Mennonite Agency Approaches and Attitudes toward Muslims and Islam, 1949–1995." MA thesis, Lutheran School of Theology, 1995.
———. "Response: Mennonite Engagement of Islam." *Mission Focus Annual Review* 6 (1998) 31–36.
Makhubela, L. M. "Conflict Resolution in Somalia: Learning from Failed Mediation Processes." PhD diss., University of Pretoria, 2010.
Mantzikos, Ioannis. "An African Version of the Taliban?: The Islamic Courts Union in Somalia (2006) and the Taliban Afghanistan (1996)." *Comparative Islamic Studies* 4 (2008) 113–29.
Marchal, Roland. "Islamic Political Dynamics in the Somali Civil War." In *Islamism and its Enemies in the Horn of Africa*, edited by Alex De Waal, 114–45. Bloomington, IN: Indiana University Press, 2004.
Maren, Michael. *The Road to Hell: The Ravaging Effects of Foreign Aid and International Charity*. New York: Free, 1997.
Martin, B. G. "Shaykh Zayla'i and the Nineteenth-Century Somali Qadiriya." In *In the Shadow of Conquest: Islam in Colonial Northeast Africa*, edited by Said S. Samatar, 11–32. Trenton, NJ: Red Sea, 1992.
Menkhaus, Kenneth John. *Somalia: State Collapse and the Threat of Terrorism*. New York: Oxford University Press, 2004.
Metz, Helen Chapin. *Somalia: A Country Study*. Washington, DC: U.S. G.P.O., 1993.

Miller, Gerald L., and Shari Wagner. *A Hundred Camels: A Mission Doctor's Sojourn and Murder Trial in Somalia*. Telford, PA: DreamSeeker, 2009.

Miller, Harold F. "The Peace Church Experience in Conflict Resolution." Paper presented at the Joint Conference on Church and Development, St. Augustin/Bonn, Germany, 1992.

Miller, Orie O. "The Biblical Imperative." In *Called to be Sent: Essays in Honor of the Fiftieth Anniversary of the Founding of the Eastern Mennonite Board of Missions and Charities, 1914–1964*, edited by Paul N. Kraybill, 23–30. Scottdale, PA: Herald, 1964.

Miller, Rachel Beth. "Learning Peace." *A Common Place*, September 2002.

Moeller, Susan D. *Compassion Fatigue: How the Media Sell Disease, Famine, War, and Death*. New York: Routledge, 1999.

Mohamed, Jama. "Kinship and Contract in Somali Politics." *Africa* 2 (2007) 226–49.

Mouw, Richard J. *Calvinism in the Las Vegas Airport: Making Connections in Today's World*. Grand Rapids: Zondervan, 2004.

———. *When the Kings Come Marching In: Isaiah and the New Jerusalem*. Grand Rapids: Eerdmans, 1983.

Murphy, Patrick. "Somalia: Militarism vs. Democracy." *Christian Century*, April 26, 1978.

Newbigin, Lesslie. *Honest Religion for Secular Man*. London: S.C.M., 1966.

Niebuhr, Reinhold. "Why the Christian Church is Not Pacifist." In *War and Christian Ethics: Classic and Contemporary Readings on the Morality of War*, edited by Arthur Frank Holmes, 301–13. Grand Rapids: Baker Academic, 2005.

Olfert, Eric. "Somalia Report." *Gospel Herald*, January 5, 1993.

Parke, Natalie. "Terrorizing Aid to Somalia." *Foreign Policy*, October 30, 2009. Online: http://www.foreignpolicy.com/articles/2009/10/28/terrorizing_aid_to_somalia.

Peacebuilding 2.0: Mapping the Boundaries of an Expanding Field. Alliance for Peacebuilding, 2012.

Peachey, J. Lorne. "Feeding the Hungry with Messy Theology." *Gospel Herald*, January 12, 1993.

Peterson, Scott. *Me Against My Brother: At War in Somalia, Sudan, and Rwanda*. New York: Routledge, 2000.

Philpott, Daniel. *Just and Unjust Peace: An Ethic of Political Reconciliation*. New York: Oxford University Press, 2012.

Prendergast, John. "Applying Concepts to Cases: Four African Case Studies." In *Building Peace: Sustainable Reconciliation in Divided Societies*, edited by John Paul Lederach 153–180. Washington, DC: United States Institute of Peace, 1997.

Rayale, Siham. "Participation through Peacebuilding: Somaliland Women's Experiences of Peace Initiatives in Somaliland since 1991." *Somaliland Journal for Peace and Development* 1 (2011) 24–40.

Redekop, Calvin Wall. *The Pax Story: Service in the Name of Christ, 1951–1976*. Telford, PA: Pandora, 2001.

Reed, Harold. "Believers Fellowships: The Somali Experience." In *Anabaptists Meeting Muslims: A Calling for Presence in the Way of Christ*, edited by James R. Krabill et al., 396–406. Scottdale, PA: Herald, 2005.

Reimer, Margaret Loewen. "MCC Board Discusses Somalia, Approves New Peace Statement." *Gospel Herald*, March 16, 1993.

"Relief and Diplomacy in Africa." *Christian Century*, December 23, 1992.

Rempel, John D. "Ambiguous Legacy: The Peace Teaching, Speaking Truth to Power, and Mennonite Assimilation Through the Centuries." In *At Peace and Unafraid: Public Order, Security, and the Wisdom of the Cross*, edited by Duane K. Friesen and Gerald Schlabach, 349–63. Scottdale, PA: Herald, 2005.

Royer, Howard E. "Relief Work in Somalia: Armed to the Teeth." *Christian Century*, November 18, 1992.

Ruth, John L. *The Earth is the Lord's: A Narrative History of the Lancaster Mennonite Conference*. Scottdale, PA: Herald 2001.

Rutherford, Ken. *Humanitarianism Under Fire: The US and UN Intervention in Somalia*. Sterling, VA: Kumarian, 2008.

Sahnoun, M. M. "Prevention in Conflict Resolution: The Case of Somalia." *Irish Studies in International Affairs* 5 (1994) 5–13.

Salvadori, Cynthia. "St. Ivel: An English Holy Man Among the Somalis." *Old Africa* 16 (2008).

Samatar, Ahmed I. "The Curse of Allah: Civic Disembowelment and the Collapse of the State in Somalia." In *The Somali Challenge: From Catastrophe to Renewal?*, edited by Ahmed I. Samatar, 95–146. Boulder, CO: Lynne Rienner, 1994.

Samatar, Ahmed I., ed. *The Somali Challenge: From Catastrophe to Renewal?* Boulder, CO: Lynne Rienner, 1994.

Samatar, Said S. "Historical Setting." In *Somalia: A Country Study*, edited by Helen Chapin Metz, 3–53. 4th ed. Washington, DC: U.S. G.P.O., 1993.

———. "Poor Somalia . . . " In *Fifty Years, Fifty Stories: The Mennonite Mission in Somalia, 1953–2003*, edited by Omar Eby, 80–81. Scottdale, PA: Herald, 2003.

Sauder, J. Paul. "The Witness Grows." In *Called to be Sent: Essays in Honor of the Fiftieth Anniversary of the Founding of the Eastern Mennonite Board of Missions and Charities, 1914–1964*, edited by Paul N. Kraybill, 55–65. Scottdale, PA: Herald, 1964.

Schaup, Darren. "The People of God (POG)." In *Anabaptists Meeting Muslims: A Calling for Presence in the Way of Christ*, edited by James R. Krabill et al., 392–4. Scottdale, PA: Herald, 2005.

Schlabach, Gerald. "Just Policing and the Christian Call to Nonviolence." In *At Peace and Unafraid: Public Order, Security, and the Wisdom of the Cross*, edited by Duane K. Friesen and Gerald Schlabach, 405–21. Scottdale, PA: Herald, 2005.

———. "Tracing the Grain of the Universe: Project Overview." In *At Peace and Unafraid: Public Order, Security, and the Wisdom of the Cross*, edited by Duane K. Friesen and Gerald Schlabach, 21–33. Scottdale, PA: Herald, 2005.

Schlabach Gerald, ed. *Just Policing, Not War: An Alternative Response to World Violence*. Collegeville, MN: Liturgical, 2007.

Schwartzentruber, Mary Mae. "Canada." In *Anabaptists Meeting Muslims: A Calling for Presence in the Way of Christ*, edited by James R. Krabill et al., 191–6. Scottdale, PA: Herald, 2005.

Segal, Ronald. *Islam's Black Slaves: The Other Black Diaspora*. New York: Farrar, Straus and Giroux, 2001.

Seiple, Chris. *The U.S. Military/NGO Relationship in Humanitarian Interventions*. Carlisle Barracks, PA: Peacekeeping Institute, Center for Strategic Leadership, U.S. Army College, 1996.

Seiple, Robert. "Should America Stay the Course in Somalia?" Interview by Randy Frame. *Christianity Today*, November 22, 1993.

Sensenig, Pearl. "Relief Agencies and Military Involvement in Somalia." *Brotherhood Beacon*, February 1993.

———. "Somali Elders Meet to Thresh Out Reconciliation." *Gospel Herald*, March 16, 1993.

Sharp, John E. "The Voice of God or an Old Man?" *Mennonite World Review*, August 6, 2012.

Shenk, David W. *God's Call to Mission*. Scottdale, PA: Herald, 1994.

———. *Journeys of the Muslim Nation and the Christian Church: Exploring the Mission of Two Communities*. Scottdale, PA: Herald, 2003.

———. "A Study of Mennonite Presence and Church Development in Somalia from 1950 Through 1970." PhD diss., New York University, 1972.

Showalter, Jewel. "Eternal Home for a Somali Nomad: Ahmed Ali Haile Dies at 58." *Eastern Mennonite Missions News*, May 5, 2011. Online: http://emm.org/index.php?option=com_content&view=article&id=743:eternal-home-for-a-somali-nomad-ahmed-ali-haile-dies-at-58-&catid=109&Itemid=124.

Shuria, Halima A. O. "Final Word: A Genuine Peace Builder." In *No Failure in Peace Work: The Life and Teaching of Dekha Ibrahim Abdi*, edited by Patricia DeBoer, 135–37. Siem Reap, Cambodia: Centre for Peace and Conflict Studies, 2012.

Sider, Ronald J. *Just Generosity: A New Vision for Overcoming Poverty in America*. 2nd ed. Grand Rapids: Baker, 2007.

———. *Rich Christians in an Age of Hunger: A Biblical Study*. 1st ed. Downers Grove, IL: InterVarsity, 1977.

———. *The Scandal of Evangelical Politics: Why Are Christians Missing the Chance to Really Change the World?* Grand Rapids: Baker, 2008.

Smoker, Dorothy, and Merle W. Eshleman. *God Led Us to Somalia*. Salunga, PA: Eastern Mennonite Board of Missions and Charities, 1956.

"Somalia Update." *Missionary Messenger*, 1953.

Stassen, Glen H. "Jesus Is No Sectarian: John H. Yoder's Christological Peacemaking Ethic." In *John Howard Yoder, The War of the Lamb: The Ethics of Nonviolence and Peacemaking*, edited by Glen H. Stassen et al., 7–24. Grand Rapids: Brazos, 2009.

———. "Just Peacemaking as Hermeneutical Key: The Need for International Cooperation in Preventing Terrorism." *Journal of the Society of Christian Ethics* 24 (2004) 171–191.

———. *Living the Sermon on the Mount: A Practical Hope for Grace and Deliverance*. San Francisco: Jossey-Bass, 2006.

Stassen, Glen H., ed. *Just Peacemaking: Ten Practices for Abolishing War*. Cleveland, OH: Pilgrim, 1998.

Stassen, Glen H., and David P. Gushee. *Kingdom Ethics: Following Jesus in Contemporary Context*. Downers Grove, IL: InterVarsity, 2003.

Stone, Ronald H. "Realist Criticism of Just Peacemaking Theory." *Journal of the Society of Christian Ethics* 23 (2003) 255–67.

Stremlau, John. "Ending Africa's Wars." *Foreign Affairs* 79 (2000) 117–32.

"Struggling for Peace in Somalia." *MCC Peace Office Newsletter*, April–June 2003.

Stutzman, Ervin R. *From Nonresistance to Justice: The Transformation of Mennonite Church Peace Rhetoric, 1908–2008*. Scottdale, PA: Herald, 2011.

"Sudan—the Next Somalia?" *Christian Century*, April 7, 1993.

Terry, Fiona. *Condemned to Repeat?: The Paradox of Humanitarian Action*. Ithaca, NY: Cornell University Press, 2002.

Toft, Monica Duffy, et al. *God's Century: Resurgent Religion and Global Politics.* New York: W. W. Norton, 2011.

Van Lehman, Dan, and Omar Eno. *The Somali Bantu: Their History and Culture.* Culture Profile. Washington, DC: Center for Applied Linguistics, 2003.

Volf, Miroslav. *Exclusion and Embrace: A Theological Exploration of Identity, Otherness, and Reconciliation.* Nashville, TN: Abingdon, 1996.

Wachira, George Mukundi, et al. *Citizens in Action: Making Peace in the Post-Election Crisis in Kenya—2008.* Nairobi: Nairobi Peace Initiative—Africa, 2010.

Walker, Bridget Ann. "Some Approaches to Peacebuilding in the Work of Dekha Ibrahim Abdi." In *No Failure in Peace Work: The Life and Teaching of Dekha Ibrahim Abdi,* edited by Patricia DeBoer, 11–30. Siem Reap, Cambodia: Centre for Peace and Conflict Studies, 2012.

Walker, Peter, and Daniel G. Maxwell. *Shaping the Humanitarian World.* New York: Routledge, 2009.

Wall, James M. "Nation-Building Deferred: Crises Ahead." *Christian Century,* November 3, 1993.

Walzer, Michael. *Obligations: Essays on Disobedience, War, and Citizenship.* Cambridge: Harvard University Press, 1970.

Weaver-Zercher, David L. "A Modest (Though Not Particularly Humble) Claim for Scholarship in the Anabaptist Tradition." In *Scholarship and Christian Faith: Enlarging the Conversation,* edited by Douglas G. Jacobsen et al., 103–17. New York: Oxford University Press, 2004.

Weaver, Alain Epp. "Meeting Jesus in the Borderlands." In *Borders and Bridges: Mennonite Witness in a Religiously Diverse World,* edited by Peter Dula and Alain Epp Weaver, 11–16. Telford, PA: Cascadia, 2007.

Weaver, Alain Epp, and Sonia K. Weaver. *Salt & Sign: Mennonite Central Committee in Palestine, 1949–1999.* Akron, PA: Mennonite Central Committee, 1999.

Weaver, J. Denny. "We Must Continue to Reject Just War Thinking." *Gospel Herald,* April 27, 1993.

Wenger, A. Grace. *A People in Mission: 1894–1994.* Salunga, PA: Eastern Mennonite Missions, 1994.

Wenger, Chester L. "The Christian Faith and Islam." *Missionary Messenger,* May 1960.

Westermann, Claus. "Peace (Shalom) in the Old Testament." In *The Meaning of Peace,* edited by Perry B. Yoder and Willard M. Swartley, 16–48. Louisville: Westminster John Knox, 1992.

Wheeler, Nicholas J. *Saving Strangers: Humanitarian Intervention in International Society.* New York: Oxford University Press, 2000.

Wilde, Margaret D. "Getting the Guns Out of Somalia: Appropriate Force." *Christian Century,* January 20, 1993.

Woodberry, J. Dudley. Preface to *Teatime in Mogadishu: My Journey as a Peace Ambassador in the World of Islam,* edited by Ahmed Ali Haile and David W. Shenk, 9–10. Harrisonburg, VA: Herald, 2011.

Woodhouse, Tom, and Oliver Ramsbotham. *Peacekeeping and Conflict Resolution.* Portland, OR: F. Cass, 2000.

"World Concern Office in Somalia Bombed." *Missionary Messenger,* April 1994.

"Xog Warran—Discourse." *Ahmed Haile: In Memory of a Legendary Peacemaker,* January 1, 2012. Online: http://ahmedhaile.blogspot.com/2012/01/xog-warran.html.

Yoder, John Howard. *Body Politics: Five Practices of the Christian Community before the Watching World*. Nashville, TN: Discipleship Resources, 1992.
———. *The Christian Witness to the State*. Newton, KS: Faith and Life, 1964.
———. *For the Nations: Essays Evangelical and Public*. Grand Rapids: Eerdmans, 1997.
———. "How H. Richard Niebuhr Reasoned: A Critique of Christ and Culture." In *Authentic Transformation: A New Vision of Christ and Culture*, edited by Glen Harold Stassen et al., 31–89. Nashville, TN: Abingdon, 1996.
———. *The Politics of Jesus; Vicit Agnus Noster*. Grand Rapids: Eerdmans, 1972.
———. *The War of the Lamb: The Ethics of Nonviolence and Peacemaking*. Grand Rapids: Brazos, 2009.
Yoder, Richard A., et al., eds. *Development to a Different Drummer: Anabaptist/Mennonite Experiences and Perspectives*. Intercourse, PA: Good, 2004.

General Index

Abdi, Hawa, 215–16
Abu-Nimer, Mohammed, 142–43
Adam, Hussein, 153, 155, 159, 179–80
Adan, Edna, 211–12
Afghanistan, 69, 117, 191, 194
Afrax, Maxamed D., 80, 154
African Union Mission in Somalia (AMISOM), 118, 129, 131, 194, 205
agriculture, 5, 50, 57, 86–87, 96, 98–99, 153, 197, 223
aid, 74, 84, 142; and armed security, 111–15; during Somali civil war, 107–11, 119–22, 134; Mennonite Central Committee, 50, 56–57, 89, 91, 138, 160, 164–67; Mennonites and USAID, 204–5, 217; military, 127–28
Aidid, Mohamed Farah, 105, 108, 116–17, 120, 125–26, 168, 173
Alexander, Paul, 44n11
Ali, Khadija, 205, 230
alternate service, 13, 45; 1-W service, 11; Civilian Public Service, 8; Pax service, 11, 45, 99
al-Itihaad al-Islamiya, 188, 194
al-Qaeda, 80, 117, 128–29, 183, 191–94
al-Shabaab, 79, 171, 205, 215; decline of, 146, 154, 194–95; engagement with, 131–32, 157, 195–96; origins of, 80, 118, 128, 192–194; recruitment, 194–95; regional activity, 118, 129, 195
Amish, 29, 56, 84
Amoud University, 138
Anabaptism, 1, 3, 15, 30, 42, 44–48, 56, 82, 203; and Islam, 69–70, 172; and Reformed tradition, 95–96
Anderson, Mary B., 111
Andrzejewski, B. W., 198–99
Ansel, Douglas, 132
Appleby, R. Scott, 90–91, 140

Bahadur, Jay, 128n90
Baidoa, 105, 119
baptism, 32–33
Barre, Mohamed Siad, 28, 35, 50, 52–58, 105, 124, 126–27, 155, 182, 188–90, 200, 214; and clan, 143–44, 146, 153; and Mennonite Mission, 6, 35, 45, 50
Beachy, Bertha, 1, 8–9, 13–15, 19–20, 28, 29, 38, 67–68, 70, 169, 203, 223, 227
Bender, Harold S., 47
Bergey, Bonnie, 15, 55, 70–71, 90, 112–14, 138, 157, 166–69, 177, 210, 214, 221–22, 224–25, 226–28, 234–35
Bible, and mission, 3, 11, 61–62, 86, 91; and Somalis, 4–5, 6, 20, 23, 25, 33, 65, 68, 86, 173
Black Hawk Down, 117, 123, 125–26

Bonhoeffer, Dietrich, 94
Borama Peace Process, 151, 163–64;
    Mennonite involvement, 137,
    167, 176, 233–34; and women,
    210–11
Boutros-Ghali, Boutros, 116, 123–24,
    126, 191
Bradbury, Mark, 145–46, 234n43
Brislen, Mike, 74, 149, 221
Burkholder, J. R., 46, 108–9
Bush, George H. W., 106, 116, 123
Bush, George W., 117, 180, 192–93

camels, 1, 148, 196–97, 218; as
    compensation, 18–19, 152–53;
    MCC breeding project, 57–58
Catholicism, 3n4, 4, 24, 54–55, 58, 69,
    107, 200
Cheese, John Ethelstan, 198, 198n72
Chenoweth, Erica, 103–4
Christian Century, 107–8, 122n70
Christian Peacemaker Teams, 45, 47,
    109
Christianity Today, 48, 107–8
Civil Rights Movement, 43
clan. *See* kinship.
Clinton, William J., 106n10, 117, 123
Clos, Ryne, 195
Cold War, 106, 123, 126–27, 155
Colenso, Bishop John, 81–82
Colombo, Bishop Salvatore, 58, 200
colonialism, 52, 77–82, 92, 126, 134,
    143, 148, 185, 188; Arab, 30,
    178–79, 181–82, 188, 229;
    British, 4, 30, 78–79, 178–79,
    204; French, 78, 179; Italian,
    3n4, 4, 22, 24, 26, 37, 78, 178,
    181–82; neocolonialism, 125;
    post-colonialism, 104; and race,
    78, 80–82
Cook, Martin L., 111–12
Cragg, Kenneth, 13, 30, 39, 64–65, 71
culture, and elicitive peacemaking, 138–
    43; Mennonite/Amish, 1, 29,
    73–74, 84–85, 231; sensitivity,
    16–18, 32, 71–72, 85, 89–90,
    120–121, 223; Somali. *See*
    Somalia; theology of, 95–97, 137

Cyrus, 132–33

democracy, 32, 62, 127, 133–34, 162,
    207; post-independence, 16,
    52; and Somali culture, 104,
    155–59; top-down approach,
    106, 124–25
dialogue, 47, 50, 85, 91, 100, 165, 218,
    225; Muslim-Christian, 58–59,
    71–72, 75, 87–88, 177–78
diya (blood compensation), 150–53,
    197, 232
Djibouti, 117, 118, 149, 152, 158, 194,
    208, 233; Mennonite presence,
    30, 69, 74, 87, 138, 171
Docherty, Jayne, 212–13
double vision, 104–5, 126, 130
Dowden, Richard, 119, 143–44, 147, 155
Driedger, Leo, 42–45
Drysdale, John, 105n8, 114, 120, 130–
    31, 155n76, 163, 234n43
Dula, Peter, 100

Eastern Mennonite Missions. *See*
    Mennonite Mission.
Eastern Mennonite University (EMU),
    8, 12, 13, 16, 64, 70, 165, 229,
    230; Center for Justice and
    Peacebuilding, 45, 85, 131,
    202–4, 206, 212–15, 217–19;
    partnership with University
    of Hargeisa, 160, 202, 205–6;
    Summer Peacebuilding Institute,
    205–6; Women's Peacebuilding
    Leadership Program, 212,
    215–17, 233; World Missions
    Institute, 64
Eastleigh Fellowship Center, 58–60,
    72; Kenya security forces, 129;
    People of God course, 59, 72;
    Somali believers fellowship, 15,
    59, 89, 166, 172–73
Eby, Omar, 11–12, 22–23, 63, 66, 224
ecclesiology, 7, 10–14
Egypt, 5, 23, 30, 127, 181, 188, 189
elders assembly (*guurti*), 32, 120, 149–
    52, 153, 183; and Mennonites,

GENERAL INDEX

31, 32, 138, 160, 163–65, 168, 170–71, 218, 233–34
Elizabethtown College, 206–7
Elmi, Afyare A., 146
English language, 4, 11, 20, 51, 52, 55, 65, 67, 78, 82, 98, 138, 204, 229
Ergada, 56, 137, 159, 164–66, 173
Eritrea, 127, 129
Eshleman, Merle, 4
Ethiopia, 4, 7, 10, 24, 50, 61, 64, 69, 106, 121, 165, 178–79, 189, 198; Addis Ababa peace process, 125, 163, 168–69, 233; Meserete Kristos Church, 21–22; military, 80, 117–18, 126–29, 131–32, 151, 180, 191–92, 194–95; Ogaden, 50, 56, 78, 105, 143, 146, 184, 189, 194
evangelism, 37, 39, 74, 83–87, 90–91, 100–101

famine, 6, 23, 51, 165, 192, 211; as pretext for military intervention, 105–7, 118, 119–22
Farah, Nuruddin, 145, 156
female genital mutilation (FGM), 24, 208, 211
forgiveness, 5, 17, 21–23, 142, 187, 224
Frey, Marvin, 112, 114, 167, 169
Friesen, Duane K., 45, 111, 115
Friesen, Leroy, 87–88

Galaal, Musa Haji Ismail, 67–68
Galkayo, 6, 23, 38, 52, 75, 86
Gandhi, Mohandas, 47
Gardiner, Judith A., 203
Garissa, 60, 113, 129, 132
Gbowee, Leymah, 212, 215
Gedi, Ahmed, 25–26, 53
Gehman, Mary, 8, 12, 20, 28, 32, 35, 64, 65, 67
Gettleman, Jeffrey, 124
Gladwin, Bishop John, 99
Good, Leon and Elaine, 138
Gopin, Marc, 84–85, 140–42, 144
Gospel Herald, 108–11
Greene, Ashley Lyn, 231
Grill, Peter, 57–58

Griswold, Eliza, 192
Grove, Merlin and Dorothy, 5, 8, 22–23, 67
Gulf War, 116
Gushee, David P., 2, 36, 83, 94–95, 97–98

Haile, Ahmed A., xxv–xxvi, 20, 58, 59, 171–75, 230, 235
Hargeisa, 159, 167–69, 188, 197, 211, 225, 229, 235; Institute of Peace and Conflict Studies, 160, 202, 205–7, 212, 217, 222; war in, 45, 50, 54, 158, 214
Harper, Mary, 80, 118, 148, 195, 234n43
Hart, Barry, 206
Hartford Seminary, 70–71
Hassan, Mohammed Abdullah, 78–79, 178, 187
Hauerwas, Stanley, 39, 93, 228
Hawiye clan, 105, 146–47, 173
Hege, Nathan, 30
Hershberger, Guy F., 46–47
Hess, Mahlon, 4
holistic character ethics, 1–2, 1n2, 7, 222
Holy Spirit, 11, 16, 19, 87, 174, 226; and Sufism, 60
Hoover, Jon, 70, 70n97
Hostetler, Marian, 55
Howe, Jonathan, 116–17, 120, 126
Huebner, Chris, xxii, 100, 136

Ibrahim, Dekha, 217–19, 235
Ignatieff, Michael, 128, 133–34
Ilesanmi, Simeon O., 111n29
Iraq, 117, 193, 226
Iran, 69, 177–78, 188, 189
Islam, 30, 53, 61, 69, 80, 98–99, 172, 181–84, 204; and Mennonites. *See* Mennonite Mission; and peacemaking, 104, 142, 144, 149, 152–53, 174, 177–81, 199–201, 229; Prophet Mohammed, 62, 65, 170, 184, 185, 197, 198; *sharia*, 174, 179, 183–84, 186, 191; as state religion, 5–6, 22, 24–25, 33; and women, 208–9, 214, 219

Islamic Courts Union, 80, 118, 126, 128, 131, 155, 190–94
Islamism, 79, 118, 155, 178, 182–83, 188–90; militant. *See* al-Itihaad al-Islamiya, al-Qaeda, al-Shabaab, *jihad*; Wahhabism, 53, 54–55, 182, 183, 188, 192, 194
Israel, 80–81, 94–95; modern state, 53, 88–89, 88n34

Jacobs, Donald, 70, 86, 98
Jamama, 5–6, 23, 33, 38, 52, 208, 223
Jardine, Douglas James, 78–79
Jenner, Janice, 202, 204, 212–14, 217
Jennings, Willie James, 78–82
Jesus, xxiii, 3, 8, 11, 13, 16, 20, 21, 25, 39, 41, 68, 84–85, 91, 100, 103; in Somali context, 15, 22, 25, 34, 60, 64, 67, 72, 86–87, 90, 170–71, 172, 227; and Israel, 81; and peacemaking, 47–48, 76, 115, 171; as prophet, 95; teachings. *See* Sermon on the Mount.
Jibrell, Fatima, 157, 203, 235
jihad, 179, 193; and Sufism, 178, 182, 199
Johar, 6, 20, 38, 67, 113, 204, 224, 231, 232, 235
just peacemaking. *See* peacemaking.
just policing, 115

Kanagy, Conrad, 73–74
Kapteijns, Lidwien, 183, 189, 208–9
Kataregga, Badru, 59, 71
Keener, Clayton and Martha, 10
Kenya, 6, 20, 54, 55, 78, 137–38, 160, 169, 173, 194, 218–19, 227; Eastleigh. *See* Eastleigh Fellowship Center; EMM/MCC Nairobi office, 166–67, 203, 227; military, 118, 129, 131–32, 154; Northeastern Province. *See* Garissa, Wajir.
King, Martin Luther, xxvi, 43
King-Grosh, Ann and Jerry, 169, 171
kinship, 137,143, 144–49, 153–54, 174, 185; and adoption, 231–32; and marriage, 151, 208–9; and social contract. *See xeer*.
Kismayu, 50, 118, 129, 131–32, 154, 171, 194
Koontz, Ted, 45, 108–9
Kraybill, Donald B., 42–45
Kraybill, Paul N., 10–13, 37, 66
Kutty, Vinodh, 79, 149, 179–80, 182–83, 190, 195

Lafoole College, 26, 52–53
Lapp, John A., 69, 98
lawsuits, 19–20
Leaman, Hershey, 110
Leaman, Ivan and Mary Ellen, 9, 13, 23–24, 27, 29, 37, 38, 52, 54, 64, 68, 75, 86
Lederach, Angela J., 90–91, 100, 163–64
Lederach, John Paul, 36, 82–83, 94, 97, 115, 138–44, 159, 160–62, 163–66, 169, 195–96, 210, 233–34
Leeuwen, Arend Theodoor van, 98
Lehman, Chester, 8, 16
Lewis, I. M., 65, 145, 147, 184, 186, 234n43
Life and Peace Institute, 151, 159–60, 165–66, 168–69, 195, 210, 234
Lind, Rhoda and Wilbert, 3–5, 12, 20, 24, 25, 31, 34, 51, 63–64, 221
Logan, Chantal and Mark, 30, 66, 72, 75, 87, 157, 158, 169–71, 221, 222–23, 225–26, 227, 234, 235
Lutheran World Relief, 107
Lybarger, Loren D., 77–78, 85–88

Mahaddei Uen, 5, 6, 18, 19, 31, 32, 35, 37, 38, 51, 67, 113, 224
Mahdi, Ali, 105, 124–25, 173, 200
Marchal, Roland, 190, 191–92
media, 80, 106, 117, 121–23, 169
Mennonite Board of Missions (Elkhart), 7, 69, 88n34
Mennonite Mission, 1n2, 4, 16, 31, 39, 41, 53, 98; early attitudes toward Islam, 61–69, 74–75; Lancaster Conference Board of Bishops, 6, 63, 65–66; openness to Somali authorities, 29–36; peace clan,

xxiii, 76, 92, 100, 142–43, 220, 230–235; reputation, 57, 84, 170–71, 202, 204, 221–22; schools, 5–6, 17–18, 20–27, 32–33, 35, 49, 67, 99, 224, 228–29, 232; teaching Islam, 5–6, 21, 25–26, 63, 65–66, 200; women, 14–15

Mennonite Central Committee (MCC), 7, 10, 43, 45, 50, 55–58, 69, 110–11, 112, 137–38, 159–60, 164–65, 167–68, 171, 203, 219, 226, 229, 233–34, 235; Mennonite Conciliation Services, 47, 50, 165; Nairobi office. *See* Kenya; Peace office, 47, 56, 111, 160; tension with EMM, 87–91

Mennonite Church USA, 49

Metzler, Marilyn, 167

Miller, David, 23

Miller, Fae, 9–10, 13, 14, 17, 19, 21, 29, 37, 52, 63, 65, 68, 70–71, 75, 87, 208, 223

Miller, Gerald L., 18–19, 152–53

Miller, Harold F., 50–51, 57, 166, 219

Miller, Orie O., 4, 7, 10–14, 37, 88, 88n34, 175

mission creep, 125–26

Mogadishu, 126, 132, 147, 181, 216; during war, 105n8, 116–18, 125, 128–29, 200; Mennonite presence; 4, 21, 23, 33, 36, 50, 51–55, 57, 137, 138, 167–68, 172–73, 203, 229

Mohamed, Jama, 143

Mohamed, Mohamed Abdi "Gandhi," 229, 235

Mohamud, Hassan Sheikh, 205, 230

Mouw, Richard J., 96

Newbigin, Lesslie, 71, 98

Niebuhr, Reinhold, 135

Nissley, Kenneth and Elizabeth, 13, 17–18, 25–26, 53, 65, 70, 86, 90, 172, 174, 217, 223, 232

non-governmental organizations (NGOs), 51, 114, 121, 162, 168, 190, 204; and military intervention, 107–8, 110, 119

Ogaden. *See* Ethiopia.

Olfert, Eric, 110

Operation Restore Hope. *See* United Task Force.

pacifism, 42–46, 73, 84, 102–3, 131, 135, 224–28; and armed security, 112–15; Christian. *See* Jesus; and necessity of force, 108–11, 213; and nonresistance, 39–40, 43, 46–49; and two-kingdom theology, 46–48, 109

Pakistan, 116, 120, 188

Palestine, 43, 69, 88

peacemaking, xxii–xxiii, 235; elicitive approach, 93–97, 115–16, 138–144, 169, 174; just peacemaking, 39, 42, 45–47, 73, 83, 111–12, 201; and peacebuilding, 47, 162; *Peacebuilding 2.0*, 207; theology of. *See* Jesus, pacifism.

Peachey, J. Lorne, 110–11

Peachey, Paul, 48

Peachey, Urbane, 87–88

Peterson, Scott, 148, 234n43

Philpott, Daniel, 162

pietism, 8–10, 67

piracy, 79, 122, 128n90, 192, 215

Plank, Carolyn, 10

poetry, 29, 68, 70, 157–59

Prendergast, John, 151–52

presence, theology of, 13, 30, 37–39, 85–87, 98, 137

Protestantism, 3, 107

Puntland, 134, 226

qat, 18, 113, 160, 164, 208

Qur'an, 25, 71–72, 178, 199–201

radio, 158–59, 228–29

Ramadan, 64, 87

Rayale, Siham, 210–11

Reed, Harold, 70, 115, 166

Reformed tradition, 69, 95–96

Rhodes, Gloria, 216, 225

Rissler, Ed, 57
Roth, Glen and Annabelle, 20–21, 65, 230
Rudy, Jonathan, 45–46, 89–90, 158, 206–7, 214, 221, 226–27, 232–33, 234
Ruth, John, 7–8, 10–11
Rutherford, Ken, 114, 125–26, 133
Rwanda, 111n29, 117, 123, 159

Sahnoun, Mohamed, 116, 120, 124–25, 165–66
Salafism. *See* Islamism.
Samatar, Ahmed I., 104, 146, 153
Samatar, Said S., 159, 228, 230
Sauder, J. Paul, 36–37
Saudi Arabia, 30, 53, 61, 155, 189, 194, 214
Sayyid Qutb, 188
Sayyid Abul A'la Maududi, 188
Schlabach, Gerald, 111, 115
secularism, 98–99, 100, 177, 182, 185, 189
Seiple, Robert, 108
September 11, 2001, 49, 111, 117, 193
Sermon on the Mount, 30, 46, 92–98; transforming initiatives, 16–17, 21, 83
sharia, 174, 179, 183–84, 186, 191, 209
Shenk, Calvin, 87
Shenk, Clyde and Alta, 9
Shenk, David W. and Grace, 33–34, 39, 52–53, 58–60, 70–72, 98–99, 173, 185, 187
Sider, Ronald J., 1n2, 48
slavery, 52, 62, 181–82
Somali believers fellowship, 15, 59, 89
Somali National Movement, 50, 188
Somali Youth League, 35, 37
Somalia; Bantu minority, 28, 61, 146, 154, 171, 232; Christians, 5, 6, 21, 22, 24–25, 33, 38–39, 53, 59, 93, 166, 172; clan. *See* kinship; constitution, 5, 24, 33, 148, 163, 208; customary law. *See xeer*; ecological issues, 50–51, 57, 105, 128n90; language, 38, 61, 65, 71, 82, 98; Mennonite ethnography, 28–29, 61–63; orality, 29, 146, 157–58, 222; pastoralism, 147–48, 150, 156; peacemaking practices, 27–29, 142–159; pre-Islamic, 174, 182; revolutionary government and scientific socialism, 6, 49, 52, 143, 182, 188–89; women, 24, 28, 64, 156–57, 203, 208–11
Somaliland, 4, 50, 54, 80, 138, 153, 167, 204, 206, 214, 234; independence. *See* Borama Peace Process; Islamism in, 177, 183, 188, 194; Sufism in, 78–79, 197
Soviet Union, 52–53, 106, 126–27, 194, 214
Stassen, Glen H., 2, 36, 45, 83, 94–95, 97–98, 103
Stauffer, Elam, 7
Stauffer, Harold, 13, 22–23
Stephan, Maria, 104
Stone, Ronald H., 112
Stutzman, Ervin R., 42, 44, 48, 73, 101
Sudan, 122, 122n70, 128, 165, 188, 189, 193, 204
Sudan Interior Mission (SIM), 5–6, 21, 25, 86
Sufism, 184–87; Ahmadiyah, 59, 184; *baraka*, 60, 185, 196; Barkhadle, Sharif Yuusuf, 197; Dervishes, 79, 178, 184, 188; and Islamism, 181–84; "Mad Mullah." *See* Mohammed Abdullah Hassan; Qadiriyah, 59, 179, 184–85, 187, 198; saints, 196–99; Salihiyah, 60, 178, 184, 187; *tariqa*, 59–60, 184–85; Zayla'i, Sheikh 'Abdirahman, 196–97
Sunday school movement, 3–4, 7
Swedish Lutheran mission, 3n4, 5, 24, 89

Tanganyika, 4, 7, 9, 66
Togane, Mohamed, 232, 235
Transitional Federal Government (TFG), 118, 127–28, 132, 190–91

trauma, 205, 217, 229
truth-telling, 29–36

Uganda, 129, 191
Unified Task Force (UNITAF), 102–3, 107, 114, 116, 124, 130–31
United Nations, 4, 115, 165, 206, 233; UNHCR, 57, 169
United Nations Operation in Somalia (UNOSOM), 105–8, 116–17, 120, 123–26, 133–35, 163, 166, 193
United States, 20, 27, 52; military involvement. *See* UNITAF; Somali community in, 194–95; USAID, 204, 205, 217

Vietnam War, 7, 13, 43, 48, 99, 108
Volf, Miroslav, 104

Wachira, George Mukundi, 219
wadaad (sheikh), 148–49, 156, 183, 185–86
Wajir, 113, 217–19
Walker, Bridget Ann, 219
Walzer, Michael, 147
War on Terror, 49, 126, 180, 193
Ward, Ron, 60
warlords, 79–80, 111, 116, 124–25, 131, 165, 190–91, 200, 234
weapons, 107, 126–28, 167, 225

Weaver, Alain Epp and Sonia K., 49, 76, 88
Weaver, J. Denny, 109
Weaver, Verda, 167
Weaver-Zercher, David, 44–45
Wesselhoeft, Carl and Leota, 8, 13, 18, 23, 31, 32–33, 35, 37–38, 51, 67, 113, 224
Wheeler, Nicholas J., 116, 134
Witmer, Barbara and Lamar, 53–54, 86–87, 157
Women's Peacebuilding Leadership Program. *See* Eastern Mennonite University.
Woodberry, J. Dudley, 172
World Concern, 108, 167
World Vision, 107–8, 203n4
World War II, 43, 46–47, 51, 185
Wursame, Abdul-Cadir, 21

xeer (customary law), 137, 143–44, 152–54, 163, 186, 197, 206, 208–9

Yemen, 129, 194
Yoder, John H., 43, 46, 48, 96–97, 103, 132–33

Zanzibar, 181
Zimmerman Herr, Robert and Judy, 109
Zwemer, Samuel, 61, 64

Scripture Index

Old Testament

Genesis

1:28	95–96

Deuteronomy

32:35	133

Isaiah

2:1–5	137
2:4	97
2:5	94–95
9:1–2	94
42:6	95
49:6	94, 95
45	133
60:1–3	95
60:11	96

Jeremiah

29:7	114

Micah

4:1–5	95

New Testament

Matthew

4:15–16	94
5:9	xxii
5:13–16	92, 97, 100
5:13	92, 136–37
5:14–16	95, 137
5:14	93, 94
5:25	18
5:37	30
5:38	83, 227
5:44	83
6:1	99
7:5	17
7:21	98
7:24–26	93
7:24	98
20:26–28	95
25	86–87
28	8

Mark

13:11   19

Luke

4:24   93
14:25–35   22

John

10:7   20

Romans

11:29   9
12:19   133
13   115
13:2–4   133

Ephesians

6:12   97

Philippians

2:1–11   174

Colossians

2:15   97

1 Peter

3:15   87
5:10   23

Revelation

21:24–26   95
21:24   96